MW00989409

Glenwood Springs

THE HISTORY OF A ROCKY MOUNTAIN RESORT

By Jim Nelson

Western Reflections, Inc.
Ouray, Colorado

GLENWOOD SPRINGS
The History of a Rocky Mountain Resort

Copyright ©1999 Jim Nelson
All rights reserved in whole or in part.

ISBN 1-890437-39-5

First edition

Western Reflections , Inc.
PO Box 710
Ouray, CO 81427

Cover and text design by Lead Dog Communications
Printed in the United States of America

Contents

AUTHOR'S FOREWORD

Small towns possess a unique atmosphere. They may not contain the cultural opportunities or the shopping meccas of the cities, but those deficiencies are far outweighed, at least in my opinion, by the more relaxed atmosphere, by the sense of belonging in the smaller community.

My wife, Mary, and I both grew up in small towns in Nebraska. After graduating from Denver University and living in Denver for some twelve years, it was a desire to regain the small town values that led us to Glenwood Springs.

We had never laid eyes on the Western Slope of Colorado, but we knew that we were ready to escape the traffic, the increasing crime rates, the air pollution of Denver. We accepted an invitation from college friends to visit Glenwood on Easter weekend of 1973. In anticipation of that visit, I searched the library for information on the town, and came away with *Glenwood Springs: Spa in the Mountains,* by Lena Urquhart.

I held in my hands the history of an area, a collection of memories that represented the infancy, the exuberant formative years, the sometimes sad, sometimes joyful maturation of a Colorado mountain town. It immediately became obvious that the author held a deep affection for the town, an intimate knowledge of the events and of the personalities that brought Glenwood Springs to the late 1960s.

I started work in Glenwood on May 15, 1973. We fell in love with Glenwood Springs on that long-ago Easter weekend, and have never regretted moving here. Then, after the formation of Defiance Community Theater Company in 1976, it was my privilege to act in *Arsenic and Old Lace.* The cast included two older women, one of whom was played by Lena Urquhart, the author who had introduced Glenwood Springs to us. I remember her as a delightful little person with pure white hair and a perpetual smile. She had a wonderful sense of humor, and I consider myself fortunate to have known her.

This book is not meant to replace *Spa in the Mountains.* I would never presume to do that. Rather, I hope to present a different viewpoint, an elaboration on the milestones leading up to the publishing of her book, and a detailing of the events since then.

Hopefully, Lena would approve. It is my honor to dedicate this work to her memory.

INTRODUCTION

The story of Glenwood Springs necessarily revolves around the town itself; the mountains and rivers that surround and bisect it, the buildings that house its businesses and its residents, and the dreams and ambitions of the men and women who created it.

However, a complete picture of the community cannot stop at the city limits. Over the millions of years required for the formation of the mountains and canyons, the thousands of years of occupation by the original inhabitants, and the 150 or so years of habitation by the white man, many outside influences have affected the growth of the community.

The modern tourist, relaxing in the world's largest natural hot springs swimming pool, is warmed as a result of volcanic activity that occurred many thousands of years ago. The rusty red cliffs south of town along Highway 82 and the alluvial fan on the north face of Red Mountain show the remains of the Ancestral Rockies, enormous mountains that were created 300 million years ago.

An ancient lake in the mountains north of town left a layer of carbonate, a mineral sometimes associated with rich deposits of silver. That formation drew the attention of prospectors, which led to the founding of the first county seat of Garfield County at an elevation of nearly 10,000 feet. The primordial swamps that once covered the area provided raw material for the seams of coal that run through the Grand Hogback not far to the south and west of Glenwood Springs. That coal attracted entrepreneurs and investors from as far away as England.

As was the case with much of the western United States, the promise of riches from various mineral deposits initially drew the white race to the Western Slope of the Rocky Mountains. The mineral exploration resulted in fabulous wealth for a fortunate few, and in years of backbreaking labor and bitter disappointment for most. Today it is the breathtaking beauty of the area, the clouds hanging below the mountaintops after a rain, the surprise of a soaring bald eagle, that bring people to Glenwood Springs.

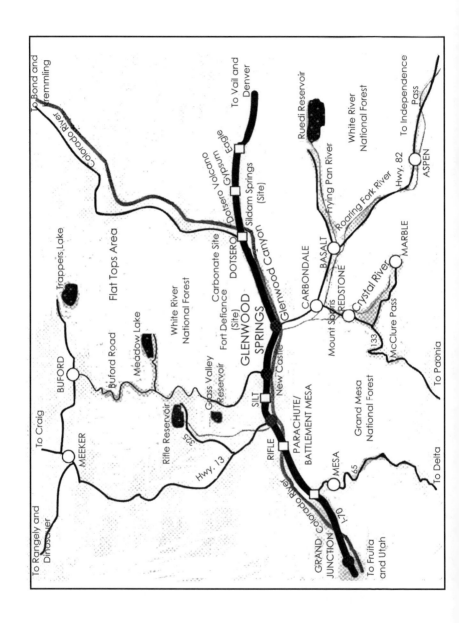

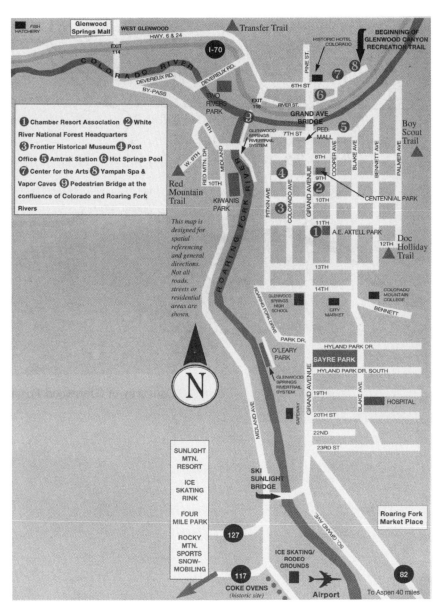

(Map courtesy Glenwood Springs Chamber of Commerce)

CHAPTER ONE

From The Beginning to The First Inhabitants

"We measure minutes. The river ignores millenniums. In its time the whole continent has been submerged under the sea at least seven times. And each time that it has risen anew the river has resumed its task. Patiently it has carried back to the ocean floor the seashells beached on the summits of the loftiest peaks."

Frank Waters, in The Colorado—Rivers of America Series

The crust of the earth is composed of gigantic slabs of rock known as tectonic plates. These plates float on the upper surface of the magma, the molten rock that makes up the core of the planet. There are many of these plates, some small, some the size of continents. As they slowly drift upon the surface of the magma, they slide ponderously past each other. Ideally, the movement is slow enough to allow the overlying surface to accommodate the changes.

However, sometimes the edges of the plates catch against each other. When this happens, the irresistible forces continue to build up until the plates suddenly break free, causing earthquakes. At other times, the plates will bump into each other. When this happens one or both edges are pushed upwards, creating mountain ranges.

Scientists believe that the earth of 300 million years ago looked much different than it does today. There is some disagreement as to the makeup of the early continents. One theory has it that there were once two giant continents, Laurasia in the Northern Hemisphere and Gondwanaland in the south. They believe that these continents were separated by a body of water that they call the Tethys Sea. Another hypothesis has it that there was only one supercontinent, known as Pangaea.

Whatever the truth, the area that is now Colorado was then covered by a vast inland sea. It was populated by some quite imaginative early experiments in the world of fish. There were sharks that may have reached fifty feet in length, and fish that sported very impressive armor, perhaps to guard against the sharks. The inland sea existed until two of the underlying tectonic plates collided, pushing their edges many thousand feet into the air. Some estimates place the elevation of this new mountain range at between 25,000 and 35,000 feet. These enormous spires formed what were to become known as the Ancestral Rockies.

These mountains were largely red in color, because of a high content of iron oxide. The mountains themselves are long gone, but we know their color because we can see their remains. The majestic mountains stood for many millions of years, but the forces of erosion began working on them as soon as they reached their ultimate height. The relentless actions of rainwater, wind, glaciers, and freezing and thawing, began their task of eroding the mountains. As each pebble, each bit of rock was loosened, it was used to disturb, to abrade other rock. The air or water or ice-borne grains gradually wore scratches, then grooves, then canyons in the underlying rock. Over the next 240 million years or so, the Ancestral Rockies were worn down completely. As they diminished, their material was spread over the areas which were to become Colorado, Utah, and much of Nebraska and Kansas. The sediments were laid down in thick layers that eventually became the red sandstones that are so prominent in Southern Utah as well as in many areas around Glenwood Springs.

The sandstone is not the only rock evident in the Glenwood Springs area. The inland seas, mentioned earlier, contained billions of tiny creatures whose lot in life was to serve as a food source for many of the other residents. In an effort to ward off some of the attention, many of them developed hard shells made of calcium carbonate. As they died, their shells settled to the bottom of the shallow sea, forming layers many feet deep. These layers were in turn covered by sediment washed down from the mountains, and the resultant pressure changed the shells into limestone. Layers of the grayish stone are visible on the north bank of the Colorado River, while the rocks on the south bank are of the red sandstone.

At about the time the Ancestral Rockies finally were worn down, some sixty million years ago, the movement of the tectonic plates tore the existing continent (or continents) apart. North America broke away from Europe, and South America separated from Africa. At approximately the same time, there was a massive upheaval in the area of the now stunted Ancestral Rockies. This uplift formed the

White River Plateau, a high, level area west of the present Rocky Mountains. To the east of the plateau, rocks were again tilted and pushed skyward, creating the peaks which would come to be known as the Continental Divide.

During this geologically busy time, the plates cracked in many places, allowing the superheated magma to surge toward the surface. In many places, the magma found a route to the open air, bursting forth as lava and forming volcanoes and cinder cones. At the east end of Glenwood Canyon, near Dotsero, the remains of an ancient volcano are visible from Interstate 70. The Dotsero area is littered with dark, porous "lava rock," and the highway rises gently as it crosses the lava flow which once blocked the course of the river. The nearby hills exhibit the gray stripe of the ash deposit.

The Caldera, or cone of the volcano just north of Dotsero. (Courtesy of Al Maggard)

In many instances, the upsurge of magma did not reach the surface. Rather, the millions of tons of magma elevated the overlying rock and dirt, sometimes pushing the overlaying rock many thousands of feet upward. When this happened, the magma solidified, forming the core of a new mountain. This core is known as an "igneous intrusion," or "lacolith." Mount Sopris, twelve miles south of Glenwood Springs, is a classic example of such an intrusion.

The majestic twin peaks of Mount Sopris that we see today are the intrusion itself, the overlying rock having long since eroded away.

No one knows how many mountain ranges grew and were worn back down by erosion, how many primordial seas filled and were in turn pushed aside by the next upthrust. Parts of the Rocky Mountains show evidence of lifting, folding, and tearing, of the rock layers. Seams of rock that lay flat for eons now stand almost vertical, forming "book

Mount Sopris, volcanic "igneous intrusion" some twelve miles south of Glenwood Springs. (Courtesy of Al Maggard)

cliffs." Faulting, or the cracking and slipping of rock layers, is the bane of coal miners. A coal seam may extend underground for hundreds of feet, and then disappear suddenly only to reappear several feet or yards higher or lower.

The area that contains northwest Colorado has been built up over the last billion years or so. The repeated uplifts and the relentless erosion gradually built up layer upon layer of rock. The grains of sand, the volcanic ash and hardened lava, the shells and skeletons of millions of generations of sea creatures, and the vegetable matter from ancient swamps, each added to the vast number of layers that make up the geology of the White River Plateau.

When the plateau was originally pushed up, it formed a level area of many hundred square miles. The elevation of the plateau was roughly 10,000 feet. Consequently, it was not long before the snows of winter covered the newly formed high country. Spring brought warmer weather and the snows melted, creating millions of gallons of water with nowhere to go. Gravity took over, and trickles became streams, which became creeks, which grew into rivers. The infant waterways wandered at first, seeking always the path of least resistance. As the rushing waters sought out the softer of the rocks and began to wear them down, they formed the pathways that would gradually grow into the tributaries of the Colorado River. The plateau continued to push upward for some time. As it did, the creeks and rivers cut deeper into the multiple layers, changing course where necessary, but always working their way downward.

Since the crust of the earth solidified some 4.5 billion years ago, innumerable layers of rock have been deposited, one above the other. Those layers that have not been worn away by erosion form a

Evidence of sedimentary layers laid down and compressed into rock over millions of years. (Photo by the author)

permanent history of the period of time in which they were formed. Many of the sedimentary layers contain not only the remains of the minerals of the period, but also a chronicle of the plants and animals that inhabited the earth during the time of the deposition. This evidence ranges from microscopic organisms to the massive skeletons of dinosaurs. The fossil record waits in its captive layers for examination and interpretation. Unfortunately, the vast majority of that information is forever buried hundreds, perhaps thousands, of feet deep.

In a few special places on earth, forces have conspired to cut down through the layers, to expose the edges of those layers to open air. Glenwood Canyon, the two thousand foot deep canyon sliced through the White River Plateau by the Colorado River, is one of those places. In sites deep within the canyon, it is possible to see, and to touch, pre-Cambrian granite, rock that began forming literally billions of years ago. Above that lies a 500 foot thick formation which began as a massive layer of sand. The sand was cemented into sandstone by silica dioxide and then metamorphosed by heat and pressure into quartzite. Deposits of quartzite have survived for so long for two reasons. They tend to occur deep within the earth, due to the their age, and they are extremely tough. The layer of quartzite that has been exposed in Glenwood Canyon is called the Sawatch Formation. There are massive formations of quartzite in the Sawatch Mountains, hence the name. *Saguache,*

The Colorado River, formerly known as the Grand, continues its erosion of the canyon. (Courtesy of Frontier Historical Society)

which has been corrupted to Sawatch by the white race, is an attempt to reduce a spoken Ute word to writing, as the Utes had no written language. The meaning of the word was "waters of the blue earth," which is thought to refer to the fact that the San Luis Valley, which lies at the south end of the Sawatch Range, once contained a large lake.

As the Colorado River enters Glenwood Canyon, it carries the drainage of nearly 4,500 square miles. It of course contains a tremendous amount of sediment, and continues to wear away at the riverbed. Even so, it has taken most of the last sixty million years to carve the majestic canyon that we see today. Dams and other water projects have affected the flow of the river, but it is still capable of carrying flows of 22,000 cubic feet per second, which equates to 165,000 gallons per second. These flows are reached only occasionally after years of unusually heavy snowfall.

At both ends of Glenwood Canyon, mineral-rich hot water bubbles to the surface along the banks of the Colorado River. After the last period of volcanic activity, many of the deep vents never completely closed. Water that fell on the White River Plateau some 20,000 years ago has spent the intervening centuries seeping down through rock layers to the still hot regions far underground. The sulfur-scented springs are a complicated soup of dissolved minerals. It is estimated that the springs along what is now called the Colorado River pour 303,000 tons of dissolved salts into the big river each year. There are numerous springs along the river. A group at the east end of the canyon became known as the Siloam Springs, and would later be the focus of development plans. They were to fade into insignificance, however, in comparison to the much bigger Yampah Springs at the west portal. The hot springs and the vapor-filled limestone caves along the river just to the west of the canyon were to attract the attention of the earliest inhabitants of the area.

CHAPTER TWO

From 18,000 B.C. to 1700 A.D.

"The Ute Indians are the oldest continuous residents of Colorado and the only truly native tribe; before the opening of the West to settlers and the discovery of gold, silver, and coal beneath their lands, they lived a nomadic existence throughout the 150,000 square miles of this beautiful mountain wilderness, the Ute's Shining Mountains."

Dorothia Farris, Chief ColorowThe Life and Times of a Ute Chieftain; Old Roaring Fork *magazine, Volume I, Issue IV*

Some say that Paleo-Indians, the old ones, were in the Americas as early as 20,000 years ago. No one knows when human eyes first gazed upon the valley of the hot springs, but it is known that many generations of Ute Indians spent at least part of each year here. The Utes called themselves "Nuciu," their word for "the people." Yampah, the name that we use for the springs, is a Ute word meaning "big medicine." The Ute tribe considered the springs to be sacred, a gift from Manitou, their deity. The "medicine" meant spiritual power to the Utes. To them, big medicine meant the ability to connect with a power higher than themselves.

The hot pools along the edge of the river and the vapor caves certainly warmed and relaxed the Utes, but that was not all. The Utes knew little of the mineral content of the hot waters and steam, but they did know that the application of the water, both externally and internally, made them feel better. They were convinced that the sacred springs helped wounds to heal, cured internal discomforts, and made them stronger.

Popular conjecture has it that early humans arrived on the North American continent between 20,000 and 30,000 years ago. An archeological site in the Yukon has been dated to around 27,000 years "B. P." (Before Present, in archaeological terms.) It is generally believed that these Stone Age peoples crossed a land bridge over the Bering Strait between Siberia and Alaska, following the big game that formed a large part of their diet. The bridge, uncovered by the lower sea level brought on by the growth of the continental ice sheets, has long since disappeared, but is believed to have existed several times over the last 40,000 years.

After crossing the fifty or so miles of the bridge, the ancient hunter/gatherers were free to spend the next 10,000 years or so spreading across the areas which would be known as North and South America. It is assumed that the animals that preceded the hunters into the "New World" included such now extinct species as the woolly mammoth, the giant sloth, and a version of the camel. We know, from the evidence of ancient kill sites, that the earliest Americans dined on these species as well as a giant form of bison and a type of horse.

The proximity of animal bones with stone projectile points proves that the early hunters used spears to subdue their quarry. They also killed the larger varieties of game by stampeding them over cliffs. They rigged traps and snares and used rocks and throwing sticks to harvest smaller animals. Later, they developed the atlatl, or spear-thrower. The implement was about two feet long and had a hand grip at one end and a hook, made of wood or bone, at the other. The hook fit into a socket at the end of the spear

The remains of a Ute wikiup, a temporary dwelling. (Courtesy of Frontier Historical Society)

shaft, and was used to propel the spear with greatly increased force. The bow and arrow were invented rather late in the period of development of the Indians of the Americas.

There is no real evidence as to the origin of the Ute Indians. The Utes themselves believed that they had always lived in the territory in which they were "discovered" by the Spaniards. One origin legend tells of Sineuwa, the Creator, cutting sticks and placing them in a bag. The Coyote, the trickster, was a compatriot of the Creator and somewhat his nemesis. Curious, the Coyote opened the bag. People of many different languages ran out, scattering in every direction. When the Creator returned, he was angered to discover just a few people remaining in the bag. He had planned to distribute the people equally all over the world, to prevent wars between peoples over the land. The Creator then called the remaining people Ute, and He proclaimed that they would be brave and able to defeat the rest in battle.

The Ute language is from a language group known as Shoshonean or Uto-Aztecean. It has similarities to the language of the Aztecs of Central Mexico. They share the language group with the Piutes, the Pimas, the Comanches, and the Hopi. The Navajo and the Apache speak variations of an Athabascan tongue, and it has been established with a degree of reliability that they crossed the land bridge sometime later than did the hypothetical ancestors of the Utes. It is unknown why there are similarities between the Aztec language and that of the Utes. Perhaps those who were to become Aztec split off from their northern cousins at some point in the distance past and moved, for whatever reason, several hundred miles south. Another more popular theory is that the Utes left Central America and migrated to the Rocky Mountain region of the American West. According to at least one modern Ute, a member of the Ute Mountain Reservation, their language contains a word for "monkey." To him, that is proof enough that they came from the south.

Whatever their route, the Utes lived in and controlled almost all of Colorado, most of Utah, and parts of Wyoming and New Mexico for hundreds of years. It cannot be said that they "owned" the territory in which they resided. Their beliefs held no concept of ownership of the land. They believed that the earth was the property, perhaps the embodiment, of a deity, and that they were responsible for its care. The products of the earth, the animals and the plants,

Mule deer, a part of the food sources for the Paleo-Indians, and later, the Utes. (Courtesy of Frontier Historical Society—Schutte Collection)

were to be used for survival, but each of them was believed to hold its own spirit.

By necessity, ancient peoples were predominantly hunter/gatherers, following what is known as a flexible subsistence system. They followed the herds as the animals moved with the seasons. They followed the seasons as the various berries, grasses, and tubers, matured. To do anything else meant starvation. They were very much children of nature. As nature prospered, as the rains came and the edible plants flourished, so the people thrived. When drought withered the grasses and the bushes, and the animals starved, so did the people. Many of them did not survive the bad times.

Over the centuries, some of the groups of people, the ancestors of the Indian tribes, turned to crude forms of agriculture as a means to supplement their diets. They planted and raised maize, squash, and beans. Some of them domesticated turkeys and dogs. These activities naturally tied them to a specific area, at least for part of the year. The transition from hunter/gatherer to farmer seemed to be a natural progression. The Utes, however, never made the change.

The fact that the Ute Indians remained in the more "primitive" lifestyle had nothing whatsoever to do with their intellect. Rather, it was a direct result of the land in which they lived. Much of their territory was composed of rugged mountains and canyons. The seasonal changes were dramatic, the summers baking under a high altitude sun, the winters bringing snows that drove most of the animal life out of the high country. The serviceberries, raspberries, wild rose hips, and other small berries ripened at different elevations at varied times. The sunflower and grass seeds were harvested during the summer as they dried, and the yampa tubers and wild carrots and onions were unearthed with the aid of digging sticks.

Pinecones were beaten to remove their nuts, and protein-rich pinon nuts were gathered to be eaten raw, roasted, or beaten into a meal that was mixed with water and baked. In addition to gathering the vegetable products, the women and children caught ants, crickets, grasshoppers, and caterpillars, as well as snakes and lizards. Very little was overlooked in the constant search for food. Popular legend has it that Indians wasted nothing in their use of wild game, and that legend is at least partially true. Under most circumstances, every part of the animal was utilized for food, clothing, shelter, tools, decoration, or products such as glue. However, at other times, a great deal of waste was necessary. If a small group of Indians was successful in stampeding a herd of bison or antelope over a cliff, they might have been faced with a literal mountain of meat and hides with no way to either process or preserve them. In such an instance, a great deal of life-giving animal products would fill the bellies of the coyote and the magpie.

Again because of the uncertainty of food sources, the early Utes lived and traveled in small extended family groupings of twenty to thirty individuals. It was not until the encroachment of the white race, beginning in the middle 1800s, that it became necessary for them to form larger groups. Each of these groups depended on a leader to negotiate with the representatives of the United States Government.

For many centuries, the small groups of hunter/gatherers spent the great majority of the year wandering their territory, confronting other family groups only by chance. However, a few days were set aside each spring to gather in much larger groups. This was the time of Mamaqui Mowats, the Bear Dance. While not the only ceremonial dance of the Ute people, the Bear Dance is considered to be

Cave paintings from a cave near Glenwood Canyon - presumably Ute. (Courtesy of John Tindall)

the most important. Traditionally, the bear holds a special relationship with the Ute. Legend tells of a Ute brave of many centuries ago who had a dream about a hibernating bear. The brave came upon the bear late in the spring, and reasoned that the bear might starve if he did not awaken soon. The Brave woke the bear, and in appreciation the bear took the young man to a secret place deep in the forest where the bears were holding their spring dance. They taught the dance to the brave, who in turn taught it to his tribe. The dance is a celebration of the coming of spring, the rebirth of life. It is a time of coming together for the older members of the tribe, a time of courting for the young. The dance itself is held inside a circular area, surrounded by a brush fence. The single opening faces the morning sun. A group of musicians sits at one side of the enclosure, beating drums, singing, or playing the "morache," or "bear growler." This instrument is made of a notched stick or the jawbone of an animal. A hard stick is drawn across the irregular surface, making a rasping noise. In addition to providing the rhythm for the dancers, the musicians are also charged with waking the bears from hibernation with their music.

The dancing is between men and women. The women invariably are the instigators, inviting the men to dance. To refuse an invitation is considered to be a great insult and is not tolerated. A dance leader, armed with a willow whip, is charged with disciplining males who do not stay in step or who are slow to accept an invitation. The discipline is a source of amusement to the audience. If a woman asks a man to dance several times, it is considered to be an open invitation for a relationship. A poster announcing a bear dance on the Ute Mountain Ute Reservation in 1997 contained the standard disclaimer, with a notable exception. To paraphrase, it denied responsibility in case of "theft, injury, or divorce."

Prior to the middle 1600s, the small groups of Utes traveled and hunted on foot. The burden of carrying the essentials of life, the small tools and extra clothing and cooking utensils, fell on the women and the domesticated dogs. Most of their containers were woven baskets or pouches made of the hides or the intestines of animals. Pottery was rare for these travelers because of the danger of breakage. Shelter was normally made of the materials at hand to eliminate the need to carry extra gear from place to place. The dwellings, usually rounded brush and mud-covered structures or conical shelters made of long poles, were known as wikiups.

The Utes, never more than 8,000 to 10,000 in number, successfully defended their vast territory against other tribes for many centuries. The Apaches and the Comanches to the southwest, the Shoshones to the north, and the Arapahoes and the Cheyenne of the eastern plains coveted the land occupied by the Utes. The Utes were never a warlike people, being more concerned with the tasks of survival, but they excelled in defending their land.

In 1609, a Spaniard named Don Pedro de Peralta established La Villa Real de la Santa Fe de San Francisco at the foot of the Sangre De Cristo Mountains. The "Royal City of the Holy Faith of St. Francis," or Sante Fe, was to become a center of Spanish habitation just a couple hundred miles to the south of the home of the Utes. Confrontation was inevitable. As they had done for many centuries, the Utes defended their territory against the strange new interlopers. However, there was something different about the strangers. They arrived astride large animals, the likes of which the Utes had never seen.

As mentioned, the Paleo-Indians had eaten the last of the "American" horses many eons previously. It was therefore with a great sense of wonder that the Utes observed these "magic dogs," as they called them. To the consternation of the Spanish, many of the confrontations with the "Mountain People" resulted in the Utes "borrowing" several of their horses.

The acquisition of the horse transformed the lifestyle of the Utes. Horses became a measure of wealth, a source of pride for the Ute families. They became expert horsemen, accomplished veterinarians and horse breeders. They could now travel much farther and faster in the search for game or edible plants. They could more easily defend their territory against both white and Indian intruders. They could chase the bison or the antelope and kill them with spear or arrow from horseback, or herd the animals into a brush corral or deep snow, or drive them over a cliff.

The large animals enabled the Utes to carry much more equipment on their seasonal movements. Just as they "borrowed" the horse from their Spanish neighbors to the south, they adopted the idea of the tepee from the plains Indians. The large conical structures, made of a circle of long poles crossed at the top and draped with the hides of the elk or the bison, could be carried quite easily through the use of the horses. For hundreds of years, they had used a carrying device called a "travois." It consisted of two sticks, crossed over the back of a dog and dragging behind him. The items to be transported were lashed to the sticks behind the animal. After acquiring the horse and adopting the tepee, the much longer lodge poles were used to create a bigger travois, which was in turn used to carry the skin coverings of the dwelling, as well as household goods, children, and the elderly or infirm. The Utes still did not create pottery in any abundance, preferring to rely on skin or basketry for container materials.

It should not be assumed that the Utes were at constant odds with the Spaniards to the south. Rather, much of the interaction between the two was friendly and cooperative. On occasion, the Indians would even trade horses to the Spaniards in exchange for beads, metal knives, guns and ammunition, and other trade goods. The fact that the horses involved in the transaction were likely descendants of animals originally stolen from them did not apparently disturb the Spaniards.

The Spanish were explorers, largely due to the urging of their church. Exploration for the sake of discovery was a part of the impetus, but colonization and the spreading of the "word of God" played a major role. Consequently, the Spaniards made several ventures into Ute country, mapping the terrain and naming geological features as the spirit moved them.

In 1604 one such explorer named Don Juan de Onate, came upon a river which was running a dull red from the remains of the Ancestral Rockies picked up by snowmelt. He named the river "Colorado," Spanish for "red." The name was not to stick for very long, however. In 1605, the Spanish Governor renamed the big river that had created several magnificent canyons on its path from the snowfields of the mountains to the Gulf of California. He called it Rio Grande de Buena Esperanza, or "The Grand River of Good Hope." Over time, the name was shortened to the "Grand," a name that was to stick until 1921, when the United States Congress officially changed the name back to "Colorado." It is to be hoped that the ghost of Don Juan de Onate felt vindicated.

CHAPTER THREE

From 1700 to 1850

"A grand bed of snowcapped mountains rose before us, pile upon pile, glowing in the bright light."

> From the journals of Brevet Captain John C. Fremont,
> recording his 1843–1844 expedition.

The Ute Indians first encountered the Spaniards early in the 1600s. They coexisted with them for over two hundred years, fighting with them, trading with them, and stealing horses from them. However, the introduction of the new people into their world had little effect on their day-to-day lifestyle, with the notable exception of the addition of the horse. There were simply too few Spaniards with any interest in encroaching upon Ute territory. It is safe to say that the vast majority of the Utes lived their entire lives without ever laying eyes on anyone of another race. This was to remain true until the middle of the 1800s.

As the Declaration of Independence was being signed many hundreds of miles to the east on July 4, 1776, two Franciscans were making plans to leave Sante Fe on a historic trek to the northwest. Father Francisco Atanasio Dominguez and Father Silvester Velez de Escalante, at the direction of their church, were making ready to set out on a search for an overland route to the missions of Monterey, California. The expedition initially headed northwest to avoid two obstacles: the yawning chasm of the Grand Canyon, and a tribe of Indians in the vicinity of the canyon who had been reported to be cannibalistic. The chosen route took them directly into the heart of Ute country.

The "Yutas" were known to be largely peaceful toward the Spaniards, and a Ute brave who introduced himself as "the Left-Handed" was hired to guide Dominguez and Escalante and their party through Colorado and Utah. The guide persuaded them to turn toward the east, in order to visit his people, who were camped on top of the Grand Mesa. Few of the Utes had ever seen a white person, and they were warmly welcomed. Not one to miss an opportunity, Father Dominguez distributed gifts and then spent several hours preaching to them through an interpreter. He told them of the great power of the white man's God, and the Utes listened politely. They could readily grasp the concept of an all-encompassing God, believing as they did that everything held its own spirit.

Some historians believe that the Utes grew so fond of the friars that they led them on a roundabout route through their territory, rather than losing them. Finally, the expedition made it as far as the Great Salt Lake in Utah, then known as Utah Lake. They did not reach the lake until September. Many in the party felt that Monterey could not be more than another week's travel away. However, Captain Miera y Pacheco disagreed. He had only sketchy reports from wandering Indian traders to rely on. Nonetheless he accurately calculated that California was at least several hundred miles to the west. Had they started from Sante Fe earlier in the year, and had the Utes not delayed them, they might have had a chance to successfully complete their journey. As it was, they regretfully turned back south toward Sante Fe.

The return route took them across the rugged canyonlands of southern Utah and the high deserts of northern Arizona. It was an incredibly difficult trip. Some of the horses were killed and eaten when wild game could not be found. They did not make it back to Sante Fe until January 2, 1777.

Although the expedition was considered a failure, a waste of the church's money, Father Escalante's detailed journals proved to be quite valuable in later mapping of the Ute country. Also, and equally as important, the relationship developed between the members of the excursion and the Utes served to solidify the friendship between the two peoples. Oxcarts filled with trade goods traveled north from Sante Fe and Taos into the fringes of the Ute nation. The iron cooking utensils, guns, mirrors, knives, and wool blankets, were traded for buffalo hides and buckskin which were in great demand by the Spanish.

In the early 1800s, there was very likely a scattering of mountain men living in western Colorado. These self-sufficient loners, prospectors or trappers or simply adventurers, lived off the land as did their Indian neighbors. Some of them eventually returned to "civilization," some died alone in the wilderness, and a few lived with the Utes.

Between 1810 and 1813, a band of Utes raided a Comanche village. Among other plunder, they came away with a child, supposedly named Too-p'-weets. It was not unusual for Indians to kidnap children and adopt them into their tribe. This child grew to be taller than the Ute children, with lighter skin. There were some who said that his mother had been from the Jicarilla Apache tribe. He was later to become known as Colorow, a war chief of the White River Utes. Sometime during his youth, he and his band were involved in a battle with the Arapaho at a place called Red Hill, about twelve miles south of the site of Glenwood Springs. It is said that he won his status as Chief of the Northern Utes because of his courage during that victory over the enemy.

Around 1825, beaver hats became all the rage in European society. Since the forests of eastern North America had been largely depleted of game by that time, the change in fashion was to have an effect on the Utes of western Colorado. American, French, Mexican, and British fur trappers began to appear along the streams of Ute territory. As the Utes were relatively few in number and generally spread thinly over their vast dominion, encounters were few in the early years. When the whites were discovered by the Utes, the meetings were usually friendly. Trading posts, and forts to guard them, were established on the edges of Ute country. Some of the Utes joined the whites in trapping the beaver, adding the dark brown pelts to their stock of trade goods.

One trapper by the name of Uncle Dick Wooten became famous for being the first person to negotiate his own treaty with the Utes. As a result, he was given safe passage throughout western Colorado for many years. Another trapper, Bill Williams, had a similar agreement with the Utes. He traveled among them and lived with them for several years. Unfortunately, he was shot and killed by a Ute war party who did not recognize him. Jim Bridger and Christopher "Kit" Carson appeared in the area in 1834. Carson worked as a fur trader for John Jacob Astor's American Fur Company.

On November 13, 1833, an event took place that momentarily demanded the attention of everyone, regardless of their other troubles. That event was the Leonid meteor shower, a brilliant display of an estimated 200,000 "falling stars" in one night.

The same year marked the birth of Ouray, who was to become the most successful and renowned of all the Ute chiefs.

Fashion, as fashion is wont to do, again shifted around 1840. Chinese silk became the covering of choice for men's hats, and the demand for beaver pelts dropped accordingly. The Utes were beginning to grow weary of the intrusions of the fur trappers anyway, and demonstrated their feelings by burning the trading post of Antoine Robideaux near the Gunnison River. Most of the fur trappers cleared out, but the Utes did not realize that the trappers had been just a symptom of things to come.

In 1845, Kit Carson acted as a guide for the John C. Fremont exploration party. At that time, Fremont was a topographical engineer, who he was mapping western Colorado. He crossed what was to be known as the Flat Tops Wilderness area some twenty-five miles north of the present site of Glenwood Springs.

On January 28, 1848, an employee of Sutter's Mill in California made a discovery that was to change the face of not only California, but also of much of western North America. Over the next year or so, the lure of gold drew many thousands of eager treasure seekers. Many of the hopeful prospectors made their way to California by way of Colorado. Inevitably, some of them stopped their journey in the mountains of Ute country, and some of those who were disappointed in California retraced their steps back to Colorado. Every rock outcropping, every hidden valley, every stream bed, was to eventually draw the attention of these fortune hunters. A few, a very few, found fabulous riches. The vast majority found only backbreaking work and bitter disappointment. The Utes watched with growing apprehension.

The Treaty of Guadelupe-Hidalgo was signed in 1848, ending the Mexican-American War. As part of the treaty, all of New Mexico and the southern part of Colorado was ceded to the United States Government. The United States Government shortly requested a meeting with representatives of the Ute tribe, and the first treaty conference between the Ute Nation and the United States government was held in December of 1849. The resulting treaty called for an annual payment of $5,000 to the Utes, in exchange for the agreement of the Utes to accept the authority of the United States government in the area. No mention was made of territorial boundaries for the territory of the Utes, but it was said that they would possess their lands in Colorado "for as long as the rivers should run and the grass grow."

Trapper's Lake, high on the Flat Tops, was deep in the heart of Ute country. (Photo by the author)

CHAPTER FOUR

From 1850 to 1870

"Agreements the Indian makes with the government are like the agreement a buffalo makes with the hunter after it has been pierced by many arrows. All it can do is lie down and give in."

Chief Ouray

The Fremont expedition, up and over the Flat Tops north of the valley that would hold Glenwood Springs, was one of the earliest attempts by the United States Government to survey and map the rugged lands to the west of the Rockies. The fact that the lands in question were, by tradition and treaty, the "property" of the Utes seemed to make little difference. Eight years later, another survey party led by Captain Gunnison worked their way across the Uncompahgre Plateau to the south and west of the site of Glenwood. The Utes observed them working with a transit and other surveying tools, marking (blazing) trees, and leaving survey markers, in their wake. They crossed the Ute lands unmolested, but then they crossed the Grand River near the present site of Grand Junction, and moved on into Utah. The Piute Indians they encountered took a somewhat dimmer view of their activities, and massacred the entire party.

In 1850 and 1851, two people were born on opposite sides of the earth who were to become acquainted some thirty years hence. Mary Katherine Horony, later to be known in parts of the western United States as "Big Nose" Kate, was born in Budapest, Hungary in 1850. A year later, in 1851, John Henry Holliday was born near Griffin, Georgia. He would become a dentist, a gambler, a gunfighter, and a drunk. He would gain fame, some might say notoriety, as "Doc" Holliday, and would end his days in a hotel in Glenwood Springs, Colorado.

William Gant, a fur trapper and prospector, made his way up the Crystal River Valley, some miles south and west of Glenwood Springs, in 1859. He was one of the first white men to enter that part of the state. He found a rusted coffee pot near the Crystal River, then known as Rock Creek. The utensil was probably left by one of the "forty-niners" who worked the valley on their way to California.

Gold was discovered near Pike's Peak in 1858, and prospectors began arriving at Cherry Creek near the eastern foothills of the Rockies in 1859. Two of these men were to continue on to western Colorado and would play quite different roles in the history of Glenwood Springs. Isaac Cooper, from Joliet, Illinois, spent that year prospecting the Colorado high country. He was enraptured with the clear air and the endless vistas, and vowed then to return to the mountains some day. His path would take a treacherous road through the misery and death of the Civil War, but he was to return.

The other man was Captain Richard Sopris. Originally a railroad contractor from Indiana, he left home at the age of forty-five to seek his fortune in Colorado. Hearing of the strike near Pike's Peak, Sopris and two companions set out for the Rocky Mountain West. They reached the brand new town of Denver on March 15 of 1859, and prospected along the Platte River and into the foothills to the west. The next spring, he returned to Indiana in order to bring his family to Colorado.

In July of 1860, Sopris led an expedition of fourteen men into what was to become western Colorado. (It was still Utah Territory at that time. Colorado was not established as a territory until 1861.) They crossed South Park to the area where Breckenridge now stands, then trekked down the Eagle River to where it joined the Grand. Not far to the west of that confluence, the Grand River disappeared into the mouth of a foreboding canyon. The sheer walls, rising some 2,000 feet straight out of the river bottom, prevented even the Indians from entering it. Two possible routes presented themselves to the explorers. The first was an ancient, but still well used Indian trail that led up onto the mountain range to the north. The other route led to the south, over what would later be known as Cottonwood Pass. This trail led to the Bunkara River, later the Thunder River, still later the Roaring Fork.

Sopris and his party chose the southern route, and as they topped the pass and dropped down toward the river valley, they were greeted by the sight of a magnificent, twin-peaked mountain. Sopris had heard of the mountain from the Utes, and he was so taken by it that he wrote, *"Touching is the majesty of this peak, so long a landmark of the Indians."* The men in his party were recording the journey in detailed notes and maps, and they honored their leader by naming the mountain after him.

The magnificent mountain which was named for Captain Richard Sopris.
(Courtesy of Scott Leslie)

There are differing stories regarding Richard Sopris'
subsequent journey down the Thunder River to its confluence with
the Grand, not far from where the big river exited that foreboding
canyon. One story has it that they found little in the way of
prospecting possibilities around the base of the big mountain and
were merely seeking new territory. The other anecdote tells of Sopris
falling ill, and of his men taking him to the site of the healing hot
springs at the recommendation of the local Utes.

Whatever the truth, Sopris and his men did venture downriver.
They built a raft to cross the Grand, and spent several days relaxing
and soaking in the hot mineral waters. On July 23, 1860, they carved
the date and each of their names in a large cottonwood tree beside
the river. Sopris named the area "Grand Springs," which was to
stick until about 1885.

The party of men returned to Denver without the gold for which
they had been searching. However, the maps which they had created
were used by Colorado Governor Gilpin in developing the first map
of the state. Richard Sopris entered politics, and served as Denver
County Sheriff and later as Mayor of the city. He was the major
promoter of Denver City Park, at the time referred to by the press as
"A City Park in the Boondocks."

On April 12, 1861, artillery of the Confederate Army fired on
Fort Sumter in Charleston, South Carolina. The act of aggression

against the United States Army was the beginning of the American Civil War. The conflict was to last for four years, and would split the United States into two factions. The "Confederate States of America" consisted of eleven states, and sought to create their own sovereign nation. The remaining twenty-three states, the "North," supported the federal government.

The Civil War is normally equated with the question of slavery, and that was indeed a large factor in the hostilities, but it was not the only area of dispute between the two factions. The North favored an interpretation of the United States Constitution that would allow the federal government expanded power in the areas of road and railroad construction, while the South preferred the "States Rights" approach. In addition, the South disagreed with the government's handling of the opening of the West. It was felt that the distribution of the lands in small plots favored the "free" farmer, rather than the plantation owner. Tariffs were another source of conflict. The South favored a lower tariff, so that they could trade cotton for cheap foreign goods. The North, on the other hand, felt that the northern manufacturers would benefit from high tariffs.

The overshadowing issue, however, was slavery. The south feared that the federal government would prohibit slavery in the western part of the United States—the territories. If this happened, the Southerners reasoned, the number of "free" states would far outnumber the slave states, thereby endangering the lifestyle and property of existing slaveholders.

The War Between the States resulted in hundreds of thousands of deaths, many of them agonizing. The conditions under which the soldiers of both sides were forced to live contributed to sickness and infection. One of the worst hellholes in a hellish war was a twenty-six acre expanse of swamp in the backwoods of Georgia known as Andersonville. It was a Confederate prison camp, "home" to thousands of Union soldiers. The conditions were hideous. At one time, more than 3,000 prisoners died each month.

One of the legions of miserable inmates was twenty-five year old Isaac Cooper. He spent his days trying to survive amidst the filth and starvation of the camp and his nights dreaming of the Colorado Rockies where he had prospected in 1859. He prayed for deliverance from the incarceration and for a return to his childhood home. He was to realize both wishes. At the end of the war in 1865, he left Andersonville weak, half-starved, but alive. He traveled to

Glenwood, Iowa, where he met Sarah Field. They were married in about 1871.

By the 1860s, the Ute tribe had formed into seven more or less distinctive bands. The separate clans met at a rendezvous at least once a year to trade goods and information, hold ceremonies, and to provide the opportunity for courtship between the young people. They also joined forces in times of conflict with other tribes, and to stage extended hunts, especially into enemy territory. There was much cooperation between the bands, but it was considered disrespectful to hunt in the territory of another band without express permission.

Two early inhabitants of the Roaring Fork Valley. (Courtesy of Frontier Historical Society)

The Weeminuche band lived in the San Juan River Valley, in northwestern New Mexico, and in southeastern Utah. The Capote clan occupied the San Luis Valley, and the Mouache covered south central Colorado and northern New Mexico. The Tabeguache band lived on and near the Uncompahgre Plateau in western Colorado, as well as in the Gunnison River Valley. The Parianucs moved up and down the Grand River with the seasons, and the Yampa band occupied the Yampa River Valley. The Unitah band lived between the Great Salt Lake and the Unitah River in Utah.

Ouray, a Tabeguache Ute, was universally recognized by the whites as the most influential leader of the Utes. He was the man who spoke for the tribe in dealing with the white man's government. He had risen to leadership of the Tabeguache clan after the retirement of Nevava, the old chief. Ouray was highly intelligent, and spoke Apache, Spanish, and English, in addition to Ute. He was instrumental, from 1859 on, in all of the Ute's various treaties. Even though the treaties became more and more restrictive of the Ute's freedom, it was generally felt that Ouray's negotiating skills won more concessions for his people than would have been possible under other leadership.

In 1863, John Evans was the governor of Colorado Territory. He and his associates negotiated another treaty with Ouray and the Utes. The gist of the agreement was that the Utes would surrender a large tract of land west of the Continental Divide. They had already been pushed out of most of eastern Colorado by the influx of prospectors into the Front Range of the Rockies. However, the Utes still held a huge area embracing the entire southwestern corner of the Colorado Territory.

Governor A. C. Hunt and his followers negotiated yet another treaty in March of 1868, fixing the east line of the reservation as the 107th meridian and the north boundary as a line fifteen miles to the north of the fortieth parallel. The 107th meridian ran about ten miles

Ute Indians in full ceremonial regalia. (Courtesy of Frontier Historical Society)

to the west of Ute City, later to be called Aspen. Consequently, Ute City and the upper Roaring Fork Valley were outside the reservation, while the remainder of the valley, including the site of Grand Springs, was still Ute territory. Ute City was beginning to attract the attention of the prospectors, due to the appearance of silver ore in a few of the diggings. The new treaty legitimized the prospecting in the hills around Ute City, but the lower reaches of the valley were legally off limits. This fact did not prevent the occasional foray onto the reservation, but the attitudes of the Utes were beginning to change toward the trespassers. They had already been pushed out of many of their ancestral hunting and gathering places in their beloved mountains.

The 1868 treaty was generally viewed as a victory by Chief Ouray, even though it further limited the territory of the tribe. The treaty was considered to be the most favorable ever negotiated by an Indian tribe. This viewpoint stemmed from the fact that the treaty called for the barring of all non-Utes from entering much of the Western Slope of Colorado, and further dictated the eviction of those already there. At a time when most other tribes had already been relegated to reservation life, the Utes roamed at least part of their former hunting grounds unimpeded.

Chief Ouray had traveled extensively, and had seen the steady increase in prospectors, settlers, trappers, and explorers. He had no illusions about the fickle nature of the white man's government. Nonetheless, the whites had been banned from his homeland, and for a time, the Utes continued their free lifestyle relatively unmolested.

In 1868, an Indian agency was established on the White River some sixty miles northwest of the location of Grand Springs. The agency, one of several to be set up across the west around that time, was intended to offer aid to the Ute tribe. Eleven years later, the White River Agency was to be the location of an incident that changed forever the future of the Ute Indian tribe.

CHAPTER FIVE

From 1870 to 1880

"The Utes must go!"

The rallying cry of the Denver newspapers,
most notably the *Denver Tribune*

By 1870, the relentless migration of whites had reached the Continental Divide, and more and more of them were trickling down the Western Slope of the Rockies. A small group of prospectors, mindless of the government's ban, built a cabin on Rock Creek, later called the Crystal River. They lived there for some time, before the Utes drove them out and burned their cabin to the ground.

What has become known as the "Hayden Survey" was performed in western Colorado in the early 1870s. Ferdinand Vandiveer Hayden directed a group of surveyors who measured, mapped, and even named much of the area around the future site of Glenwood Springs. They noted the presence of coal and oil shale deposits, took the first accurate measurements of Mount Sopris, and named the Grand Hogback. They reported on the geography, the geology, the animal life, and the vegetation of the area. The maps that resulted from the extensive survey were the first introduction to western Colorado for many of the eventual settlers in the area.

Western photographer William Henry Jackson was roaming the area with the Hayden Survey party, using glass plate negatives to capture much of the scenic beauty. Reportedly, Jackson went to the effort of climbing many of the peaks to obtain panoramic views. Unfortunately, as the story goes, he was using a mule named Gimlet to carry the glass plates. Gimlet managed to fall somewhere in the Roaring Fork Valley and break most of them.

Meanwhile, John Henry Holliday graduated from the Pennsylvania College of Dental Surgery, and opened his first dental office in Atlanta, Georgia. Holliday was, by all accounts, a true southern gentleman. He was about five feet ten inches tall, slender, well dressed and soft-spoken. Unfortunately for his dental career, he contracted consumption, which we know today as tuberculosis. His weak lungs were further aggravated by the warm, humid climate of his home state. His uncle, John S. Holliday, originally diagnosed his disease and recommended that "Doc" seek a drier climate. It was not long before he did just that, heading for the American West.

By 1874, the discontent of the Utes was increasing. Gold had been discovered in the San Juan Mountains, which of course lured another flood of eager fortune seekers into the area. Many of the Utes favored violent retaliation, but Chief Ouray insisted that his people would be better served by peaceful negotiation than by armed conflict. This attitude did little to pacify many of the Utes, including Colorow, who was by now Chief of the "White River" Utes, a splinter group of the Yampa clan.

The government felt that another treaty was in order. They proposed that the Utes give up almost four million acres in the middle of the San Juan Mountains, which was coincidentally in the middle of the remaining Ute lands. A delegation of Utes, including Ouray, was escorted to the nation's capital and treated like royalty. They received full state protocol, gifts, and decorations, were wined and dined, and generally shown off to Washington society. The Utes dressed in white man's finery for the ceremonies. However, Chipeta,

Colorow and part of his White River band of Utes. Colorow is seated in the center of the picture. (Courtesy of John Tindall)

Chief Ouray and his wife Chipeta, seated in the center of the front row, other members of the Ute tribe and various white dignitaries during treaty negotiations in Washington, D.C. (Courtesy of Frontier Historical Society)

Ouray's wife, dressed in white buckskins. She was the darling of the Washington social set.

In return for the relinquishment of their land, the Utes were promised some $60,000 in annuities and allotments, (which they never received). There was much resistance to the signing of the document, but what was to be known as the Brunot Treaty was finally signed by Chief Ouray. Unfortunately, as part of the government's concessions, Ouray was awarded a salary of $1,000 a year, a house, and 160 acres of land near present-day Montrose. Chipeta was given new furniture for their home. In the eyes of many of the Utes, Ouray had sold out to the whites. He was accused of treason, and there were several attempts on his life. Discontent was again growing.

In 1875, Isaac Cooper finally returned to the mountains of Colorado. He had spent the previous few years in business in Glenwood, Iowa, saving against the day when he could return to the west. He began mining and promotional work in the mountains to the west of Denver, in Boulder, Clear Creek, and Gilpin counties.

Colorado became the thirty-eighth state on August 1, 1876. It was a time of great change, of high excitement in the new state, indeed in the entire

Chipeta, wife of Ouray. (Courtesy of Frontier Historical Society)

country. Thomas Edison was just about to demonstrate the first incandescent light and was adapting the mysterious force of electricity for home use. The twin steel ribbons of railroads were creeping all across the eastern third of the nation, and the population of the United States was approaching fifty million.

Perhaps it was a portent of things to come when the Cheyenne and Sioux Indians of Montana annihilated General George Armstrong Custer and 264 men under his command. Custer was a national hero, and the news of the massacre both terrified and enraged the white settlers and prospectors who continued to "invade" Colorado.

Another development that was to have far-reaching effects on the relationships between the whites and the Ute Indians occurred in 1878. Nathan C. Meeker was appointed as Indian Agent for the White River Agency on March 18 of that year. Meeker, an Ohio native, had been working for the *New York Tribune* when he was assigned the task of writing an article about Utah. While traveling to the western state, his train was halted in Wyoming by a November snowstorm. He changed his plans and returned back east to Cheyenne. While there, he spawned a plan to create a "Union Colony of Colorado." He envisioned a community of people with "good moral character," a cooperative society dedicated to temperance. Each person would be required to deposit $145 to a fund that would be used to purchase a tract of fertile land. They would build a town, and each of the residents could buy up to 160 acres for farming. Horace Greeley, the editor of the *New York Tribune,* liked the scheme, and threw his support and influence behind Meeker. Meeker named the resulting town Greeley, after his benefactor.

Meeker was not held in favor by many of the residents of the new town on the high plains of Colorado. He insisted on an almost impossibly high moral structure, and his "holier-than-thou" attitude annoyed the settlers. After Horace Greeley died in 1872, Meeker found himself in financial difficulties. He owed Greeley's estate $1,000, and he had no means to repay it. The trying times brought out the worst in him. He became even more brusque and tactless. It seemed as though he was striving to be unpleasant. In an attempt to obtain funds, he applied for a position as an Indian Agent, and was successful. He left Greeley on May 3, 1878 for the White River Agency.

High in the Rockies, long-ago geological forces had formed a layer of limestone many feet thick. The limestone was made of calcium carbonate, and was subject to "intrusions," or voids that contained veins of other minerals. Some of these intrusions contained such things as lead and gold and silver ore, which naturally attracted a great deal of attention. The word of huge deposits of precious metals brought hordes of hopefuls to the new mining camp of Leadville, Colorado. Isaac Cooper joined the throngs, and lived and prospected in Leadville for about two years. Leadville, which sits at an elevation of 10,200 feet, was aptly named "The Cloud City." The rarefied air, ample snow during all but a few of the summer months, and the raw north wind combined to make living and working conditions challenging, at the very least. Notwithstanding the brutal environment, the rush to Leadville was on, and there seemed to be no stopping the stampede. It was estimated that, by 1878, as many as 5,000 immigrants were pouring into Colorado on a daily basis. Of those, approximately 500 per day were making their way to Leadville.

Other prospectors who had not "struck it rich" in Leadville moved down to the Eagle River Valley, just to the east of the big canyon that engulfed the Grand River. John Blake, "Frenchy" Cleiopfar, and W. M. Bell then proceeded to follow an ancient Indian trail up onto the Flat Tops. They were searching for signs of precious metals, evidence of gold or silver-bearing ore. Not far up the trail, they met a man named George P. Ryan. Ryan was from Philadelphia, and was a wealthy hunter and adventurer. He had spent some time wandering about in the Ute Reservation, high in the Flat Tops, and he told them of a discovery he had made at an elevation of almost 10,800 feet. A prehistoric lake had left a three inch layer of carbonate that spread over a large area. He and his three new-found friends were excited by this discovery, because the cap of carbonate resembled a similar layer at Leadville. Having arrived in the Cloud City too late to capitalize on the fabulous riches that were being pulled from the ground there, Cleiopfar, Bell and Blake felt certain that they had discovered another bonanza. Ill-equipped to survive the winter at the site of their discovery, they all left the Flat Tops that autumn. Ryan headed back east to "civilization," and the other three men made their way back to Leadville. They were surprised to find that the population had grown from around 500 to nearly 20,000.

Unbelievably, the population of Leadville was to reach 40,000. The resultant sprawl of humanity obviously resulted in appalling living conditions for the majority of the populace. There was no room left for the latecomers to live or to prospect. A few of the more opportunistic turned to other pursuits to earn a living; hunting, fishing, or providing goods and services to the remainder of the residents. One of these entrepreneurs was James M. Landis. He owned several head of donkeys, and he harvested grass hay with a hand scythe in the meadows of the mountains and utilized them to haul it back to Leadville to be sold as horse feed. In 1878, he worked his way over Hunter Pass, (later to be known as Independence Pass), and down the Roaring Fork Valley into Indian country. He met no opposition, so he continued on down the river to where the Roaring Fork met the Grand River. He had heard of the place which Richard

Sopris had named Grand Springs, but this was the first time he laid eyes on it.

There was deep grass hay in abundance, but that was not all. The wild hay gave way to sagebrush, then to scrub oak. Higher, tall pines covered the surrounding mountains, dotted with patches of aspen. The Grand River appeared out of a deep canyon to the east, swallowed the waters of the Roaring Fork in the middle of the valley, and disappeared between almost vertical slabs of sandstone to the west. There were few passable routes into or out of the valley. One was the route that Landis had used, the Roaring Fork Valley. What appeared to be an ancient Indian trail climbed the high, flat-topped mountains to the north. A couple of smaller cuts, made by what were to be known as Three Mile Creek and Four Mile Creek, led up into the mountains to the south and west of the valley.

The resident Utes welcomed Landis, and invited him to use the structure that they had built over one of the hot springs. Landis contrasted this inviting valley, the lush vegetation, the hot springs, and the warm, soft air to the harsh, bitter wind and the bustle of Leadville. He vowed then and there to return to the valley of Grand Springs and to make it his home. The following spring, in the year of 1879, he did just that. Although the land of the valley still "belonged" to the Indians, Landis returned and built a small log cabin. It is not recorded what the attitude of the Utes was to this trespassing, but he was apparently accepted by them.

Word of the carbonate deposit high in the Flat Tops spread, and the spring of 1879 found an eager group of miners camped at the east end of the Grand River Canyon, waiting for the winter's accumulation of snow to melt enough to allow them access to the high country. The camp took on the name of Dotsero. There are at least three theories about the origin of the name. One has it that a "witness" corner, or a "dot zero" (.o) had been established at that location. A witness corner is a reference point used in surveying and mapmaking. Another story claims that dotsero is an Indian word meaning "new earth," referring to the volcanic crater that is still visible to the north of the interstate highway that bisects the valley today. Still another story claims that the town was named for the daughter of an Indian chief. It is likely that the name did in fact come from an Indian word, for it appears that the name was originally used in about 1883. The survey crews did not begin working in the area until 1885.

Whatever the derivation of the name, it stuck. As the miners waited for warmer weather, they spent part of their time establishing a set of rules of conduct for themselves and those to come later. They declared that the legal size of any claim was to be 300 feet by 1500 feet, and also that such pastimes as claim jumping would be dealt with harshly.

In addition to the miners, other entrepreneurs arrived in the new little camp. Nels and Doc Yost brought in a freight wagon of liquor, and established a saloon. Ellen O'Neal freighted in the supplies and equipment to open a restaurant, and Frank Belding started a dry goods and general merchandise store. By the time the snows finally receded enough to allow passage to the site of the new bonanza, they had become so well established that they stayed, and the town of Dotsero was born.

The camp of Dotsero was outside the boundaries of the Ute Reservation, but most of the old Indian trail and certainly the site of the ancient lake bed were well within Indian lands. This fact obviously did not deter the eager prospectors, but they did build a log fort near a tributary of the Grand River called Wagon Gulch. The fort was some distance from the lake bed, but it was felt that the location was less vulnerable. They named it Fort Defiance, quite probably to express their attitude toward the Indians in general and the United States' treaties in particular.

In June of 1879, prospecting also began at the site of Ute Spring, up near the headwaters of the Roaring Fork River. The miners were finding mostly silver which of course brought another hungry flood of prospectors. The resultant camp became known as Ute City, and later Aspen.

By 1879, the new state of Colorado was the scene of almost frantic prospecting and mining activity. More and more hopefuls were pouring into the state from the eastern United States, from Europe, from Canada and Mexico. It is hardly surprising that there was great resentment among the immigrants that a large portion of the western and southwestern parts of the state was still held by the Indians. There was increasing oratory and numerous newspaper editorials calling for the removal of the "savages" from Colorado. "The Utes Must Go!" was the rallying cry, and it was being heard more and more frequently.

Then, on September 29, 1879, a relatively small group of Utes was to inadvertently seal the fate of the entire tribe. Nathan Meeker, the Indian Agent at the White River Agency, was not looked upon with favor by very many of the Utes under his care. Meeker's attitude, indeed the prevailing attitude of the United States Government, was that the Utes should be trained to be farmers. By tilling the soil, it was reasoned, the Indians could produce foodstuffs to support themselves. Not only that, but an Indian busy plowing a field or harvesting the fruits of his labors would not be an Indian out running around in the hills, annoying the ever-increasing population of white prospectors and settlers. They could not understand why a people who had spent the last few thousand years hunting and gathering, wandering free through their mountains, could not be persuaded to cheerfully put down their spears and bows and pick up a hoe or a plow handle.

Because of Meeker's insistence that the Utes submit to what amounted to domestication, there was a great deal of unrest and resentment toward him. In August of 1879, a Chief by the name of Jack, or Captain Jack, traveled to Denver to complain to Governor Pitkin about Meeker. When Meeker found out about the complaint, he told Jack that he should be hanged for disloyalty.

The large herd of horses that were owned by the White River Utes was another problem for Meeker. The Indian ponies required several acres of pasture along the White River, land which Meeker felt could be put to better use as farmland. In September he ordered one of his men, Shadrach Price, to plow up 200 acres of the lush pasture, to be used for the planting of winter wheat. It was obviously meant to be a test of wills.

Two of the Utes named Jane and Antelope immediately protested to Meeker, who chose to ignore them. Not long after that a few rifle bullets were fired out of the sagebrush, narrowly missing Meeker's plowman. Price declined to do any more plowing until the matter was settled.

For most of the next week, meetings were held between Meeker, Jack, and another chief named Douglas. The situation became even more heated when a Ute medicine man named Johnson came to Meeker's office to complain. Meeker met Johnson's protests by telling the medicine man that he had too many ponies, and that perhaps some of them should be killed. At that, Johnson physically attacked Meeker, pushing him out through the door of the office and against a hitching rail outside. Two of the White River Agency employees restrained Johnson, and the angry Ute stalked away.

The next day, Meeker wrote to both Governor Pitkin and to Senator Teller, informing them of the incident. He also sent a telegram to United States Commissioner Hayt, requesting armed protection. In response, orders were sent to Major Thornburgh at Fort Steele, Wyoming Territory, to immediately move toward the White River Agency. They moved out toward the agency on September twenty-third. The expedition consisted of 153 soldiers and twenty-five civilians. It took them several days to reach the reservation boundary at Milk Creek. When they crossed into Indian territory, the Utes took that action to be an act of war and attacked the soldiers. There were an estimated 300 to 400 Indians, led by Jack and Colorow, well-positioned in the hills above the soldiers, and they began firing on the troops. The soldiers circled their wagons and used flour sacks and bedding for additional fortification. Early in the battle, Major Thornburgh was killed by an Indian marksman while trying to ride back to the circled wagons. The siege lasted for most of a week, with many casualties on both sides. During a forced march to lend assistance to Thornburgh and his men, Captain James McCann and his Rocky Mountain Rifle Mounties camped at the site of the courthouse in present day Glenwood Springs. Finally a relief column arrived at Milk Creek on October 5, and the Utes faded back into the hills.

At about the same time as the initial attack on Major Thornburgh's party, events were coming to a head at the agency. As one of the white women, Flora Ellen Price, walked across the compound of the agency, she saw Chief Douglas and several other Indians. She was disturbed to see that some of them were armed. As she watched, the Utes raised their rifles and fired upon some of the white employees who were working on the roof of a new building, hitting at least two of them.

In the ensuing melee, another of the employees named Frank Dresser, Meeker's wife Arvilla and his daughter Josie, and Flora Price and her two children took refuge in an adobe milkhouse. They hid there for several hours, listening to the gunfire outside. Arvilla was greatly concerned about the fate of her husband. At dusk, the fugitives made a break for it, running across a plowed field toward the sagebrush beyond. The Indians gave chase, firing in their direction. Arvilla Meeker was struck in the leg by a bullet, and the Indians captured them. They took them back to the agency where some of the buildings were on fire. Dresser was able to escape across the fields while the Utes were occupied with the women.

Arvilla saw a body on the ground, and as they approached it, she saw that it was her husband. He had been shot in the side of his head. One account of the incident claims that Nathan Meeker had been pinned to the ground by a stake driven through his mouth, "to silence his infernal lying." However, journals later written by Arvilla Meeker make no mention of it.

The Utes killed eleven other whites besides Meeker and looted and burned the agency. Taking their captives, they left the area and headed southwest. They traveled through western Colorado for twenty-three days before they were finally persuaded to release their prisoners. It was a mutual effort of Chief Ouray and several white officials that finally won their freedom. There are differing accounts as to the treatment that the white women suffered at the hands of the Indians, but they did survive. Ouray was in ill health at the time

Monument erected by Rio Blanco County commemorating the Meeker Massacre. (Photo by the author)

of the "Meeker Massacre," and the incident greatly saddened him. It was said that he considered suicide when he heard of it.

Not surprisingly, the Meeker Massacre was the catalyst that resulted in the ouster of the Ute Indians from western Colorado. The white settlers were of course incensed, and felt quite vindicated in their attitudes toward the Indians. Under some duress, a great many of the Utes signed the resultant relocation agreement with the United States Government. According to one source, a government representative paid two dollars to each man who would sign the agreement. Governor Pitkin sent a courier to the Roaring Fork Valley to warn whites of the dangers of Indian attack. All but two of the residents of Ute City left, only to return after things settled down a bit.

There is a story about the Smuggler Mine near Ute City, which may or may not be true. According to this account, a prospector shot at a deer near his camp. He missed, and the deer ran toward Smuggler Mountain. He followed it and succeeded in killing it. As he was dressing the animal, he noticed a promising outcropping of rock and staked a claim on it. Just then another prospector happened by on a mule. The two struck up a conversation, and the deer hunter was persuaded to sell the claim to the other man for fifty dollars and the mule. The Smuggler Mine and related properties eventually produced about $97,000,000 in ore, including the largest silver nugget ever mined. It weighed 1,840 pounds.

CHAPTER SIX

From 1880 to 1885

"On the morning of September 7, 1881, the last of the Utes were passed in junction of the Colorado and Gunnison Rivers—if one stood on Pinon Mesa, what a march of retreating civilization he could have seen! Here was the last defeat of the red man. Here the frontiers of the white man met, crushing the Utes in its mighty embrace. What a sight to see the vanquished shift from the last scene of action."

> Walker D. Wyman, in what has been called the classic description of the Utes' forced march to the reservation in Utah

B. Clark Wheeler was known to be a venturesome promoter. He and Charles A. Hallam had acquired an option on several properties in and around Ute City. He arrived in Leadville in 1880, and made it known that he planned to snowshoe over Hunter Pass. The pass, just to the west of Leadville, climbed to around 12,000 feet, well above timberline. On the other side lay Ute City, later to be called Aspen, site of several silver strikes. Wheeler had made a down payment on the mining properties sight unseen, and he wanted to take a look at them. Isaac Cooper offered to accompany him. Leadville was terribly crowded, and Cooper wanted to take a look at the largely unexplored areas to the west. He had heard tales of hot springs and a vapor cave near where the Roaring Fork River fed into the Grand. He was aware that it was still Indian country, but he had to see the place for himself.

Wheeler, Cooper, Dr. Richardson, and Jack King left Leadville in February. It took them ten days to traverse the sixty miles to Ute City. The snowdrifts were huge, the temperature well below zero, and the trail nonexistent. When they finally reached Ute City, they found a population of thirteen.

In the spring of 1880, James Landis returned to the valley of Grand Springs and "squatted," or filed for squatters' rights on 160 acres of land at the confluence of the Roaring Fork and the Grand rivers. The Utes were still in residence, but they were accustomed to Landis and his cabin by then, and there was no effort to "evict" him, even though Colorow and Captain Jack spent much of 1879 and 1880 roaming the Roaring Fork Valley, running off settlers and prospectors.

Later in 1880, the Ute lands were formally opened for settlement. The Meeker Massacre had served to hasten an action that was probably inevitable, given the crush of white humanity seeking "greener pastures" in the west. The proclamation by the government brought a fresh influx of hopefuls, while legitimizing the likes of Landis, Bell, Blake, Cleiopfar and the others who were already in residence.

Even though it was still difficult to get to the Grand Springs Valley, Landis was not to be the only white resident for long. Perhaps it was the aftermath of the Meeker Massacre, perhaps it was a sort of grudging acceptance of the intrusion of the white man into their world, but the Utes and the very earliest white settlers to the Grand Springs area apparently coexisted quite peacefully. The Utes had built a hogan on the south side of the river, covering the entrance to a limestone cave. The cave contained hot mineral springs, from which issued strong-smelling but comforting vapors. The Utes had used the cave for centuries to relax them, to cleanse them, and to heal their aches. They also on occasion used the cave as a medium of punishment for recalcitrant braves. It was no doubt terrifying to be trapped in the cave with no light or ventilation, and it was reportedly quite effective.

With the opening of the Ute lands, little stood in the way of white settlement. The canyon on the Grand River, between Grand Springs and Dotsero, remained impassable. However, both ends of it were to see the encroachment of white settlement. A large expanse of grass and sagebrush to the south of the Grand and just inside the east entrance of the canyon was settled by Ike Barrier in 1880. The resulting property was eventually to become the Bair Ranch.

Just inside the west end of the canyon, east of the dramatic curvature of the Grand River known as Horseshoe Bend, a small town was established in 1880. It was initially called Cobblehurst, but it was destined to acquire another rather odd name. One version of the story says that when the Colorado State Government sent out questionnaires to the numerous small communities that were dotting the state, there was apparently some uncertainty as to the official name of Cobblehurst. In any event, the questionnaire was returned to the state offices with "No Name" written in the space reserved for the name of the town. In a remarkably early example of governmental lethargy, "No Name" was dutifully recorded, and the name was to stick. Another version of the origin of the name of the little settlement claims that it was named for nearby No Name Creek. Whatever the source of the strange moniker, it has provided a chuckle for several generations of travelers.

By the middle of 1880, Chief Ouray was quite ill. However, he was to be subjected to one more treaty. With a negotiating position crippled by the Meeker incident, the Utes had little choice but to sign the new agreement. The document further defined boundaries for the Southern Ute Reservation, and forced the Northern Ute bands to release their already weakened hold on Colorado and to move to a reservation in Utah. It was to be one of the final official acts for the chief who had served his people for so long. Ouray died on August 24, 1880. He was succeeded by Ignacio as overall chief of the Utes.

Frenchy Cleiopfar had a disagreement with his two partners, Blake and Bell. He moved farther down another of the creeks that cut the north rim of the great canyon and built his own cabin there. The creek, not far from the eastern end of the canyon, became known as French Creek. Near the west end of the canyon, Grizzly Creek got its name in 1881 when George P. Ryan killed a particularly large bear near the waterway. Ryan was a hunter, prospector, and rancher, and was one of Garfield County's early commissioners.

Meanwhile, John Blake and W. M. Bell, with the help of James Landis, Joseph Long, D. Cole, C. C. Davis, Rufus Coates, and Henry Blake, filed for a townsite to be called Defiance. The 640 acre Defiance development took in not only the original Fort Defiance but also a great deal of territory on both sides of the Grand River. The plat of the townsite mentioned the fact that Grizzly Peak was visible to the west of the site's location. Promising outcroppings of rock prompted the town's founders, as well as several others, to file claims in the area, which was located some six miles east of Grand Springs. They advertised in the Leadville newspaper, offering free lots to the first to make their homes in the community. They predicted a population of 5,000 by the fall of that year. They were, as it turned out, quite overly optimistic. Little was to come of their grandiose plans.

Mrs. E. M. Landis, James' mother, sold her farm in Kansas and moved to the Grand Springs Valley in the spring of 1881, bringing milk cows and needed supplies to what was to become her new home. She thus became perhaps the first white woman to ever see the valley, and certainly the first to settle there.

According to the agreement reached in 1880 between the Ute chiefs and the Unites States Government, the Utes were to move to the reservation in Utah in 1881. All of the Utes moved to eastern Utah except the Uncompahgres and the Southern Utes. The Uncompahgres were to have been moved to designated spots along the Grand River near the western border of Colorado, but they refused to do so. Finally, they were forced to move to the reservation with the others. Repeated unsuccessful attempts were made to move the Southern Utes out of the state.

According to the *Ouray Times* the movement of the White River Utes consisted of, "1458 braves, women and children, with 10,000 sheep and 8,000 ponies." Colonel MacKenzie from Fort Garland, along with nine companies of infantry and nine companies of cavalry, were assigned to ensure that the move took place with no resistance. Even then Colorow and about fifty braves charged the massed troops the night before the scheduled departure and had to be subdued.

It has been said, with appreciable justification, that the white man would have starved to death on the lands on which he forced the Native Americans to live.

At about this time, Kit Carson, the son of the famous mountain man and army scout of the same name, began operating a stage line over Hunter Pass from Leadville to Ute City. In the winter of 1881 his horses, as well as those of other freighters, developed a strange hoof disease that, if left unattended, would eventually cripple the animals. William Farnum, a freighter, was said to have lost his entire herd to the mysterious ailment. When Carson's horses began showing signs of the disease, he remembered tales of the Utes taking their sick and wounded to the medicinal hot springs by the Grand River. He drove his entire stock down the Roaring Fork Valley to the springs. After standing in the hot water and mud for some hours, the horses were cured. The fame of the hot springs was spreading.

Yomas (Jonas) Lindgren, one of the earliest settlers in the Grand Springs area, became the first to use the hot springs commercially. He had been born in Sweden in 1854 and had immigrated to the United States in 1877. After working at iron mining in Michigan and quartz mining in Leadville, he came to Grand Springs in 1881 to "take the waters." Jonas suffered from rheumatism, and he had heard from the Indians of the comforting qualities of the hot mineral water. There were many hot springs along both sides of the Grand at that time. Estimates range from thirteen to over fifty. The largest and hottest of these was on the north bank of the river and provided a rather impressive flow of 122 degree water. Lindgren painfully hewed a crude bathtub out of a large log. He would fill the tub partway with the steaming water and then temper it with cold water from the river. Having achieved a bearable temperature, he would immerse himself in the hot liquid and soak away his aches.

It was not long before others, settlers and stage and freight drivers, were stopping by for a relaxing soak. Jonas, spotting an opportunity, began charging ten cents for the use of his tub. For the dime admission, he provided just that, the tub. The bathers carried their own water and were offered neither roof, towel, nor privacy. Apparently no one minded all that much, as the waters were said to cure such things as influenza, croup, sinus problems, and the occasional case of lead poisoning. Reportedly, Jonas made enough from his early "hot tub" to set himself up in farming. He homesteaded in the Gypsum Valley area and ultimately owned a ranch of some 200 acres.

Dead Horse Creek, the east fork of which feeds a geological phenomenon on the north wall of Glenwood Canyon called Hanging Lake, was named in 1881. A group of prospectors who were working the north rim of the canyon lost a pack horse over a steep cliff in the area, and the creek got its name.

On October 26, 1881, one of the most famous gun battles of the old west was to take place near the OK Corral in Tombstone, Arizona. The battle was said to have taken all of twenty-eight seconds. It was between the Clantons and the McLaurys on one side, and the Earp brothers and John Henry "Doc" Holliday on the other. The Earps and Holliday were successful in killing three of the "bad guys" and also in forever ensuring their places in western history.

Ute City was incorporated as Aspen in 1881. The first issue of the *Aspen Times* was published that year, and the former mining camp continued to gain both population by the thousands and mining claims by the hundreds.

In 1882, according to local legend, pioneer Mike Callahan inadvertently discovered the properties of oil shale. There had been stories of the "rock that burns" from the Ute Indians, but Callahan gave that eventuality little thought as he built his new cabin near Parachute Creek in western Garfield County. The cabin was of course made of logs, and one of its nicest features was a handsome stone fireplace which Callahan had crafted out of local shale. The stone tended to fracture in parallel lines, so it was a simple matter to lay the flat, grayish-striped rock. Unfortunately the roaring fire that he built to celebrate his housewarming melted the oil from the shale, eventually igniting and burning the entire cabin.

Isaac Cooper had never really recovered from the physical stress and illness that he had suffered as a Civil War prisoner at Andersonville. It may have been his infirmity that lured him to the hot mineral springs of Grand Springs, but it was a vision of the future that kept him there. After arriving at the valley and sampling the hot springs and the vapor cave, Cooper determined that he had found his new home. He and several others, including John Blake, William Gelder, and Frank Anzensperger formed the Defiance Town and Land Company in 1882 and purchased James Landis' original 160 acre claim from him for $1,500.

Altogether the land company acquired some 400 acres. Cooper was the majority owner of the company, holding seven-twelfths of the stock. Since the original Defiance development had come to almost nothing, Blake and the others pulled a rather remarkable bit of sleight-of-hand. By changing the direction of the Grizzly Peak sighting on the original Defiance filing, they magically "moved" the Defiance townsite some six miles to the west. It may have been

Very early valley residents and their homes. The taller gentleman is said to be Perry Malaby. (Courtesy of Frontier Historical Society)

a bit creative, but it did eliminate the necessity of filing for a new townsite designation. They laid out the plat of the new townsite, naming the main north and south street "Cooper Avenue."

Also in 1882, James Landis filed on some additional claims along the river, including the site of the Indian's vapor cave. He also used the money from the sale of the 160 acres to Cooper and his associates to acquire a ranch in Spring Valley, to the southeast of Defiance, and also property at the site of the carbonate deposit on the Flat Tops. He then married a lady by the name of Dolly Barlow. Their first child, a son named Harry, was to be the first white child born in Garfield County. Landis built a new home for his family and established himself in business in the new town.

Initially Defiance was largely composed of tents of various sizes, plus a scattering of dugouts, log structures partially sunk into a hillside. Fred A. Barlow, Dolly's brother, opened a restaurant/hotel in one of the larger tents and later established the first post office. In fact, the new little town was known as "Barlow" on postal records for a short period of time. Miss Lucy Peebles was the first to hold

Dugout from about 1883 - believed to be that of Fred Barlow, early hotelier/ postmaster. (Courtesy of Frontier Historical Society)

classes in one of the tents, and Martin Van Buren Blood, who had built the Broken Rib Saw Mill, the first on the Flat Tops, also taught a few pupils. Blood was also a notary public, and he was kept quite busy handling the legal forms necessary for the new residents of the county to file claims to land and mines.

Isaac Cooper brought his family from their home in Glenwood, Iowa to Defiance. He had developed a vision of a world-class spa, a resort to be visited by the "rich and famous." Unfortunately, Defiance at that time was an untidy little community of haphazard tents and log structures. During much of the year, there was only one reliably usable hot spring. The openings of the others were low on the riverbank, and were usable only during times of low water. To bathe in them at other times was to risk drowning. In addition, access to the new little community was still quite limited. The big canyon to the east was still impenetrable, and "Hell's Gate," just west of town, consisted of steep sandstone slabs that began high on the mountains to each side and dove to the bottom of the river. In spite of Cooper's promotional efforts, few came to his "spa."

On February 10, 1883, a new county was formed. The new political subdivision which stretched from east of the Grand River Canyon to the Utah border was named Garfield, after James Garfield, the assassinated president. Prior to the formation of the new county

Isaac Cooper, standing at the center of the picture, had a vision of a world-class spa. (Courtesy of Frontier Historical Society)

that included the town of Defiance, the area had been part of Summit County.

The plat of Carbonate City was filed with the United States Land Office on April 5 of 1883. The fledgling town was also referred to as Carbonateville and simply as Carbonate. The townsite, which covered a full square mile around the ancient lake bed on the Flat Tops, was laid out with named streets. On April 13 of that year, the new little town acquired a post office. A sixteen mile toll road that partially followed the old Indian trail was built from Defiance to Carbonate. George P. Ryan sunk a 100 foot mine shaft near Carbonate, and several thousand prospectors made up the population of the little town. Shortly, Carbonate became the first county seat of the new county of Garfield. C. A. McBrairty, one of the major promoters of lot sales in Carbonate, became the first Garfield County clerk and recorder.

A drawing of Glenwood Springs by Flora Maxfield, dated 1883. The island shown in the Grand River was to become the future site of the Hot Springs Lodge and Pool. The tree upon which Captain Richard Sopris and his men carved their names was located on the island. (Courtesy of Frontier Historical Society)

In September of 1883, another town was incorporated next to Carbonate. It was named Siluria. There was a great deal of interest in the Carbonate area. Many people, including James Landis and B. Clark Wheeler, "declared occupancy" on 160 acre plots on the Flat Tops. The "Declaration of Occupancy" was the official document involved in establishing "Squatters' Rights." There was a lively market in mining claims for Carbonate. Many eastern investors bought and sold the claims sight unseen, much like the modern stock market.

Meanwhile down in the fledgling town of Defiance, activity was increasing. John Blake built the first real house at the corner of Seventh Street, or Riverfront, and Palmer. It was a small, two room affair, but it was an actual house. With a partner named Putnam, Blake also opened the first hardware and general merchandise store in town. Fred Barlow built the St. James Hotel, William Ragland opened a blacksmith shop, and Dick Donovan opened one of the first general stores. A Dr. Baldwin ran a pharmacy out of the back of a covered wagon, and a lady by the name of Thomas utilized one of

One of the establishments along Riverfront in 1884. (Courtesy of Frontier Historical Society)

the hot springs for a laundry. Two grocery stores opened in tents, and yet another tent with a false front served as a saloon. It was owned by Pat Carr.

A toll road was developed up the Roaring Fork Valley to Aspen, and soon Kit Carson's stage line was running a semi-weekly stagecoach on the route. Other stage lines of the day included the Barlow and Sanderson and the Western Stage Company. James Landis and Perry Malaby built the first bridge across the Grand River, and A. L. Chase built a crude ferry. Another hotel, called the Colorado, was built at the corner of Eighth and Grand.

The flurry of building in the early 1880s naturally made use of the ancient cottonwood trees that grew along the Grand River. The large tree which Richard Sopris and his party had used for their marker back in 1860 was sadly one of the first to fall.

It was at about this time that Isaac Cooper's wife Sarah grew weary of living in a town with the blustering, swaggering name of Defiance. She convinced her husband, and he in turn convinced the other city fathers, to change the name of the little town to Glenwood Springs, after their former home in Glenwood, Iowa. It is not recorded what the city officials thought of the idea, but nonetheless, the new name remained.

Walter Bourchier Devereux, his wife Mary, Walter, Jr., and William Gregory. (Courtesy of Frontier Historical Society)

The president of the Aspen Smelting Company, Jerome B. Wheeler, (no relation to B. Clark Wheeler), was faced with a problem. There was too little silver ore being produced in the Aspen area to justify the existence of his smelter. Walter Bourchier Devereux, who had been hired by Wheeler to manage the smelting operation, suggested to Wheeler that he create a market for silver ore in order to stimulate mining activity. Devereux was a mining engineer, a graduate of both Princeton and the Columbia School of Mines. He had come to Aspen in 1883, at the age of thirty. During the next two years, he was to obtain fourteen patents on inventions to improve the smelting industry.

Wheeler agreed with Devereux's plan and began purchasing ore, which initiated a great deal of activity in the mines around Aspen. He also invested in the mines themselves. Some estimates set his eventual total investment in the mining industry of Aspen at over six million dollars. Wheeler had come to Colorado a rich man and invested heavily not only in the mines but also in the Colorado Midland Railroad, banks in Aspen, Colorado City, and Manitou Springs, marble deposits up the Crystal River, and coal claims in Pitkin and Garfield counties.

By August of 1884, about a month's supply of ore had been accumulated, and the smelter was put into operation. Ore production continued to increase, and the Vallejo and the Spar mines began producing rich ore. Then, in December of 1884, a massive ore deposit was discovered in the Aspen Mine. Wheeler and Devereux formed the Aspen Mining and Smelting Company which consolidated the smelting operation with several mining properties. Walter Devereux was appointed to the position of manager of the new company.

Previously, Devereux had worked as a mining engineer in Michigan, in North Carolina, and in South Dakota. He went to Globe, Arizona in 1881 to manage the Takoma Copper Company and took with him his new wife, the former Mary Porter Gregory. They had become engaged in 1873 but were not married until October 28, 1880. Their time in Arizona was reportedly an adventurous one, as the Apache Indians were on the warpath for at least part of the two years that they spent there.

The Devereuxes had four children; Walter Jr., known as "Bourchier," William Gregory, Hester, and Alvin. Alvin was born in Glenwood Springs, while his older siblings were all born at Mary Gregory Devereux's family home in New York. All of the children

Part of the "Grand Hogback," coal-bearing formation that runs across Western Colorado. (Photo by the Author)

were born between 1881 and 1889. Hester died at the age of three in 1888.

The expanded activity at the smelter increased the demand for fuel. Coke, a product produced by heating coal under low oxygen conditions, was the ideal fuel for the smelting of ore. The heated coal basically melts, progressing through a "plastic" state, and ultimately forming a hard, porous substance which is almost totally composed of fixed carbon. When reignited, it burns hot, with little smoke. In the early days of smelting in Aspen, coke was hauled in wagons from Crested Butte, some thirty-five miles away on the other side of the Elk Mountains.

Devereux heard of coal deposits farther down the valley, and in 1886 he went in search of them. His travels brought him to the rather shabby little frontier settlement of Glenwood Springs. Isaac Cooper, never one to miss an opportunity, approached Devereux with his idea of a resort. Devereux had his mind set on coal exploration however, so he was less than receptive.

It did not take long for the young mining engineer to realize just how extensive the coal deposits were. A coal-bearing formation known as the Grand Hogback ran from southwest of Marble, north and west past New Castle and on to near Meeker. The Hogback boasted a thick seam of coal that ran through much of its length. Devereux explored the area of the Hogback and filed on numerous claims all along the seam. He then either developed them himself or leased the claims to towns or coal camps such as New Castle, South Canyon, Sunlight, Marion, and Spring Gulch. He was one of the principals in the Grand River Coal and Coke Company, and he hired F. H. A. Lyle to run the new company. They built fifty coke ovens, and wagonloads of coke were soon arriving at the smelters in Aspen.

It shortly became evident however, that even the six and eight-horse teams were not going to be adequate to haul the amount of coke needed to process the small mountains of ore that were being produced. A railroad, it was reasoned, would make it feasible to haul the ore to smelting plants better equipped to handle the volume. Also it appeared that the developing coal mines could produce sufficient amounts of coal to develop a coke production industry. The coke could also be shipped on a railroad to the same smelters, increasing the profits of the company. A railroad was sorely needed.

The Colorado Midland Railroad Company was incorporated, with John J. Hagerman, a wealthy entrepreneur from Colorado Springs, as president. Jerome Wheeler was vice-president, and many of the directors were residents of Colorado Springs who recognized the value of a rail line to the ore-rich mines of Aspen. They arranged a contract for the construction of a standard-gauge railroad from Colorado Springs on the eastern slope of the Rockies over Hagerman Pass and thence up the Roaring Fork Valley to Aspen.

At about the same time, the Burlington Railroad began preparing a railroad grade along the north side of the Grand River, heading east into the canyon. They graded to the present location of the highway tunnels and even started a tunnel before the project was abandoned due to massive costs.

The still-booming town of Leadville needed a coal supply for its smelters. They contacted the Denver & Rio Grande Railroad Company about building a rail line to the Glenwood Springs area. After much consideration, it was decided to build a narrow gauge line from Leadville, over Tennessee Pass, and down the Eagle River. That was the easy part. The final leg of the construction, the last eighteen miles or so, would have to go through the Grand River Canyon, which no human being had ever traversed from end to end.

It has been written that the Defiance Town and Land Company dug a second vapor cave on the south side of the river in 1883. The new cave was about 100 feet west of the original one. It was driven about 125 feet into the hillside, where a large spring was encountered. The original Indian cave, which was known as "Cave Number 1," had been increasingly utilized by the whites after the Meeker Massacre and the ouster of the Utes. In the name of modesty, the caves were used by the men in the mornings and by the ladies in the afternoons. The fee of admission was 25 cents. There is some question as to whether the second cave, imaginatively named "Cave Number 2," was ever completed.

All was not well in Carbonate. C. A. McBrairty, the Clerk and Recorder for Garfield County, was suspected of joining two other men, "Dad" McMullen and "Scarface Bill" Case, (or Casa) in "salting" assay samples from Carbonate with rich ore from Leadville. He was fired by the county commissioners for dereliction of duty, and in the fall of 1883, the county records were ordered brought to Glenwood Springs for safekeeping.

Bathhouse built over the old Ute vapor cave on the south side of the river. (Courtesy of Buzz Zancanella)

McBrairty promptly moved back off the Flat Tops down to the Dotsero area. There he began promotion of a spa and resort at the Siloam Springs, named for sacred springs in the Middle East. Along with Fred Metcalf and George Rust, they formed the Siloam Springs Sanitation and Town Company. They filed a town plat showing a bathhouse, a hospital, a depot, a hotel, a bridge, and sixty-two blocks of streets. Although only one building was ever completed and little evidence now exists, they did in fact develop a spa that was described by the *Colorado Exchange Journal* as "Colorado's Choicest Summer Resort."

On November 6, 1883, Glenwood Springs was designated as the permanent county seat. Perry Malaby and Charles Brown were paid a total of $12.50 to transport the county records down to Glenwood Springs. The first repository for the records was a dirt-floored dugout owned by Nims Ferguson.

The snows came early to the high country in the autumn of 1883. Some accounts say that it snowed nonstop for forty days and nights in Carbonate. The snows ultimately reached sixteen feet in depth, driving almost everyone out of the high country for the winter. After

About the only remaining trace of Carbonate, once said to have a population of 5,000. (Courtesy of Frontier Historical Society)

the heavy winter there were tree stumps in the area some ten to fourteen feet tall, testifying to the depth of the snow when the trees were felled by the persistent miners. There is some historical disagreement as to whether the unusually harsh winter was the impetus for the movement of the county records. The next spring the runoff from snowmelt was higher than any white man had ever seen. The runoff took out the bridge that had been built by Landis and Malaby. It also washed out the foundation of the proposed hotel at Siloam Springs.

The Grand River Bridge Company was formed to build another bridge across the river. It was a toll bridge, and it connected with Cooper Avenue which was the "main street" of Glenwood Springs. The tolls collected for use of the bridge were to be used for its replacement in case of another washout. Many of the earliest permanent buildings were built along Cooper Avenue, and the tents along "Riverfront," the street which ran along the south side of the river, gradually gave way to more substantial structures.

As part of the 1880 agreement between the Utes and the government, the Utes were

Colorow in his later years. He had developed a taste for biscuits and honey. (Courtesy of Frontier Historical Society)

allowed to return to western Colorado each summer to hunt in their ancestral hunting grounds. Consequently, early Glenwood Springs was, at least during the summer months, a mixture of whites and Indians. For the most part, they coexisted peacefully, but there was the occasional complaint by white housewives about Ute braves "mooching" food from them. Colorow, for instance, had a taste for biscuits and honey which might have accounted for his somewhat portly appearance later in life.

Cooper Avenue was filling up with buildings and businesses, and construction was increasing on Grand Avenue, one block to the west. The Mirror Saloon and Wholesale Liquors building was built in 1884 at 714 Grand Avenue. The Mirror Saloon Building houses the Glenwood Shoe Service in its present incarnation, but it still sits on its original cedar post foundation. It is the oldest building in present-day Glenwood Springs. Another of the very early buildings is the brick facade across the street at 701 Grand. Originally the Topic Bar, the building has also been a restaurant, a monument shop, a shoe repair store, a photography studio, and an import shop. The portion of the shop that faces Seventh Street originally had a wooden porch for viewing the river.

The estimated 200 or so residents of Glenwood Springs in early 1884 were still predominantly male. The little town was still quite primitive, with mud streets and no running water save the rivers, but it was approaching the stage where it would be considered habitable by women and children. As mentioned, John Landis married Dolly Barlow in 1882. However, Dolly was not the first bride in the valley. That honor goes to Mrs. Perry Malaby. Malaby went back to Iowa and returned to Glenwood Springs with his new wife. He built her a new home on the present location of the United States Post Office.

Fred Barlow's wife, Ella, started the closest thing to a hospital when she began caring for the sick in her home. When they moved to a larger house on East Eighth Street, it became known as the "Barlow Hospital." Meanwhile, her enterprising husband enlarged one of his buildings and opened a restaurant that became known as the "Venison House," due to its major menu item. Another restaurant started about that time, run by a man named Ennen. The tiny establishment was named the "Delmonico," perhaps with visions of rivaling the large New York restaurant of the same name.

The next in a series of Barlow hotels was constructed in 1884. It sat at the southeast corner of 8th and Cooper, and was an imposing three story structure. Later it would be known as the Grand Hotel, the Yampa Hotel, and also as the St. Joseph's Sanitorium.

Many of the early entrepreneurs in Glenwood Springs were quick to file claim to tracts of land in and around the fledgling city. Perry Malaby and John Manning, who were said to have brought the first wagon into the valley, filed on a ranch to the west of the Roaring Fork River near the Grand. Nims Ferguson claimed a large acreage to the north of the Grand River and east of Oasis Creek. He is said to have successfully hunted bear on his property for several years, until the continued growth drove the big mammals higher into the hills. Ferguson called his spread "Echo Park." Joe Enzensperger chose the west bank of the Roaring Fork, and Judge John Noonan settled at the junction of the two rivers. Hiram P. Bennett arrived from Denver and homesteaded land south of the downtown area.

John Blake, one of the founders of Defiance and reportedly the engineer of the somewhat mysterious shift of the townsite some six miles to the west, had somewhere acquired a common-law wife named Gussie. Since the town was still largely male, the two of them saw an opportunity. Gussie established the first reported "red light" operation in Glenwood Springs. Gussie and her associates, the "ladies of the evening," or "ladies of the brick," or "ladies of negotiable affection," became one of the first tourist attractions of the new town. Miners from Aspen and Leadville were known to travel to Glenwood Springs for the hot springs, to get their laundry done, and presumably to visit Gussie and her girls.

It is said that Gussie set up her operation in a building on a corner of Bennett and Riverfront. After she left town to spend the winter in the East, her common-law husband John rented the structure to the county so that the county records could be moved out of Nims Ferguson's dugout. According to the story, Gussie returned the following spring to find her former place of business occupied. She proceeded to build a lean-to on the side of the new courthouse, and went back into business. With a degree of distaste, the county offices shared the building with Gussie and her employees until 1886. John Blake was sheriff of Garfield County from 1883 to 1884, having been appointed by Governor James Grant.

The original Colorado Hotel, which had been built at the corner of Eighth and Grand, was moved to make way for the new Hotel Glenwood. The first version of the hotel, built by Isaac Cooper, William Gelder, and Joe Enzensperger, was a fifty by fifty foot structure of two stories. It sat in the center of the lot. In that same year, H. R. Kamm built what was probably the first brick building in town on the northwest corner of Eighth and Grand and opened a store in it.

As mentioned, Cooper Avenue was named for Isaac, one of the founders of the town. The Grand River was of course the source of the name for Grand Avenue, and other streets took on the names of early businessmen. Bennett Avenue was named for Hiram Bennett. Palmer Avenue took the name of either William Palmer of the Denver & Rio Grande Railroad, or Lottie Palmer, an early "woman of color" who was reportedly brought from Aspen by miners who built her a log cabin and paid her to do their laundry and to cook for them. It is said that she was eventually able to invest over $10,000 in Aspen real estate. It is normally assumed that Blake Avenue was named for John, but there is of course the possibility that Gussie was afforded the honor.

Isaac Cooper was one of the investors in the Denver & Rio Grande Railroad. His influence helped to bring the railroad line to Glenwood Springs. He and Frederick C. Childs filed a townsite some eleven miles south of Glenwood Springs, just north of Carbondale. The site they chose was at the confluence of the Roaring Fork River and Rock Creek, later to be known as the Crystal River.

Cooper and Childs reasoned that their new town would be the ideal location for a railway station when the line continued up the Roaring Fork Valley toward Aspen. Childs constructed a large building which housed a post office and a general store, and Cooper began work on a brick building which was to be called the Hotel Moffat. Sarah Cooper filed on land in the immediate area, and all of the activity created a minor boom atmosphere until the railroad bypassed their little town and built the station in Carbondale. The settlement was originally called Coopertown, then Rockford, after Rock Creek, and later Satank, then Moffatt, and finally Satank again.

Due to the continued influx of settlers and prospectors, the first United States Land Office was opened in Glenwood Springs in November of 1884, relieving M. V. B. Blood of the responsibility of filing the minor blizzard of claims forms.

The Hotel Glenwood, built in 1885. Picture features the volunteer fire department, about 1887. (Courtesy of Frontier Historical Society)

By early 1885, the population of Glenwood Springs had grown to over 300. Newcomers were still streaming into Colorado, and the valley of the hot springs was certainly an attractive place to visit or to settle. The flow of outsiders was adequate to demand more hotel rooms, and Cooper, Gelder, and Enzensperger began an enlargement of the Hotel Glenwood. The final seventy-five foot by one hundred foot structure boasted three stories and seventy-five rooms, and cost $65,000.

After Hiram Bennett homesteaded land in the valley in 1883, he moved back to Denver for a period of time. When he returned to Glenwood Springs two years later, he found that a man named McMonagle had taken over the abandoned homestead and resold it. Bennett was unsuccessful in reacquiring the land.

Once the nearby trees had disappeared, the need for lumber was filled by a sawmill at the confluence of the Roaring Fork and the Grand, which had been built by George Bennett and J. W. Beaman. The routes that were constructed to transport logs to the mill were largely responsible for many of today's roads. Bennett and Beaman also owned and operated sawmills at Hip Roof and Boiler Creek on the Flat Tops and in No Name Canyon.

Sunshine Coal Camp - Name later changed to Sunlight. (Courtesy of Buzz Zancanella)

Fred Atkinson took over the gold claims of Dick Grant west of town. There were huge deposits of pure lime there, and he opened a quarry and built a lime kiln. He also opened two brickyards, one at the base of Red Mountain and the other at the western end of Eleventh Street.

Walter Devereux's enterprises were doing well. There were operating coal mines in numerous places, including the Sunshine Mine up Four Mile Creek, and several mines up South Canyon, west of town. South Canyon Coal Camp had a population of some 300 people, a blacksmith shop, a bunkhouse for the bachelor miners, and a library with 1,200 volumes. A small hot springs near the end of the canyon served as a bathtub for the miners.

Captain E. E. Prey, an industrialist, was the head of the South Canyon mines. He apparently did quite well financially, as he built the first large home in Glenwood Springs around 1885. The three-story brick mansion was erected on the south side of the Grand River at the base of Red Mountain. No provision was made for indoor plumbing or electric lighting, but there were fireplaces in every room. There was a stable and a servants' house. Captain Prey also built a private ferry so that he and his family and servants could gain access

Early footbridge across the Grand River, and the "Polly Pry," ferry owned by Captain Prey. (Courtesy of Frontier Historical Society)

to Glenwood proper. He named the boat the "Polly Pry," after a news correspondent of the day.

There were labor disputes in the Colorado coal industry at this time. The workers went out on strike, complaining of low wages, dangerous working conditions, and almost total control of the workers' lives by the companies. The mine owners and operators responded by importing thousands of workers from Mexico, Austria, Greece, and Italy to work the mines. The immigrants came to the United States full of hope for a better life for themselves, and eventually for their families. In many cases they found only years of grinding labor and the struggle to break away from the same company control that had driven their predecessors to strike.

The coal companies, on the other hand, reasoned correctly that the obvious language differences would help to prevent the workers from banding together to dispute their conditions. Of course the inability to communicate verbally with many of their fellow miners added a new dimension to the already considerable dangers of working underground.

In response to the burgeoning economy of the valley, George Arthur Rice and Company opened the first bank at the corner of Riverfront and Grand Avenue. The Carson Stage Line was running into Glenwood Springs from the south. The line ran from Glenwood up the Roaring Fork Valley to Aspen, then over Hunter, or Independence Pass, to Leadville. It connected with the narrow gauge

Denver & Rio Grande Railroad at Granite, some twenty miles south of Leadville. The Interocean Hotel on Cooper Avenue burned to the ground late in 1885. The Presbyterian Church was built in that year. Both Catholic and Presbyterian services had been held in tents prior to the construction of the new church.

As busy as things were in Glenwood Springs, there were other happenings in the area that were to have significant effect on the still small town. In the summer of 1885, Paul Blount, who was clerk and recorder of Garfield County, made a survey from Leadville to Grand Junction. His survey route was to become the path of the Denver & Rio Grande Railroad. Isaac Cooper invested in the Railroad Company. He knew full well what a railroad would mean to his town, and he pushed for a route that would take the rails through the Canyon of the Grand. Meanwhile the Colorado Midland pushed forward with their plans for the rail line over Hagerman Pass and into the Roaring Fork Valley.

The mid 1880s were a time of heavy investment in the United States by wealthy British capitalists. Wheeler and Hagerman had interested an Englishman named Busk in providing money for their railroad venture. Walter Devereux also had the backing of English money in his mining operations.

George Edinger arrived in Glenwood Springs in 1885, taking a job as a postal clerk. He went from job to opening small store of his own and gradually moved into private banking. A man named Russey built the first stable. Thomas Kendrick, who had been running the Clarendon Hotel in Leadville, pitched a huge tent on the corner of Riverfront and Colorado Avenue. He utilized the big structure as a hotel and eventually developed the Kendrick Cottages. The cottages were a favorite lodging place for tourists.

Interestingly, the Frontier Historical Society possesses a copy of a Certificate of Marriage dated June 29, 1885, recording the union of Frank L. Smith of Satank and a Mrs. Gussie Blake. The marriage was performed by Lyman B. Mews, Justice of the Peace, and witnessed by Florence Gray and Roxie Reed. From other records, it appears that Gussie continued her profession in at least a supervisory capacity after her marriage.

Charles, Bryan, and Henry Hubbard opened a livery stable near Emma, some distance south of Glenwood Springs. Henry established a guide service for wealthy big game hunters and homesteaded in Spring Valley. Charles housed his family in a large tent on Riverfront.

On August 25, 1885, the city of Glenwood Springs was officially incorporated, and the first election of city officials was held on September 21. Also, that fall the first newspaper office opened. The *Ute Chief* was published by J. S. Swan and W. J. Reid. Not long after that, the *Glenwood Echo* issued its first edition. The owners built a building at 732 Cooper Avenue, which housed the paper. It was edited by James L. Riland and had the financial backing of Aspen's B. Clark Wheeler. As the population of the area was still predominantly male, the *Echo* ran an ad in midwestern newspapers seeking wives, and reportedly found themselves acting as a matrimonial agency for eager bachelors.

The first tax assessment had been levied in 1884, and was collected in 1885. The funds were to be used for road improvements, principally to construct a road to the west, through Hell's Gate. If the town of Glenwood Springs was ever going to amount to anything, reasoned the city fathers, there simply had to be more ways for people to get to it. A contract was awarded to J. D. Taylor to build a wagon road from Mitchell Creek west through the "gate" to Canyon Creek. At that time, anyone approaching Glenwood Springs from the west had to either travel up and over the Flat Tops, or leave the Grand River at Ferguson, (later Silt), and follow Divide Creek up into the mountains to the southwest and then follow Four Mile Creek down into Glenwood. A route through Hell's Gate would cut many arduous miles and countless hours off of the trip.

Of all the activity in Glenwood Springs in the few years up to and including 1885, perhaps the most significant in terms of importance to the future of Glenwood Springs was the return of Walter Bourchier Devereux. Devereux had by that time made a rather impressive fortune in silver and coal, and he remembered the dream of Isaac Cooper to turn Glenwood Springs into a luxurious resort, a world-class spa. When he again came to Glenwood Springs, he was ready to turn that dream into a reality. He was very aware of the growing competition of the two railroads to be the first to reach Glenwood and the resultant lucrative coal-carrying contracts, and he was also aware of the plans to hack a road through Hell's Gate. He knew what those advances would mean to the little town, and he intended to capitalize on them.

Devereux had four brothers: James Henry, Horace K., Alvin Jr., and Paul. Alvin suffered from mental illness, and Paul died of "consumption" (tuberculosis) in 1895. Walter brought Horace and

The Devereux brothers: from left to right, Paul, Horace, James, Walter, Alvin. (Courtesy of Frontier Historical Society)

James to Aspen to share in the wealth available in the still booming mining town. The brothers both held lucrative mining positions. Walter was ready to move on, to throw himself into the development of his new project. He was instrumental in forming the Colorado Town and Land Company, and in the incorporating of the city. He purchased the ten acres surrounding the hot springs from Isaac Cooper for $125,000.

CHAPTER SEVEN

From 1886 to 1890

COLOROW THE UTE IS DEAD
Pneumonia takes him to the Happy Hunting Grounds
Protests to the last that he was
Cheated out of White River Country
A TROUBLESOME REDSKIN
Died Dec. 12, 1888
Deaf—Over Weight
Since exciting 1887 Indian War, Colorow, under espionage of military authorities has been away from the Agency only on hunting trips. Became surly when debarred from "His Country" which he has ever contended the whole White River Valley to be. He was never an amiable Indian, and previous to being so effectively driven out of Colorado, he was a continual menace to all settlers in the country to which he claimed title.

News of Colorow's death spread rapidly among the Utes, and particularly the Unitah, and they have been indulging in the wildest manifestations of grief. The Ute women have, in many instances, cut off their hair and assumed other evidences of mourning. Thirty horses were at once killed by the young bucks, to accompany the old man to the Happy Hunting Grounds. He was buried yesterday with the most lavish pomp of savage funeral exercises. In his grave were placed blankets and stores ad libitum, which, in accordance with the Indian idea, he will have use for in his spiritual abode.

Colorow's obituary, as printed in the Denver Republican, *December 13, 1888.*

As of 1886, the population of Glenwood Springs had reached almost 700. On the other hand, the population of Carbonate was on its way back down. Its post office was removed during that year, and the number of residents was dwindling.

During that year, coal was discovered near the present site of New Castle. The town had originally been called Grand Buttes. The name was later changed to Chapman, and then to New Castle. Samuel Wraith, the superintendent of one of the mines, had been born in New Castle, England, and he was responsible for the final name change.

Walter Devereux, having purchased a large chunk of Glenwood Springs, wasted no time whatsoever in making his mark. He began by organizing the Glenwood Light and Water Company. He served as president, and his major shareholders were the Rathbone brothers of London. The new company promptly built a hydroelectric plant on the north side of the river and provided electric lights for the town, making Glenwood Springs one of the first to boast that distinction, even beating New York City. Most towns of the day gradually moved from kerosene lamps and candles to gas lamps, and finally to electric lighting. Glenwood was able to skip the gaslight period completely.

Interior of the hydroelectric plant built by Walter Devereux's Glenwood Light and Power Company. (Courtesy of Frontier Historical Society)

Next Devereux formed the Colorado Land and Improvement Company, which in turn began work on what was to become the centerpiece of his development, the hot springs pool. The plans called for a hot mineral water pool some 150 feet wide and 600 feet long, a large bathhouse, and a "sweat cave." The pool was to become the world's largest natural hot springs pool. The Yampah Spring was the largest of the springs that bubbled up near the river, and it was chosen to feed the big pool. The chosen spring flows at about 3,500,000 gallons per day, at a temperature of 122 degrees Fahrenheit, or 51 degrees Celsius. The nearest rivals in Fahrenheit temperature of their water were: King's Bath, England, at 119 degrees, Carlsbad, Germany at 113 degrees, and Vichy, France, at 108 degrees. Under its modern incarnation, the big pool changes water completely every six hours, the small pool every two.

The big Yampah Spring came from the north bank of the Grand, just across from a large island in the middle of the river. It appeared that it would be necessary to divert the entire flow of the river to the south of the island, so that the island would become a part of the north bank. That would allow the necessary room to build the planned pool and related buildings. Much of the labor involved in moving the many tons of rock for the diversion was provided by the inmates of the local jail. There was apparently no shortage of inmates, because the influx of wealth into the area naturally brought with it those who would attempt to obtain that wealth by less than honest means. Many of the patrons of the saloons and gambling halls that lined Riverfront Street probably wound up working on Devereux's wall.

Judge John T. Shumate came to Glenwood Springs in 1886. He served as judge for the 9th Judicial District and also as a state legislator. Will Parkison came to town from Central City and opened the Pharmacy. Drugstores in the late 1800s carried some "patent" medicines, pre-made, pre-packaged pills, capsules, and the like. However, many of the doctors of the day prescribed the so-called "crude" drugs, and such, which would be ground or liquified by the pharmacist.

The new edition of the Hotel Glenwood opened in 1886, featuring lavish appointments. Isaac Cooper and his partners had added a third story. Outside balconies and wrought iron were to be added later. The hotel boasted electric lights and hot and cold running water. There was not a city water system as yet, so the water was pumped from the Grand River. It was a favorite lodging place for

The Hotel Glenwood after the addition of balconies. (Courtesy of Al Maggard)

visiting dignitaries, mine owners, and celebrities. H.A.W. Tabor, wealthy owner of the Matchless Mine in Leadville, and his second wife Baby Doe were frequent guests.

J. D. Taylor and Jay Cox, his engineer, directed the crew that hacked and blasted a crude shelf road through the slabs of red sandstone that lined the Grand River west of town. The road was a minor nightmare to maintain, susceptible to falling rocks, but it was a godsend for the people of Glenwood Springs. At last, Glenwood was accessible from the west without taking a long, arduous route up and over the surrounding mountains. Ranchers in the west end of the county were now able to drive their herds directly through town on their way to market.

The opening of Hell's Gate also aided Captain Prey and his South Canyon coal mines. However, the canyon led south from the Grand River, and the new road was on the north side. To get the coal shipments to the road, he moved his ferry, the "Polly Pry," from its berth by his mansion. The ferry was used to haul coal and passengers for some time until a bridge was finally built at the South Canyon location.

It was about 1886 when Captain Prey inadvertently caused an uproar among the local populace. Dissatisfied with a succession of female cooks, he brought in Chang, a male Chinese chef. He was merely trying to satisfy his gourmet appetite, but the action was viewed as an insult to the local women. "All hell broke loose," resulting in the calling of a meeting of the citizenry to determine whether the "Chinaman" would be allowed to remain in Garfield County. Another faction, slightly more direct in its approach, called for the lynching of the unfortunate cook. Chang left town, and the *Ute Chief* came out as "strongly opposing the introduction of Chinese labor."

The Catholic Church was established in 1886. The same year, Attorney Charles Darrow opened the Fairy Caves. The Darrow family had homesteaded the land which included the caves in the late 1880s. The caves, high on the side of Iron Mountain to the north of Glenwood Springs, wind under the mountain for almost two miles, although only some 1,000 feet had been discovered at that time. It is one of the largest caves in Colorado and is filled with fanciful mineral formations, stalactites, and stalagmites that gave the cave its name. The largest chamber was some twelve feet wide and two hundred feet long. Darrow began developing the caves for public

Early visitors to the Fairy Caves, located in Iron Mountain north of Glenwood Springs. (Courtesy of Frontier Historical Society)

tours, installing electric lights and blasting a tunnel that connected the main cave with a smaller one that opened onto a breathtaking view of the Grand River, 1,200 feet below in the canyon. Both the lighting and the tunnel were completed by 1897. Another cave, called "Alexander's Cave," was discovered by a crew of railroad surveyors about one and one half miles inside the west end of the Grand River Canyon. The newly discovered cave was opened to tourists in competition with the Fairy Caves.

The population of Glenwood Springs was burgeoning rapidly. By early 1887, some 1,200 souls called the scruffy little town home.

During construction of the hot springs pool. (Courtesy of Frontier Historical Society)

With the opening of Hell's Gate, the heavy investments of the Devereuxes and their English backers, and two railroad companies competing to be the first to reach Glenwood Springs, excitement was high. There was a great deal of building going on, not the least of which was the big hot springs pool.

The rapid growth was not without its problems, however. There was still no water or sewer system, and the air was frequently fouled with the odor of human and animal waste. The two big rivers that flowed through town provided plenty of water, but the Roaring Fork was becoming increasingly polluted with the leachings from the piles of mine tailings upriver in the Aspen area. The waters of the Grand flowed reasonably clear much of the year, save the occasional mudslide upriver. However, obtaining the water for domestic use required either hauling it oneself or buying it at ten cents a bucket or a dollar a barrel from F. M. "Daddy" Green and his water wagon.

While Green was plying the streets with his water wagon, S. W. Nott delivered milk from his dairy on Mitchell Creek. His wagon was known as the "Silver Chariot." During the summer, H. B. Walz delivered ice that he harvested during the winter and stored under layers of insulating sawdust and straw in a building on the west bank of the Roaring Fork. Most of the groceries that were purchased in early Glenwood Springs were delivered to the homes of the buyers on horse-drawn wagons.

After buying the hot springs and the surrounding ten acres from Cooper, Walter Devereux rented and then purchased Captain Prey's mansion on the south shore of the Grand River. His wife, Mary, renamed it Cedarbank. His brother, Horace, purchased 320 acres across the Grand River, with plans to plant the tract as an orchard. He also established an elk ranch, and constructed an early fish hatchery on Mitchell Creek west of town. The Devereuxes then purchased another ten acres along the east bank of the Roaring Fork, under the name of the Colorado Land and Improvement Company. This company, like their others, was backed with a great deal of English money. The ten acres was destined to become a racetrack and, in an effort to bring a bit of civilization to their town, a polo field. They also purchased much of the land that was later to hold Cardiff and the coke ovens.

The Christian Church was formed in 1887, and a new schoolhouse was erected at a cost of $25,000. The old school had

been located on Cooper Avenue, not far from the saloons and brothels of Riverfront. This was of course considered unsuitable, undesirable, and probably unsanitary. The new school was located on

The mansion of Captain Prey which was purchased by the Devereuxes and renamed Cedarbank. (Courtesy of Frontier Historical Society)

the corner of Eleventh and Blake.

With the rapid increase in population came those who would provide services of a more basic nature. The saloons, the brothels, and the gambling houses proliferated. With the added humanity

A view of Riverfront in the early 1880s - stores, saloons, gambling halls, and brothels. (Courtesy of Frontier Historical Society)

came the inevitable problems. The first shooting in Glenwood Springs was credited to Elijah Cravens. Cravens and George Ford became involved in a quarrel and wound up fighting. Cravens went home, procured his gun, and returned. He again confronted Ford, but this time he settled the argument for good by shooting and killing him. Chester Baker was involved in another altercation with a fellow gambler in Hawley and Reese's Saloon. Baker, who was also known as the "Texas Kid," fired at his antagonist twice, missing him both times. He did, however, succeed in killing two innocent onlookers, F. M. Smith and Joseph Mathison.

One of Gussie Blake's "sporting girls," a young lady named Florence, was killed in a dispute over a handsome miner from Aspen. Another of the "ladies of the brick" brained her with a heavy water pitcher. According to Lena Urquhart in *Roll Call — The Violent and Lawless*, it was Gussie herself who performed the deed, killing the girl with an ironstone pitcher. Her all male jury ultimately ruled that the death was accidental, and Gussie was acquitted. There is little or no record of the alleged homicide, so any theories about the deed are conjecture, nothing more. However, it is tempting to surmise

John Henry "Doc" Holliday - dentist, gambler, gunfighter. An early graphic artist had apparently decided that Doc would look better in dark hair. His hair was really ash-blond. (Courtesy of Frontier Historical Society)

that the "Florence" who was the victim of the altercation was the same lady as the Florence Gray who is listed as a witness on Gussie's 1885 marriage license. After all, Glenwood Springs was home to only about 1,200 people at that time. The chances of Gussie Blake having two close acquaintances named Florence seem minimal at best.

It was this rough-hewn atmosphere that greeted a thirty-six year old former dentist when he arrived in Glenwood Springs in May of 1887. There are differing stories as to why John Henry "Doc" Holliday came to Glenwood. He had been suffering from tuberculosis, or "consumption" for several years, and many believe that he came seeking the healing effects of the hot mineral springs.

Another story tells quite a different version of his arrival. The fact that Doc Holliday and Wyatt Earp had become fast friends is not a subject for debate. Wyatt is quoted as saying:

"Doc was a dentist whom necessity had made a gambler; a gentleman whom disease had made a frontier vagabond; a philosopher whom life had made a caustic wit; a long, lean ash-blond fellow nearly dead with consumption and at the same time the most skillful gambler, and the nerviest, fastest, deadliest man with a six-gun I ever knew."

Doc had spent the previous few years wandering around the new west, building a reputation as a gambler and a gunfighter. He spent time in Texas, Arizona, Kansas, South Dakota, and Colorado. Occasionally, he performed a bit of dentistry but spent most of his days dealing or playing poker and faro. Estimates of the number of men who died at his hand range up to twenty-five or so. The true number is almost certainly a great many less than that. Doc was about five feet ten inches in height, but he was slender and somewhat weakened by his lung disease. It no doubt served his purposes to perpetuate the image of a quick, deadly gunfighter.

Doc had made the acquaintance of a prostitute named "Big Nose" Kate during his travels, and the two of them carried on a frequently tumultuous relationship for several years. She was suspected of visiting him in Glenwood Springs.

The other version of Doc's arrival speculates that he and Wyatt had been "offended" by a couple of men, and that they followed them through Aspen, down the Roaring Fork Valley, through Glenwood, and up onto the Flat Tops. There, according to this portrayal, Doc and Wyatt found them camped by a lake, "put their lights out," and left them there. Upon returning to Glenwood

Springs, Doc was too sick to travel farther, so he stayed in the little town and Wyatt went on.

Whatever the truth, Doc Holliday took up residency in the newly refurbished Hotel Glenwood. He dealt faro and poker in some of the local gambling halls, performed a little dentistry, and reportedly drank heavily. The fact that anyone would submit to tooth repair by an active consumptive perhaps speaks to the scarcity of dentists in Glenwood Springs at the time.

As part of their development plans, the Devereux brothers spent some $40,000 in the excavation of another "vapor cave," this time on the north side of the river. The tunnel followed the hottest of the springs into the solid limestone of the mountain. They dug in some thirty-five feet, and excavated three large rooms.

Interior photo of the new vapor caves showing the marble benches. (Courtesy of Frontier Historical Society)

The hot mineral water was diverted to run through the rooms, thus creating another underground steam bath for tourist and resident alike. Where the original caves on the south side of the river were somewhat primitive, the new cave complex boasted an enclosed entrance, marble benches, and electric lights powered by the hydroelectric plant just to the west. Both the old cave (No. 1) and the new caves were used for a time, but then the old cave gradually fell into disuse. The old cave was eventually sealed over and blended in with the roadbed for the Denver & Rio Grande Railroad.

The patrons of the new caves were a bit more modest than had been the customers of Jonas Lindgren. Both sexes wore heavy linen bags, open at both ends, with a drawstring at the neck. They were certainly proper, if not terribly fashionable. The customers could time their stay in the caves by the use of a large hourglass that was provided for them.

In 1887, Grand River Coal and Coke Company filed the plat for the town of Cardiff. The new town was to grow up on the west bank of the Roaring Fork River, on land owned by the Devereux brothers, some three miles south of Glenwood Springs. Cardiff, named for Cardiff, Wales, was developed with a single purpose in mind; to produce coke. Certain grades of bituminous coal are suitable for the making of other products. The soft coal may be used in its original form for home heating, but it may also be heated under low oxygen conditions to produce coal tars, gases, and a hard, grayish-black substance known as coke. When ignited, coke produces intense heat with little or no smoke. It is ideal for the smelting of metals such as the silver ore being produced up the valley in Aspen.

Walter Devereux and other entrepreneurs such as John Osgood, the coal baron of Redstone, found the coal deposits of the Grand Hogback to be largely of excellent coking quality. Thus Cardiff was, in fact, formed with one purpose in mind; that of processing bituminous coal into coke. Ultimately there would be a total of some 249 coke ovens, 199 traditional beehive-shaped ovens, and fifty rectangular Belgium or "stack" ovens. The interiors were shaped to concentrate the heat of the coking coal and lined with firebrick to withstand the intense heat of the process. The few remaining ovens exhibit an interior surface with an almost glass-like consistency, the ends of the bricks fused together. The ovens served coal mines of Sunlight, Marion, Spring Gulch, and South Canyon.

In its heyday, Cardiff held around 150 residents and contained a thriving business district and some fifty cabins, plus another thirty or so rental cabins for the workers. In addition to the Midland Railway Station and accompanying round-house, there were several mercantile establishments, including the Railroad Inn and the Hotel DeCardiff. It was said that the glow from the coke ovens

The town of Cardiff just south of Glenwood Springs. (Courtesy of Frontier Historical Society)

The Cardiff Coke ovens in operation. (Courtesy of Frontier Historical Society)

could be seen at night from as far away as New Castle. In fact, one of the more popular tours for visitors was a ride up Lookout Mountain to view the sunset, followed by the sight of the glowing ovens as darkness descended.

In July of 1887, Isaac Cooper's health was deteriorating, but he was still quite active in the development of his town. He had been planning a water system for Glenwood Springs, and the town board accepted his offer. Cooper supervised the laying of pipe in an effort to bring water from No Name Creek, which is located not far inside the west portal of the canyon. He investigated the Roaring Fork River as a water source, but it was too polluted to be used for domestic purposes.

At about the same time, thirty-five men organized the first formal fire fighting unit in town. It was originally named the Glenwood Hook and Ladder Company. Since there was still no water system, water to fight the fires came from whichever source was handy, usually one of the rivers. In honor of Cooper, once the water system was established, the name was changed to the Isaac Cooper Hose Co. Number 1. Soon after, another company named the Rough and Ready Hose Company Number 2 was formed. The firemen were needed, for most of the buildings were still made of wood, and kerosene lamps and candles were still being used to some extent for lighting. A new building at 822 Grand Avenue, containing a furniture store, also housed the first fire bell. Prior to its installation, firefighters were summoned by volleys of pistol fire. There were known to be side bets on which hose company would reach a fire first.

The corner of Eighth and Grand in 1891 - The Hotel Glenwood is on the left, First National Bank is on the right, and the Hotel Barlow, later St. Joseph's Sanitorium, is in the background. (Courtesy of Al Maggard)

Building continued at a frantic pace throughout 1887. The First National Bank was formed by James L. Hagerman, its first president, Walter Devereux, vice president, and J. H. Fesler, cashier. The bank was organized with $100,000 capital, an impressive amount at that time. The bank originally opened in a one-story frame building on Eighth Street. They soon began construction of a three-story, fifty by one hundred foot building at the corner of Eighth and Grand. They spent another $40,000 on the building.

A few months later, the Glenwood National Bank opened. It was located a few doors down the street at 828 Grand Avenue. It also boasted $100,000 in capital. John L. McNeil was the president, J. L. Osgood was vice president. C. N. Greig was cashier. The Glenwood National was largely financed by backers of the Denver & Rio Grande Railroad. Isaac Cooper had also invested in the Denver & Rio Grande. Devereux, Hagerman, and others with more of an "up-valley" background were either investors in, or supporters of, the Colorado Midland Railroad. As 1887 progressed, a real rivalry developed between the two rail companies, each of them predicting that they would be the first to reach Glenwood Springs.

A large two-story stone building was erected on the western side of Cooper Avenue. Known as Hyde Hall, it was to house the

Glenwood Opera Company. However, the hall was also used for just about anything that was in need of a venue. The hall featured dances, prize fights, dog and pony shows, various citizens' meetings, and church services. There were also talent shows, visiting clairvoyants, and palm readers.

The eminent arrival of two railroads and the construction of the big pool spurred even more construction in the hotel industry. The Yampah Hotel, the Williams Hotel, the Denver, and the Star all grew out of the hodgepodge of tents and dugouts that had infested the Riverfront area. The Kendrick Cottages also opened for business.

The *Glenwood Echo* began publication, with B. Clarke Wheeler as manager. Also, the *Daily News* opened, with H. J. Holmes as editor and publisher. Three attorneys came to town, by way of Leadville and Aspen. They were Joseph Taylor and his two nephews, Charles and Edward. Edward Taylor became district attorney of the Ninth Judicial District not long after his arrival. His new position gave him authority over water rights for the Grand River, the Roaring Fork River, and the White River. He would become known as the "Father of Water Rights on the Western Slope." Seeing the exhilaration caused by the approach of the rail lines, Taylor began to develop a vision; a concept of a wagon road through the formidable Canyon of the Grand.

The original Glenwood Springs jail, a twelve by twelve foot cube of concrete. (Courtesy of Frontier Historical Society)

Since the Garfield County records were moved from Carbonate, they had resided in several locations around town. First kept in the dugout of Nims Ferguson, they were moved to John Blake's building, and finally to the upper floor of a building on Grand. Then a real courthouse was erected on the southwest corner of Eighth and Pitkin. The building also contained a jail, replacing an unlovely concrete cube that had been used for that purpose for some time. The original jail, a twelve square foot concrete structure which had been erected on Blake Street between Eighth and Ninth, was moved to Rosebud Cemetery and served for some years as a tool shed. It has since been moved to Veltus Park on the west side of the Roaring Fork River.

A man named Andrew Hyde, for whom Hyde Hall was named, opened a flour mill some distance south of town on the east bank of the Roaring Fork. It was a small custom mill, catering to farmers who would bring their wheat to him and have it ground into flour. The mill was later sold to W. W. Livingston. The new owner enlarged the mill and began marketing under the brand name of "Yampah Flour." He also sold another brand known as Columbine Flour, as well as a packaged cereal.

Up until 1887, the Utes were still returning each summer to visit their sacred springs and to hunt in their ancestral hunting grounds. That was to be the last year of their pilgrimage, however, due to an incident that occurred in August of that year. A Ute named Augustine had reportedly been murdered near Rangely. Colorow, old and still portly, accompanied a small band of Utes into the White

A shipment of Yampah Flour. (Courtesy of Frontier Historical Society)

River country to camp, hunt, and to protest the killing of one of their own. On his last visit to Glenwood Springs in 1887, Colorow was described as having poor posture and hearing, and to be suffering from depression, senility, and the burden of some 275 pounds on his five foot eight inch frame.

Jim Kendall, Sheriff of Garfield County, sought a reputation as the man who had finally rid the county of the "savages." As the Utes approached the town that was by then called Meeker, after the slain Indian Agent, there were loud and prolonged protests from the white residents about the "trespassers." Angry confrontations developed between the Utes and the sheriff's men, and Colorow began moving his people back toward the Utah border. Kendall reported an Indian uprising, and a contingent of soldiers from the Colorado National Guard in Aspen, under the command of Captain Goslin, started for the Meeker area. As they passed through Glenwood Springs, they were joined by twenty-one volunteers, including Jack (Jasper) Ward. Ward was an undersheriff and had been the founder of New Castle. Governor Alva Adams, for whatever reason, traveled to the site of the conflict, stopping at the Hotel Glenwood on his way.

At a site known as Cedar Hill, the whites and the Indians battled on August 25. In the fracas, Colorow was wounded. Jasper Ward, a National Guard Lieutenant named Frank Folsom, and a cowboy known only as "Curly" were killed. It was also reported that as many as seven Utes died that day. The remaining Utes moved on into Utah, and the posse and the soldiers collected their dead and returned to the Roaring Fork Valley. The "Colorow War" reportedly cost the state between $30,000 and $80,000, depending on the source.

According to *Colorow—The Angry Chieftain* by Lena Urquhart:

"In a few days Sheriff Kendall mysteriously disappeared. Foul play was considered responsible, but no one cared, and an investigation was never made."

Jasper Ward's body was, according to Urquhart, originally buried at the scene of the battle but was disinterred and brought back to Glenwood some ten days later. A cemetery had been established on a plot of land which sat on a shoulder of Lookout Mountain to the east of Glenwood Springs. The first grave marker was dated 1886. Jasper Ward was to be one of the first persons buried in the new Linwood Cemetery. The shoulder of the mountain which held the

A Sullivan compressor used during building of the railroad grade through the canyon. (Courtesy of Frontier Historical Society)

new cemetery became known as Jasper Mountain.

Glenwood Springs was doing its best to prepare for the influx of tourists who were sure to descend upon the valley once the trains arrived. Buildings and businesses were appearing almost overnight. By the later months of 1887, the two blocks that composed the center of Glenwood Springs held no fewer than twenty-one saloons, and an impressive number of gambling halls and sporting houses. The madams increased their staffs to fifty, then to one hundred.

Finally, after so much anticipation, the trains did in fact arrive. At least one of them did. After two years and over two million dollars in cost, the final track was laid into Glenwood Springs for the Denver & Rio Grande Railroad. The construction crews had spent the last several months blasting their way through the virgin rock that made up the south wall of the Grand River Canyon. In those days, there was little or no concern for the environment. The object was to get from point A to point B, using the most direct route possible. If a wall of rock stood in the way, they either tunneled through it or blasted it away altogether. If there was a river handy to dump the resulting loose rock into, so much the better.

Surprisingly, amidst the seeming disregard for the aesthetics of the canyon, one segment of the Denver & Rio Grande crew exhibited a remarkable degree of craftsmanship. In places near the center of the canyon, retaining walls were necessary to support either the canyon wall or the rail bed itself. With the assistance of Mexican and Chinese laborers, Italian stonemasons constructed walls of carefully fitted rock. The walls were "dry-laid," stacked and fitted so well that they still stand today, still support the massive weight of rail traffic without the benefit of mortar.

The narrow gauge tracks of the Denver & Rio Grande passed through three tunnels with a combined length of 1700 feet, plus a "half tunnel" of 185 feet. The Jackson Tunnel just to the east of the old vapor caves was 1331 feet long, and the final construction of that tunnel delayed

An engine emerges from the Jackson Tunnel just east of Glenwood Springs. (Courtesy of Frontier Historical Society)

the planned October 1 arrival of the first train.

As it turned out, it was not until October 5, 1887, that the first train pulled into town. The event was cause for extensive celebration. Schools were closed so that the children of Glenwood Springs could join in the festivities. The moment was perhaps best described by a special supplement to the *Ute Chief:*

At about 7:45 P.M. on Wednesday the special pulled in, and to say it was enthusiastically welcomed would be drawing it very mild. As the train pulled through the tunnel its two engines opened their broad throats and gave a prolonged whistle. They were answered by the Electric Light Company, supplemented by 3500 human voices and reverberations from many pounds of giant powder. Bonfires had been lit on every side, and the town was lighted by the explosion of fireworks, the burning of calcium lights, tissue transparencies, electric lights, and rows of candles (each homeowner placed a lighted candle on the walk in front of his house). For a full quarter of an hour the noise was deafening. Finally the party descended from the train, and they were welcomed in a neat appropriate speech by Mayor P. Y. Thomas. In a few minutes the party was escorted to Hotel Glenwood with the Glenwood Brass Band leading, and the citizens' committee and the citizens generally following. Several short addresses were made in front of the hotel, several selections played by the band, when the party adjourned to the capacious lobbies.

The lead engine, No. 187, was under the control of O. B. Gutshall. Despite his illness, Isaac Cooper had traveled to Leadville so that he could ride the first train into Glenwood Springs. He was joined on the "Little Giant," as the train was named, by David H. Moffat, president of the Denver & Rio Grande, by Colorado Governor Alva Adams, and by other officials of the railroad and of the state. Cooper took part in thespeeches and toasts for a while, but then was forced to retire to his rooms in the Hotel Glenwood. However, a huge banquet had been set, and the celebrations continued into the early morning hours.

The *Ute Chief* also stated:

"The arrival of the train at the foot of Grand Avenue was the supreme moment in the life of Captain Isaac Cooper. The Ute Chief expresses the hope that he lives long enough to see the country as it is pictured in his mind's eye. It was eminently proper that the founder, pioneer and benefactor of Glenwood Springs should ride the first train, and be greeted with music, cheers, exploding fireworks and giant powder."

The Denver & Rio Grande construction crews wasted no time in continuing the laying of rails up the Roaring Fork Valley toward Aspen. At the same time, the Colorado Midland Railroad was building down the same valley, aware that they had been beaten in the unofficial race with the Denver & Rio Grande, but still intent on arriving in Glenwood in a timely manner. As it turned out, it was not until December 12 that the Midland finally did so. By that time, two other events had transpired that would deeply affect Glenwood Springs. The first of these events was not to gain any appreciable degree of notice for some years to come, but the second immediately and directly affected the entire populace.

Doc Holliday took no notice of the goings-on during the arrival of the first train. His condition had worsened, and he slipped into a coma in September of 1887. He still lived in the Hotel Glenwood, and his minimal needs were met by hotel personnel and presumably by "Big Nose" Kate. On the morning of November 8, 1887, he reportedly awoke from the almost two month coma, and ordered a tumbler of whiskey. According to witnesses, he then drank it off with obvious satisfaction, said, "This is funny!" and quietly died. His last words were interpreted to mean that he considered it humorous that he was dying in bed with his "boots off." After the life he had led, filled with unpleasant gamblers, drunks, and gunslingers, perhaps his demise in bed was "funny." He was thirty-six years old.

Services were held for Doc at the First Presbyterian Church. Holliday had been raised in the Presbyterian faith, but he had received Holy Communion in the Catholic Church after his arrival in Glenwood Springs. However, Father Downey was out of town, so the Presbyterian minister performed the service. According to local legend, both Doc and another unfortunate resident died at about the same time. Due to the weather and road conditions so late in the year, the steep wagon road up to Linwood Cemetery was impassable. Consequently, the two men were buried at the base of the hill, to be disinterred in the spring and moved on up to the cemetery.

There are those who say that this indeed happened, and that Holliday's remains do in fact reside somewhere in the old cemetery. However, there are others who claim that the family of the other decedent came up with the necessary funds to move their dear departed, while no one cared enough about Doc to pay to have him moved. According to that theory, he still lies somewhere at the base of the promontory that holds the Linwood Cemetery, perhaps under someone's back porch. Yet another version of the story has it that he rested near Palmer Avenue until 1907, when he was relocated to the cemetery.

The second event involved another death. This one was of immediate concern to the people of Glenwood Springs. On December 2, Isaac Cooper passed away, also in the Hotel Glenwood. Unlike Doc Holliday, Cooper's death threw the town into mourning. Businesses were closed, and Cooper lay in state in the Hotel Glenwood. Quite fittingly, his body was transported by train to Denver, where he was buried in Riverside Cemetery. He was forty-eight.

The Colorado Midland Railroad finally reached Glenwood Springs on December 12, and there was another celebration, but i

Denver and Rio Grand tracks through the canyon. Note that the narrow gauge rails were laid on wider cross ties to allow for later expansion to standard gauge width. (Courtesy of Frontier Historical Society)

was somewhat muted in comparison to the one that had been held in October for the Denver & Rio Grande. The Midland had, after all, come in second. Also, the city was still saddened by Cooper's death.

Attorney Charles Darrow was retained by both railroads, an act which helped to establish his successful legal reputation. Darrow was to eventually serve as both city attorney and county attorney.

As predicted by Isaac Cooper, by Walter Devereux, and by many others, the arrival of the railroads did indeed transform Glenwood Springs. Almost overnight, the formerly isolated community became what Cooper had envisioned, a spa that catered to the rich mine owners, to the coal and hard rock miners of Aspen and Leadville, and to the first of millions of tourists. Both trains ran "weekend specials," or "laundry trains," from the mining communities to and from Glenwood. The miners could ride the trains into Glenwood for $1.50 round trip. Once in Glenwood, they could wash both their bodies and their clothing in the natural hot water prior to embarking on an evening of drinking, gambling, and whatever other diversions came to mind. Glenwood Springs might have become the spa for the rich and famous, but it was also still the provider of services to the riotous and bawdy.

The railroads brought not only rowdy miners. They also brought a new freedom to the miners, to the ranchers and farmers, to the merchants of the area. They provided a new and infinitely more convenient way of transporting their goods and their animals. The trains did indeed bring a new way of life to the entire area.

In January of 1888 the Cardiff coke ovens were fired for the first time. Cardiff actually had a Midland depot before Glenwood Springs, and the

The flume built for the water system. (Courtesy of Frontier Historical Society)

Midland Railroad also built their roundhouse there. John Osgood, who would later gain fame as the founder of Redstone and Cleveholm, the "Redstone Castle," came to Glenwood at about that time with Irene, his first wife. He purchased a lot at 932 Colorado Avenue, but there is no proof that he built the residence that presently sits there. It appears to have been built by a man named Sam Dougan who was the brother of lumberyard owner William Dougan.

The Glenwood Light and Water Company, under the direction of Walter Devereux, undertook Isaac Cooper's project of providing drinking water to the people of Glenwood. They took Cooper's plan to divert water from No Name Creek and carried it somewhat farther.

They filed for water rights on the clear waters of Grizzly Creek, which contained a more abundant and dependable flow than did No Name Creek. Planning to tunnel between the two creeks, in order to divert the Grizzly Creek waters into No Name Creek, they built a giant wooden flume to carry water into the city. Soon the homes of Glenwood Springs were blessed with running water for the first time.

As promised, the arrival of the railroads spurred the growth of Glenwood Springs. By the early months of 1888, the population was nearing 2,500. Glenwood boasted a courthouse and jail, two national banks, a new school building, and three three-story hotels. The Methodist and Episcopal churches opened their doors for the first time in that year. There were several doctors in town, including Dr. J. S. Manley, Dr. William Crook, and Doctors Dean, Robinson, and Dunn. They served the populace of Glenwood Springs, as well as the residents and workers in the various coal camps scattered around the mountains. Dr. Manley used a small building at the east end of Seventh Street for a crude clinic.

During 1888, the Colorado Midland Railroad extended its rail lines west to New Castle. They had been using a converted freight car that was parked on a siding on the west side of the Roaring Fork River as their depot. In 1889, they built a small depot building at the western end of Tenth Street, and built a bridge across the river for a spur line. The Denver & Rio Grande established a dispatch office in north Glenwood Springs. After the Denver & Rio Grande reached Rifle in 1889, the two former rival railroads formed a new company — the Rio Grande Junction Railway Company — with the intent of jointly extending a rail line west to Grand Junction. The companies agreed that they would split the cost of the rail construction, and that each company would hold half of the stock of the new one. As a concession to progress, the Denver & Rio Grande changed its tracks from Denver to Rifle from narrow gauge to standard gauge. This was not as large a task as might be imagined; the original rail bed and cross ties had been designed to handle either gauge.

The first part of Devereux's spa complex, the pool itself, was completed in 1888. The big hot spring was encircled with a sixty foot diameter masonry wall. The big pool, which was dubbed the "Natatorium," was built with walls of red sandstone and paved with fire brick brought from Golden. The shallow end was three and one half feet deep, and the depth gently sloped to five and one half feet at the other end. The finished pool was the largest in the world, measuring seventy-five feet wide by 615 feet long. The uncomfortably hot water from the springs was cooled to about eighty-five degrees for the big pool. A cold water fountain was installed near the deep

During construction of the stone bathhouse at the hot springs pool. (Courtesy of Buzz Zancanella)

end, and a small wooden bathhouse was built near the west end. Almost immediately, construction began on a massive sandstone bathhouse.

The Devereuxes hired an architect from Vienna, Austria named Theodore Von Rosenberg to design and oversee the construction of the big pool and of the magnificent bathhouse. Von Rosenberg had been a bridge engineer for the Midland Railroad. He chose red sandstone from the Peachblow Sandstone Quarry up the Frying Pan River.

Theodore Von Rosenberg, architect of the Hot Springs Lodge and Pool. (Courtesy of Frontier Historical Society)

An 1888 advertising pamphlet boasted that,

"The hot springs are bubbling up over a large area and both sides of the Grand River. The principal spring on the north side was said to be delivering a flow of 4000 gallons per minute at a temperature of 124 degrees."

It goes on to say,

"To the tourist seeking a cool retreat from the cares of business, Glenwood presents unusual attractiveness. The grandeur of the Canon is unsurpassed. It is a kaleidoscope of ever changing colors, shadows, and forms."

Buffalo robe, said to be that of Colorow. (Courtesy of Frontier Historical Society)

Word reached Glenwood Springs in December of 1888 that Colorow had died. Some claimed that the wounds he had received in the abortive encounter with the whites in the summer of 1887 contributed to his death.

J. C. Schwarz was the proprietor of the funeral parlor on the second floor of the building that housed the furniture store on Grand Avenue. In 1889, he purchased the Linwood Cemetery on the mountain just east of Glenwood Springs.

CHAPTER EIGHT

From 1890 to 1895

"Englishmen of every variety abound. Here, fresh from the Columbian Exposition come a German count and countess, followed by their body physician and body surgeon and a numerous retinue armed with rifles and other weapons of war. There goes a bright-eyed professor of world-wide reputation from New York. And yes, it is he, the prince of scientists, von Helmhotz, himself, who is promenading up and down the long corridor. "

From the writings of Dr. Henry M. Lyman,
a summer guest of the Hotel Colorado in 1893.

Since long before the appearance of the white man in the Roaring Fork Valley, there had been an ancient Indian racetrack on the north bank of the Grand River. It was used by the Utes and later by the white cowboys and others who fancied themselves to be horsemen. All of the Devereux brothers were accomplished horsemen, as was F. H. A. "Hervey" Lyle. The old Indian racetrack was a little crude for their tastes. While the big stone bathhouse was under

Overview of Glenwood Springs from the top of Red Mountain showing the polo grounds and racetrack at the lower right corner of the picture. (Courtesy of Frontier Historical Society—Schutte Collection)

construction, they began to build their own racetrack on their ten acres along the Roaring Fork River. Also, they planted grass for their polo field and began work on a golf course. The Glenwood Polo and Racing Association built a clubhouse and a grandstand for the observation of the sports.

The city of Glenwood Springs floated a bond in the amount of $30,000 for a beautification project to tie in with the polo ground complex. Cottonwood trees were planted along both sides of Grand Avenue leading from the downtown area to the polo grounds, and ditches were dug for street drainage.

With the polo field completed, Lyle and the Devereux brothers needed competition. The Glenwood Springs of 1890 was not exactly a hotbed of polo players, so they enlisted some of the local cowboys and taught them the rules and the finer points of the game. The cowboys were themselves excellent horsemen, and their quick, tough little ponies were often more than a match for the thoroughbreds of the "upper class. " The first game was staged in 1890, and the new and novel sport soon drew an enthusiastic audience. It did, after all, offer something new upon which to wager, as well as a new gathering place for Glenwood's elite.

The cowboys not only defeated the town team on several occasions, but they also discovered new sources of income. A good cow pony was worth a decent amount of money, from ten to fifteen dollars in 1890. That same pony, trained for polo, was worth several times that much to wealthy visitors from the eastern United States. In addition, the cowboys offered their services as guides and

F. H. A. "Hervey" Lyle - employee of and fellow polo enthusiast to the Devereuxes. (Courtesy of Frontier Historical Society)

William Cross and his taxidermy studio. His skill brought him national acclaim. (Courtesy of Frontier Historical Society)

outfitters to the visitors, charging them dearly for introducing them to the excellent hunting of the area.

Construction in the downtown area of Glenwood Springs continued. The building at 715 Cooper Avenue was completed, and housed the collection of William Cross, an internationally known taxidermist. He performed his work in the building, and his display of mounted wildlife became a nationally famous tourist attraction.

The Odeon Theater was also completed in 1890. It was built on Riverfront, but the address would eventually change to 312 Seventh Street. Originally designed to be a live theater, the Odeon was later converted to a silent movie house. Graffiti from the 1890s still exists in the upstairs dressing rooms.

The small sample room on the north side of the Hotel Glenwood was converted to a barbershop by one of the early black residents, a gentleman named Billy Stiles. The little building has housed either a barbershop or a hair salon since then.

Perhaps the most significant construction of 1890 was the completion of the big stone bathhouse at the pool. Theodore Von Rosenberg designed the magnificent building to be fabricated from red "Peachblow" sandstone from the quarry on the Frying Pan River.

The hot springs pool and stone bathhouse in the winter with the pool shrouded in steam. The three hardy souls are standing on the base of the cold water fountain. (Courtesy of Frontier Historical Society)

The stone was brought down the roaring Fork Valley by the Midland Railroad and was laid by a master stonemason named James Goldie. The massive walls were approximately two feet thick.

The final cost of the bathhouse was $100,000. When completed, It was by far the most expensive building on the Western Slope of the Rockies. Von Rosenberg was originally from Vienna, and the architecture showed an Austrian influence. The center of the building was three stories tall, while both ends were two stories. A veranda extended the full length of the building on the south side, away from the pool. Ornate cupolas on each end of the building doubled as a ventilation system. The cupolas were occasionally used to house orchestras for the enjoyment of guests.

The interior of the bathhouse was designed to exhibit the utmost in luxury. The floors were made of imported mosaic tiles. The basement contained Roman baths, equipped with English porcelain tubs and enamel-plated walls. There were thirty such baths for the men, and another twelve for the ladies, and of course separate entrances.

The ground floor housed four more baths, even more luxurious than the Roman baths one floor below. There were also well appointed parlors for both sexes, a physician's office, and the office for the bathhouse.

The second floor contained an exclusive gambling casino, which was restricted to the wealthy male patrons of the establishment. In the evenings, the gentlemen were required to be dressed in white tie and tails. It afforded the upper classes the opportunity to test the whims of luck without the necessity of rubbing shoulders with the unwashed r a b b l e across the river on Riverfront.

Just west of the circular

The main lobby of the stone bathhouse. (Courtesy of Frontier Historical Society)

The "cocktail" spring in the foreground, the Inhalatorium in the background. (Courtesy of Frontier Historical Society)

enclosure of the Yampah Spring was a smaller round stone structure that enclosed the "cocktail" spring. Here Bartow Duncan, a courteous black employee, served goblets of the hot mineral water. The liquid could be drunk, gargled, or "snuffed" by the patron. A few steps away was a vat into which one could discharge the excess.

Further east was another small building known as the "Inhalatorium." Its purpose was to provide a place where the health-seeking customer could breathe in the thick, sulfur-scented vapors from the Yampah Spring. It was adorned with potted plants, and provided quite an attractive, if somewhat malodorous respite from the cares of the world.

A smaller building was constructed at the western edge of the pool. Known as the Conservatory, it provided a place to purchase pastries, coffee, tea, and corsages. Another formal garden was constructed between the stone bathhouse and the river, complete with another fountain. Near the big pool was an enclosure that held both white and black swans, and farther west, beyond a lily and goldfish pond, was a large man-made lake that provided sanctuary for native waterfowl and fish. The lake featured an island garden.

Not long after the completion of the massive stone bathhouse, two things became obvious: first, the popularity of the big pool quickly rendered the new bathhouse too small to handle the masses of potential customers. Second, the social elite were being subjected to the multitudes who also wanted to avail themselves of the healing and recreational advantages of the pool. Consequently another building, a wooden one this time, was erected just to the east of the stone structure. It was called the Pool House. Admission to the stone bathhouse was fifty cents. Admission to the new wooden one was half that, effectively segregating the clientele. Also, since few people in that day owned their own bathing suit, the rental of proper attire

THE GLENWOOD HOT SPRINGS & HOTEL COMPANY

PRICES FOR BATHS AND TREATMENT

STONE BATH HOUSE

Roman and Douche Baths, with attendance and couch	$1.00
Plain Tub Bath	.50
Alcohol Rub	.25
Body Shampoo, in connection with bath	.25
Massage, general	2.00
Massage, local treatment	1.50
Yampah Douche	1.00

POOL FROM STONE BATH HOUSE

Suit provided	.75
Without suit provided	.50
Care of private suit, per month	.50
Care of private suit, two weeks	.25

25c BATH HOUSE

Single Bath	$0.25
Alcohol Rub	.25

INHALATORIUM

Per treatment	.25

VAPOR CAVE No. 3—NEW

Bath, with attendant and couch	1.00
Massage, general	2.00
Massage, local treatment	1.50
Body Shampoo, in connection with bath	.25
Alcohol Rub	.25

VAPOR CAVE No. 1—OLD

Single Bath	.50
Alcohol Rub	.25

POOL HOUSE

Pool, with suit provided	.50
Pool, without suit provided	.25
Care of private suit, per month	.50
Care of private suit, two weeks	.25

SPRAY TREATMENTS FOR CATARRH

Per treatment	.50

Coupon tickets at reduced rates for courses of Vapor Caves, Tub Baths, Massage and Spray Treatments for Catarrh on the basis of five baths for the price of four.

For about seven months in the year winter rates, which show a reduction of twenty per cent on single, and a further twenty per cent for courses of baths, hold good.

(Courtesy of Frontier Historical Society)

further denoted social standing. The suits rented in the stone building were made of wool, and nicely tailored. Those from the Pool House were of cotton, and tended toward baggy, especially when wet.

The resident physician was Dr. Schmitz. He was originally from Holland and had been educated in France. n avid promoter of the Yampah waters, he claimed that they could cure just about anything; rheumatism, gout, lead poisoning, catarrh, obesity, nervous strain, dyspepsia, and many other disorders and discomforts. In association with Charles F. Chandler, he built a small bottling plant near the pool. For some time, the magical water was bottled and shipped worldwide. Ed S. Hughes, who ran a wholesale and retail liquor dealership, was in charge of the plant.

The famous Yampah Hot Springs Mineral Water, said to cure many types of ailments. (Courtesy of Frontier Historical Society)

For some years, crude trails had been hacked along the north wall of the Grand River Canyon by prospectors and explorers who had descended to the floor of the canyon by way of the various creeks that cut the north rim. Some of these trails, many times little more than a faint footpath, connected the creeks with each other. In 1890, Henry Morrow used the abandoned Burlington Railroad grade on the north side of the river as a jumping-off place, and proceeded to work his way into the canyon, connecting the various trails, and creating the first wagon road from one end of the canyon to the other. It was a major accomplishment, laying as it did the groundwork for future highways, but the resultant road was extremely crude at best. For the next several years, it was negotiated on foot, by horseback, and occasionally by a wagon or stagecoach driver with more intestinal fortitude than intellect. The new road was susceptible to all manner of problems; rock slides, snowslides, and closures due to high water were common.

In accordance with the times, Morrow and his men held little regard for the native rock or vegetation. As the Denver & Rio Grande crews had done before them, impeding rock or plant life was removed by the quickest way available. The pick and shovel and liberal doses of "giant" blasting powder were applied to anything which had the misfortune to be in the way. Loose rock was unceremoniously dumped into the river. The term "environmentalist" had yet to be coined, and little thought was given to the appearance of the finished product. The prevailing attitude was no doubt efficient, but the previously untouched canyon bore the scars of the activity.

In March of 1891, Editor Holmes of the *Carbondale Avalanche* moved his newspaper operation to Glenwood Springs. He purchased the *Glenwood Echo* on May 30 and combined the two publications. The new newspaper was called the A*valanche Echo*. Holmes also started the *Daily News,* which eventually became the *Ute Chief News.*

F. A. Barlow, hotel owner and civic booster, did a great deal of advertising in 1891, promoting his hotel and claiming that the mineral-rich waters of the new pool would cure virtually anything. His claims took the form of a guarantee, and he reportedly had very few customers who disputed his assertions.

The *Avalanche Echo* reported in December of 1891 that a party of prospectors, led by John Harvey, was prospecting the volcanic crater just to the north of Dotsero. The paper reported that the prospectors were growing apprehensive about breaking through the bottom of the crater and falling, perhaps miles, down the volcanic shaft toward the center of the earth. The *Avalanche* stated that some nuggets of gold had been found in the vicinity but expressed the hope that Harvey and his crew didn't "open a new beeline route to the Chinese empire. "

A wagon on the newly constructed road through the Grand River Canyon. (Courtesy of Frontier Historical Society)

The Cooper Street Bridge across the Grand River, which had been built in 1885, was proving to be inadequate. It was a narrow affair, and the burgeoning population and activity resulted in increased traffic across the big river. A contract was awarded to the

The Grand Avenue Bridge, completed April 25, 1891, showing the pedestrian esplanade. (Courtesy of Frontier Historical Society—Schutte Collection)

Bullen Bridge Company of Trinidad, Colorado. Theodore Von Rosenberg, the architect of the Hot Springs Pool Bathhouse, was also the architect and engineer of the new bridge. There were numerous delays in the completion of the bridge, a fact that was pointed out repeatedly by Editor Holmes in his newspapers.

The new Grand Avenue Bridge was finally dedicated on April 25, 1891. Theodore Von Rosenberg designed the bridge to complement the Hotel Colorado. It featured a pedestrian esplanade that hung under the span of the main bridge, providing a pleasant walkway from one side of the Grand River to the other.

The old Cooper Avenue Bridge was moved to a location spanning the Roaring Fork River at Seventh Street, where it replaced a suspension footbridge. Mrs. Perry (Eleanora) Malaby was the last person to cross the footbridge before it was dismantled.

The *Avalanche* for May 31, 1891, reported that a figure from the past made his second visit to the area. Captain Richard Sopris, the man for whom Mount Sopris was named in 1860 and a member of the first recorded party of white men to visit the area of the Yampah hot springs, had come to town. He reportedly stayed at the Hotel Glenwood. According to the *Avalanche,* Sopris was " . . . a remarkably well preserved man looking scarcely fifty while his age is over seventy-eight. " There is no record of his reaction to the changes in the valley in the intervening thirty-one years.

In an experiment designed to provide much-needed rainfall for the arid western United States, the Agricultural Department launched a balloon into the clouds somewhere in the midwest during 1891. The balloon carried significant charges of dynamite which were timed to explode inside the clouds, thus releasing the moisture trapped therein. While it did in fact rain later that evening, there is little evidence that the experimentation was continued.

Benjamin Harrison was president of the United States in 1891. He traveled by train through Colorado that year, stopping at Glenwood Springs in May. He attended services at the First Presbyterian Church during his visit. Partly as a result of his observations during that trip, President Harrison established the White River Timber Land Reserve, the precursor to the National Forest. The Reserve was established in October of 1891.

The Glenwood National Bank, which had been established by John Osgood and John McNeil in 1887, agreed to merge with the First National Bank of Hagerman and Devereux. Also, the owners of the Hotel Glenwood sold their operation to R. J. Bolles.

With his spa complex complete, Walter Devereux turned his attention to the creation of a hotel that would match his other construction projects. He retained the architectural firm of Boring, Tilton, and Mellon from New York City. They designed a building some 260 feet deep and 224 feet wide. It was modeled after the Villa de Medici, an Italian mansion from the sixteenth century. The plans showed a massive structure in the shape of a giant "U," surrounding on three sides an open courtyard some 124 feet on each side. It would be called the Hotel Colorado.

The hotel was to be constructed partly from sandstone from Wilson's Peachblow Quarry on the Frying Pan River, as was the hot springs bathhouse, and partly from Roman brick. Construction on the new hotel actually began in August of 1892. The initial cost estimates were in the neighborhood of $400,000.

Cardiff had been established as the permanent coking operation for Devereux's Grand River Coal Company. In 1892, the Cardiff coke ovens produced 53,019 tons of coke. Since his attentions had shifted to the continuing development of the spa/hotel complex, Walter Devereux sold all of Grand River Coal's holding to the Colorado Fuel Company of John Osgood. In the fall of 1892, Osgood in turn consolidated Colorado Iron and Colorado Fuel Company, creating Colorado Fuel and Iron.

During 1892, the Colorado Land & Improvement Company acquired a $500,000 mortgage with the International Trust

The remains of a massive snowslide in the Grand River Canyon. (Courtesy of Frontier Historical Society)

Company to develop geothermal resources, including the vapor caves.

A newspaper article in March of 1892 indicates that there was still some interest in the original townsite of Defiance, some six miles east of Glenwood Springs. Roughly two feet of galena, an ore which often held precious metals, was found, and several claims were "bonded" during 1892. Apparently little was to come of the new enthusiasm.

In the winter of 1892, a massive snowslide in Glenwood Canyon trapped a Denver & Rio Grande freight train, isolating the crew for two days.

Alexander's Cave was sold to Frank Mason in 1893. He changed the name to the Cave of the Clouds, and competed with the Fairy Caves for a time. However, Mason's cave never achieved the popularity of the other attraction.

Richard Sopris, the prospector, explorer, and adventurer for whom the mountain twelve miles south of Glenwood Springs was named, and whose party was the first recorded group of white men to lay eyes on the confluence of the Roaring Fork and the Colorado Rivers, died in April of 1893. He was eighty years old.

In May of 1893, the Hotel Colorado was completed. The new hotel was one of the two most luxurious in Colorado, rivaled only

The Hotel Colorado, soon after the grand opening on June 10, 1893. (Courtesy of Don Vanderhoof)

by the Brown Palace in Denver. The final product cost nearly $850,000. According to the *Avalanche Echo* of July 16, 1893, the huge building used some three million bricks and 10,000 tons of Peachblow Sandstone. The building was framed throughout with Oregon fir, the trim and floors were hard pine, and the doors were yellow poplar. Pennsylvania slate covered the roof. The area of the Hotel Colorado's roof exceeded the area of the State Capital in Denver. Carpeting for the building exceeded 12,000 square feet.

The Denver & Rio Grande Railroad had built a special spur line to run to the hotel, and the grand opening from June 9 to June 12 drew trains from Denver, Colorado Springs, Leadville, and Aspen. Both the Denver & Rio Grande and the Colorado Midland ran special trains to the event. Several thousand out-of-town guests attended the spectacular affair. It was said that there were visitors from all over the United States. On Friday, June 11, tours were conducted to the vapor caves and of course to the pool. The Fairy Caves were electrically lit by then, and were a popular attraction. The night of Saturday, June 10 was set aside for a grand ball.

The new hotel boasted 201 Victorian guest rooms, 170 fireplaces, and 31 private bathrooms, a rarity for the day. Two matching grand stairways curved up from the lobby level, and a hydraulic elevator carried guests to the upper floors. Another handled their luggage. In what was likely a novelty for many of the guests, the hotel as well as the entire town of Glenwood Springs was lit by electric lights.

The twin grand staircases in the center of the lobby of the Hotel Colorado. (Courtesy of Frontier Historical Society)

To match the fountain in the deep end of the big pool, the Florentine fountain in the center of the open courtyard expelled a stream of water 185 feet into the air. Colored lights were trained on the fountain after dark, creating a pleasant display. The pool surrounding the courtyard fountain was stocked with trout. The landscaping surrounding the hotel and in the courtyard, done by William Pflaging, was mirrored by the greenery around the pool.

A carriage road was located just in front of the hotel, where Sixth Street now runs. A stone walkway arched above the road, spanning the distance from the front of the hotel courtyard to a promenade that led to the pool.

A view of the fountain and trout pond in the open courtyard of the Hotel Colorado. (Courtesy of Frontier Historical Society—Schutte Collection)

The north dining room, complete with waterfall and trout pond. (Courtesy of Frontier Historical Society)

Inside the hotel itself, an open lobby ran east and west, from one side of the hotel to the other. The west wing contained a large ballroom and a music room. The east wing housed the lady's billiard room, a play room and nursery for the younger guests, a dining room, and the Presidential Suite. There was another dining room across the lobby from the open south court. In the center of the room, separated from the diners by a low railing, was a representation of a sparkling clear mountain pool. The pool was landscaped to resemble a mountain clearing, and was home to very pampered native trout. The pond was fed by a twelve foot wide, twenty-five foot long waterfall on the north wall of the room. The dining rooms used Havilland china which had been made especially for the hotel.

The full basement held the men's billiard room and a bar, as well as the laundry, baths, a tunnel to the servants' quarters, and an immense room under the kitchen and central dining room that was capable of holding 300 tons of ice. At the time of its opening, the Colorado Hotel had an employment roster of 160, all of them brought in from Boston or England. It was apparently felt that the elegance of the hotel demanded the services of personnel who exhibited a refinement not found in Glenwood Springs in any great quantity.

The *Denver Times* was quoted as calling the new Hotel Colorado, *"A monument of architectural grace and elegance to the energy, business ability and taste of Walter B. Devereux and associates. "*

The *Denver Republican* enthused, *"Some of the beds have testers (canopies) on them gracefully wrought in arabesques. Each room has an extension electric globe whose height in front of the dressing-case mirror a lady can regulate. "*

There was of course a polo match on Saturday afternoon, pitting Glenwood Springs against Colorado Springs, as well as a series of horse races for the entertainment of the local populace and the visitors. An impressive pyrotechnic display was presented on the terrace of the hotel in the evening, preceding the elegant ball at 10:00 P.M. At the beginning of the ball, Mr. and Mrs. Walter Devereux led the grand march. She was gowned in an "Elizabethan costume of lavender silk combined with brocade," as well as diamond jewelry. The other guests, both male and female, were dressed in the most elegant fashions available. Abe Cohen's clothing store in the First National Bank Building, and Napier and McClure Dry Goods provided men's suits and shirts, while millinery was provided by Mrs. E. Austin. T. R. Williams and B. Silver sold gentlemen's clothing, and J. G. Silver ran a tailor shop. Many dressmakers, including Mrs. John Shelton, had been busy creating gowns for the affair. A woman named Bowker reportedly owned a dressmaking emporium that catered to both society ladies and to the "ladies of the brick. " She accomplished this with a minimum of confrontation by delivering gowns to the prostitutes' places of business for their selection and purchase.

The Hotel Colorado opening was certainly the social event of the season. With the hotel now open, the pool complex and vapor caves in full operation, and two railroads serving the community, Walter Devereux's version of Glenwood Springs was at last ready to play host to the world. In the months following the grand opening, the Hotel Colorado's register saw such names as Armour, Mayo, and Gould. Margaret "Molly" Brown, David Moffatt and "Diamond Jim" Brady were among the distinguished guests.

A scant two weeks after the opening of the Hotel Colorado, the announcement came from England's House of Lords that the mints in India had been closed to the further coinage of silver. India was

An early advertisement featuring the Hotel Colorado, the Hot Springs Pool, and an overview of Glenwood Springs. The highway/pedestrian bridge is shown closest to the camera, the Midland Railroad bridge in the background. Apparently due to the whim of the graphic artist who designed this layout, Mount Sopris has been moved to the west of town. (Courtesy of Scott Leslie)

to go on the "Gold Standard," the currency backing that had been adopted by most of the rest of the civilized world. Silver immediately dropped in value, and a meeting of the Colorado silver mine owners was held at the Brown Palace Hotel in Denver. The owners agreed to cease silver production in Colorado until it could again be produced at a profit. After a period of dire, and as it turned out, accurate predictions for the silver industry, the United States Government also abandoned silver. The resultant "Silver Panic" turned towns such as Aspen and Leadville into virtual ghost towns almost overnight. It also seriously affected the future of coal production on the Western Slope of Colorado, since so much of that coal was used to produce coke for the smelting operations. The coal for the growing steel industry was being supplied by the vast coal fields of eastern Colorado and elsewhere, so the market for Western Slope coal dropped accordingly.

Glenwood Springs was certainly affected by the change, as were many other towns that relied upon silver mining for a part of their economy. However, Devereux's efforts had turned Glenwood into a tourist attraction that continued to attract wealthy British tourists who rubbed shoulders with newly-rich Coloradans. Therefore, while many Colorado mountain towns literally died, Glenwood Springs lived on, the huge pool and the elegance of the Hotel Colorado separated from the raucous saloons and bawdy houses of Riverfront by the Grand River.

There was great concern among bank depositors due to the Silver Panic, and it appeared that the First National Bank was in danger of experiencing a "run," with bank customers demanding their money to the point of cleaning out the bank. Walter Devereux left for Denver by train to pick up $50,000 in cash to help cover the anticipated withdrawals. Thanks to a ruse by James Henry Devereux, Walter's brother, who was then bank vice President, and J. H. Fessler, the cashier, the extra money was not needed. Early the next morning as the expected crowd of depositors was gathering outside the bank, Fessler pulled up in his buckboard, in which was prominently displayed his fishing equipment. The two men remarked loudly about what a great day it was to go fishing up Grizzly or No Name Creeks and Fessler marched back out, whistling, and drove off. The intended message spread rapidly through town. If the cashier was that unconcerned, reasoned the depositors, then they obviously had little reason to worry. The crowd disbursed and people actually began redepositing their money.

In the fall of 1893, Griffith Jones and Henry Hubbard discovered a large limestone cave near the south rim of the Grand River Canyon, across from the future site of the Shoshone Power Plant. Some 3,000 feet of passages would eventually be surveyed, and it would become known as the "Hubbard Cave. " Hubbard and Jones were prospecting in the area, and were attracted by a cold draft issuing from the cave. They discovered the entrance, and proceeded to explore the twisting passages for some time. They eventually became lost and had to rely on their dog to lead them back to daylight.

October of 1893 saw a strike by the coal miners at the Vulcan Mine near New Castle. The initial complaint centered around two missed paydays for the workmen. The miners also demanded that only one person in the mine be responsible for setting dynamite charges, and that everyone be out of the mine when the dynamite

The new spa building covering the Cave Number 3, on the north side of the river. (Courtesy of Frontier Historical Society)

blast occurred. Another bone of contention was a headlamp called the Wolfe Safety Lamp. The problem with the lamp was a special mesh cover that was designed to collapse and extinguish the lamp in the presence of explosive gas. On the downside, the cover dimmed the light from the lamps to the point of making it difficult for the miners to see their work. The workers of the Consolidated Mine also went out on strike, and stayed out for some five months. The mine owners responded by boarding up the Consolidated Mine and threatening to let it fill up with water. They also hired back less than half of the original workers and lowered the wage scale of the Vulcan miners.

Late in 1893, the Hotel Colorado paid about half of its 160 employees a year's salary and terminated them, sending them back to Boston or England. The Silver Panic prevented the hotel from doing the amount of business that had been anticipated.

In 1894, a pavilion/observatory was built on the summit of Lookout Mountain. The *Avalanche* reported that a contract had been let, and that Theodore Von Rosenberg was to be the architect. The structure was to be made of vertical logs, arranged in a circular structure some eighteen by eighteen feet on the outside, fifteen by fifteen on the interior. There were also to be "toilet rooms" for ladies and men. Also that year, the foundation for the spa building was laid over Cave Number 3 of the vapor caves.

The United Mine Workers called a general strike in the summer of 1894. The miners of the Vulcan and the Consolidated mines near New Castle were hesitant to go out on strike so soon after their work stoppage of the previous October, but they joined their fellow miners. During the strike, the Midland Railroad bridge was burned by the miners to keep United States Marshals out of New Castle. Finally, the Colorado State Militia was used to ensure the safety of the trains. After the strike was over, John C. Osgood of Colorado Fuel and Iron closed the Consolidated Mine and a new work schedule of eight hour shifts was instituted at the Vulcan. Late in the year, the Consolidated miners agreed to accept the same wage scale as before the strike, and the Consolidated was reopened.

Walter Devereux, his hotel and spa complex completed, opened a mining engineering office in New York City in 1895. Even though Glenwood Springs was not immediately affected by the Silver Panic, Devereux likely had a premonition of the harder times to come. For the next several years, he wintered in New York and returned to his mansion in Glenwood Springs in the summers to play polo and to hunt and camp in the surrounding mountains. He and the rest of the family had by that time invested in mining operations all over North America as well as in Canada, Mexico, and Tasmania.

Notwithstanding the threat of economic downturn, building continued in downtown Glenwood and in the residential area just to the east. The Sheridan Building was built at 720 Cooper Avenue to house a saloon, a dairy creamery, and luxury apartments. It occupied the site of the first schoolhouse that had been abandoned due to its proximity to the "red light" district. The original Citizen's Bank Building, a frame structure, was also built in 1895. The Silver Club Building at 715 Grand Avenue was completed in the same year, and was the location of a well-appointed men's saloon and gambling hall. The existence of numerous small bedrooms, or "cribs," on the second floor hints at other uses for the building.

The Devereux brothers were largely responsible for the incorporation of the town of Antlers, a now non-existent town between Silt and Rifle.

Doctor William Crook purchased a Victorian home at 1002 Bennett Avenue in 1895. Doctor Crook, one of the town's earliest physicians and an investor in the Colorado Midland Railroad and Grand River Coal and Coke, was also a good friend of Buffalo Bill Cody. The two men had met in their youth in Fort Leavenworth,

Kansas when their families became friendly. Cody was a frequent visitor to Dr. Crook's home.

The Fairy Cave Company was formed on September 16, 1895. A pathway had been constructed from the Hotel Colorado to the caves, and donkeys were available to transport tourists up the slopes of Iron Mountain. A tunnel led from the main cave to a smaller one, the smaller cave opening onto a cliff overlooking the canyon. The view was said to be exceptional.

CHAPTER NINE

From 1896 to 1900

"The first parades had no theme and people would decorate floats with whatever was handy. They would start on Grand Avenue by the bridge and then go as far as the individual drivers of the floats cared to go. As the parade gyrated noisily through town, one by one, floats would peel off and park, or slide down side streets when they believed they'd gone far enough. Eventually the parade would just peter out. If you were watching, it made sense to stay near the first few blocks."

From *Strawberry Days Forever*, by Lisa Gerstner,
The Valley Journal, June 12, 1997

Edward Taylor, who had become district attorney of the Ninth Judicial District in 1887, furthered his political career by running for, and winning, the seat as Colorado state senator of the twenty-first district. Taylor had harbored a vision for several years; his vision involved a road through the Grand River Canyon. To be sure, Henry Morrow had carved a crude trail from one end of the canyon to the other, but Taylor envisioned a real road, a road that could be safely traveled without the danger of snow and rock slides, a road that was not subject to inundation by the waters of spring run-off. His determination to bring such a road into being was a large part of the impetus for his senatorial campaign.

To the west of the railroad freight yards was another hot spring, which had been all but ignored in the fever to develop the huge hot springs pool. Robert Ware changed that situation in 1896 when he built a large home and a small bathhouse. The buildings were surrounded with a park-like area that was planted with fruit trees and flower gardens. The bathhouse featured ten large tubs filled with hot mineral water, for the enjoyment and relaxation of the customers. Ware operated the bathhouse as a health center, and transported guests from their homes or hotels in a horse drawn ten-passenger carriage.

The seams of coal that run through the Grand Hogback from South of Redstone to north of New Castle had been mined in several locations over the years. There was a coal camp at Coal Basin, north of Redstone. A coal town was established at Sunshine, some nine miles above Glenwood Springs on Four Mile Creek. The small town, later changed to Sunlight, was located just below the present location of Sunlight Ski Area. Other mines and the accompanying towns appeared up South Canyon, at Marion, at Spring Gulch, and near New Castle. The mines varied widely in the amount of coal produced, but they did have one very important thing in common. Coal is produced when the rotted remains of plant and animal life of the ancient swamps is subjected to pressure and heat. If the heat is intense, as it was along the Grand Hogback due to volcanic activity, another substance is produced. It is a gas known as methane.

Early coal miners referred to methane as "fire damp," and cursed it for what it was, an element that added a great deal of danger to their daily work. Methane gas is poisonous. Breathing the vapors can result in sickness or death. In addition to that danger, the gas is also highly volatile. The methane tends to occur in pockets within the coal seams, and sparks from metal tools or machinery have set off many explosions, injuring or killing the miners unlucky enough to be involved. In the early days of coal mining in the area, the use of torches and blasting powder carried the added hazard of methane explosions.

Coal mining is, by its very nature, a hazardous occupation. The sometimes extremely steep angles of the coal seams in Colorado produce difficult, perilous, working conditions. The grade of the coal seams in the Grand Hogback range from around twelve degrees to over forty-five degrees. An 1888 report by the Inspector of Coal Mines reports the pitch of the coal seams in the Consolidated Mine near New Castle as being fifty-five degrees. The use of heavy machinery, sharp steel pickaxes, and blasting powder carries the threat of injury. Working deep within the earth exposes the miners to cave-ins or rockfalls, trapping or crushing them. Coal dust, created and stirred up by the mining process, is inhaled by the miners many hours of the workday. Many times, the result is the dreaded Black Lung Disease, shortening the breath and the lives of the miners. Fine coal dust is also explosive. Water from underground springs is a constant problem, flooding tunnels and making the working conditions even more unpleasant and hazardous. The removal of large quantities of coal from the core of a mountain can sometimes result in "bumps" or "bounces" as the earth rearranges itself to accommodate the cavities. These movements can range from annoying to lethal.

The possibility of employment in the coal mines of western Colorado brought many immigrants to this country, especially after the labor disputes in 1884 and 1885. In most cases, they were under contract to the mine owners. Agents in Europe offered to pay the transportation costs of Italians, Greeks,

A coal miner, his children, and a fellow worker. (Courtesy of Frontier Historical Society)

Austrians, and others to America, in return for the payment of a percentage of their earnings. The agents guaranteed to the United States Immigration authorities that the newcomers would be gainfully employed. The miners who contracted with the agents and mining companies were basically indentured servants, tied to the mines until they repaid the cost of their passage plus a large profit to their exploiters.

The coal towns of the day were frequently company towns, set up to provide for the daily needs of the miners. There were houses, usually small and utilitarian, a general store that carried food, clothing, mining tools, household utensils and other essentials of life, schools for those miners with families, and sometimes saloons, clubhouses, and other amenities. In many instances, the miners were paid at least partially in scrip that was only redeemable at the company stores, further bonding the miners to their employer. The miners were, in most cases, required to purchase the tools that they used daily to mine the coal. The average pay for a ten to twelve-hour day was around $3.00 to $3.50, yet the cost of all of the necessary picks, shovels and other mining tools could run to $75.00.

A great many of the immigrants came to the United States alone, leaving their wives and children in their native land until the miners could afford to pay their passage to America. For them, it was vital that they worked to the satisfaction of the mine owners. In the early days of coal mining in the United States there were no unions. There was no paid vacation, no unemployment insurance, no medical benefits or sick leave. There was only the opportunity to work underground for up to twelve hours a day. If a particular worker was not able to produce, he was simply replaced. There were no doubt instances of men leaving their families to come to the "new world," only to perish in an explosion or mine cave-in. Considering the lack of long distance communication of the day, the families might never learn of the fate of their loved one.

When the wives and children did arrive, it was many times their efforts that delivered the family into a semblance of financial equality with the rest of the area. Many of the wives filed homesteads on the thousands of acres that were still available in the mountains around Glenwood Springs, and sold freshly baked bread and farm products or provided laundry or cleaning services to earn the necessary money to help support the family.

As of 1896, Garfield County had ten operating coal mines. 457 men were employed in the mines, of whom 287 were employed in the mines in the vicinity of New Castle. The three largest of these were the Consolidated, across the river from the town, the Keystone, a mile and one half down river from the Consolidated, and the Vulcan, just west of New Castle. Given the level of safety considerations in the coal mining industry in the late 1800s, it was not surprising that accidents and fires in the mines were a weekly occurrence. However, on February 18, 1896, a massive explosion ripped through the Vulcan mine. Mining timbers were thrown some 400 feet away. The terrible methane blast killed 47 men and injured many others. The resultant blockage of the tunnel was so complete that it took most of the next four weeks to recover all of the bodies. The Vulcan mine was owned by the Atcheson, Topeka, and Santa Fe Railroad, one of the few mines in the area not controlled by either the Colorado Fuel and Iron Company or the Grand River Coal and Coke Company.

The telephone had been invented by Alexander Graham Bell in 1876, but the newfangled device was not to arrive in Glenwood Springs until after the turn of the century. However, Glenwood was not totally without a type of telephone communication. Will Parkison formed and lead a cooperative called the Beach Valley System which provided a crude form of verbal communication over wires. Each subscriber, of which there were about thirty, purchased a large box with a transmitter and a receiver, and with a receptacle representing each of the other stations. By inserting a key in the proper hole, the user could act as his or her own operator, causing the device to ring on the other end of the line. It was basically a form of intercom, but it served the purpose until real telephones arrived on the scene.

In 1897, the building at 716 Cooper Avenue was completed. It initially housed Ed Bosco's Saloon, and also featured furnished rooms on the second floor.

On July 20, 1897, a fire erupted in the New Castle Mine. No one was injured or killed in the conflagration, and it was extinguished by diverting an irrigation ditch into the mine. The diversion succeeded in putting the fire out, but it took a month to drain the mine and get it back into operation.

On September 3, 1897, another mine explosion jarred the mining community. The Sunlight Mine on Four Mile Creek above Glenwood Springs had been in operation since the early 1880s. The name of the town had been changed from Sunshine to Sunlight earlier in the year, because there were several other coal towns in Colorado and Wyoming called Sunshine. At about 5:45 P.M. on the day in question, what was described as a small explosion killed twelve men. They were reportedly working near the entrance of the mine when the blast hit them. Unusually strong air currents helped to feed the resultant fire.

Another weekly newspaper, the *Glenwood Post,* was purchased by Amos J. Dickson on January 1 of 1898. The newspaper was actually the result of the merging of the *Post* and the *Weekly Ledger,* two papers that had been started in the early 1890s. The *Glenwood Post* joined the *Avalanche Echo* and the *Ute Chief News.*

The building that occupies 824 and 826 Grand Avenue was completed in the late 1890s. It housed one of the first Budweiser Beer distributorships in the western United States. Also, the original frame portion of the Rex Hotel at 420 Seventh Street was constructed in 1898.

The Sisters of Humility opened Glenwood's first hospital in 1898. They purchased ten and one half acres south of town from Edgar Wilson, and hired T. J. McDermott to build the hospital building. They were able to maintain the hospital for only a few years before financial difficulties forced them to close the facility. While they were in operation, however, they helped to nurse the populace through both diphtheria and smallpox epidemics. McDermott, the carpenter to whom they owed their mortgage, finally took over the property.

Early in 1898, the Tri-County Farmers' Union members paid a call on the leaders of Glenwood Springs. The farmers' organization had been formed a few years earlier to promote the numerous productive farms and orchards that were being established in the area. There had been talk for some time about the possibility of a special day, some sort of annual observance, to stimulate demand for farm products and increase interest in the valleys of the Roaring Fork and the Grand River. They proposed that the celebration be centered around the strawberry, one of the most popular crops.

The city fathers were receptive to the notion, and it was not long before the excitement began to grow. Both A. J. Dickson, publisher of the *Glenwood Post,* and H. J. Holmes of the *Avalanche Echo* positioned themselves directly behind the project. Dickson wrote an article entitled, "Why We Should Have Strawberry Day" that was read at the courthouse during a gathering to discuss the possibilities. Holmes proposed contests featuring flower and fruit displays with appropriate prizes. The concept of "Strawberry Day" took on a life of its own. Before long, the date of June 18, 1898 was chosen for the first edition of what would become one of Colorado's oldest annual festivals.

The four months leading up to the designated day were filled with promotional activities. There was talk of recreational activities, of visitors from afar. Some imaginative soul proposed that everyone in the area include an image of a "pretty, juicy-looking strawberry" on their stationery. A special invitation was sent to Governor Alva Adams, and every newspaper in the state contained an invitation to the celebration. Both railroads promoted the festival, offering special rates to and from Glenwood Springs. The Colorado Midland also provided a band of thirty uniformed members who formed at the corner of Eighth and Grand to entertain the celebrants. Between the two trains and those visitors who arrived by carriage or horseback, the first Strawberry Day attracted some 2,500 visitors to Glenwood Springs. Miners and their families were brought into town by rail from the various surrounding coal towns, and business was brisk at the hotels, restaurants, saloons, gambling halls, and, presumably, the "houses of ill fame."

A view looking north on Grand Avenue on June 18, 1898, the very first Strawberry Day. The Hotel Colorado is visible across the bridge. (Courtesy of Frontier Historical Society)

The Hot Springs Pool gave free admission to all comers, and the Glenwood Springs team beat Leadville in an afternoon baseball game in front of an enthusiastic crowd. (The score was 6 - 5.) The Colorado Midland Band played again at a great ball in the evening. Everyone involved proclaimed the first Strawberry Day a success.

The single activity that set the new festival apart, and was to become its identifying feature, was the serving of generous portions

The beginning of a tradition - the serving of strawberries, cake, and fresh cream (Courtesy of Frontier Historical Society)

of freshly-baked cake, covered with strawberries and drowned with fresh cream. The delectable treat was free to all, as were tall glasses of lemonade. The ladies of Glenwood spent many hours preparing the cake and strawberries for the huge, appreciative crowd. They, of course, had no way of knowing that they were an important part of the first in a series of celebrations that would be continued for over one hundred years.

Another annual event was begun in July of 1898, the twenty-three mile bicycle race from near Basalt to Sixth Street in Glenwood Springs, near the Colorado Hotel and the Natatorium, or big pool. Many of the local men paid the dollar entry fee. The Colorado Midland Railway, which paralleled the road, ran a special observation train for those wishing to watch the race. The train kept pace with the race leaders all the way into Glenwood Springs. The first year the race was won in a time of one hour, twenty-six and a quarter minutes by William Broughton.

"Half-tunnel" on the Taylor State Road through the Grand River Canyon. (Courtesy of Frontier Historical Society)

In 1899, Senator Edward Taylor sponsored a bill in the Colorado state legislature, asking for $40,000 in state aid for the building of a road. A great deal of road construction occurred just before the turn of the century, but this particular road was to have a dramatic effect on the town of Glenwood Springs. The proposed road, the first continuous wagon road from Denver to Grand Junction, was to pass through the Grand River Canyon, just to the east of Glenwood Springs. It was obviously an incredibly ambitious project, but Taylor had harbored a vision of the completion of the road for years, and he was successful in pushing the bill through the state legislature. The road would follow the crude trail that had been hacked out of the canyon rock by Henry Morrow.

In a move basically unheard of in those days, the bill called for the preservation of the natural beauty along the roadway. Roadside advertising would be banned, and the existing shrubs and trees were to be protected. This unusual provision, along with the road itself, would be a monument to Edward Taylor. It was to be called the Taylor State Road.

As the Sisters of Humility struggled to survive financially while ministering to the sick, another Catholic nun

An advertisement for the St. Joseph's Sanitarium, about 1899. (Courtesy of Frontier Historical Society)

named Sister Superior Mary Agnes arrived in town. She had attended Sisters College in Ottumwa, Iowa, and became a nun in the service of the Sisters of Mary at the age of fifteen. When her father died in 1889, he asked that all of his considerable wealth be used by his daughter to establish a charitable institution of some kind. Sister Mary Agnes brought his money to Glenwood Springs and purchased the St. James Hotel from Fred Barlow. At the age of thirty-two, she established the St. Joseph's Sanitarium and Hotel. The hotel was already plush, but she spent many thousands of dollars in transforming it into a first class operation.

The first floor of the refurbished hotel/sanitarium held parlors, dining rooms, kitchen, reading rooms, and a barbershop. The second level contained private sleeping and toilet rooms, as well as a private office and parlor. Above that on the third floor were the physician's office, the surgery, laboratory, chemical storage, and a large chapel. Private apartments comprised the fourth floor. An elevator carried guests and patients between floors. Sister Mary Agnes proclaimed that no one, rich or poor, was ever to be turned away from her doors. She advertised heavily, anticipating visitors from all over America, as well as from other countries. She was never, unfortunately, to realize her dream. The location of the St. Joseph's Sanitarium and Hotel, just yards from the saloon and "red-light" district, cast a shadow over the operation, and it was to last only three years.

The treacherous Vulcan Mine was finally closed for good in 1899, with a fire in progress deep within the mine. Along the mountain to the south of the Colorado River, across the valley from New Castle, there is a broad band where vegetation is sparse, where the snow never collects. One hundred years later, as this is written, the fire still smolders along the coal seam beneath the surface.

CHAPTER TEN

From 1900 to 1905

"Alas poor equine. If the anticipations of Alexander Winton of the Winton Bicycle Co. will be ultimately realized, the horse will slowly but inevitably drop into oblivion.

Mr. Winton has succeeded in perfecting a horseless gasoline motor carriage which can be operated by a woman and which is barren of all the obnoxious appurtenances which have been objectionable in many of the horseless carriages in use in Europe and which have been indifferently introduced in this country..."

The *Cleveland Plain Dealer, October 25, 1896*

In 1900, the population of Glenwood Springs was 1,350. The Colorado Telephone Company obtained a franchise to provide Glenwood Springs with telephone service for the first time. They strung a line down the Roaring Fork Valley from Aspen and offered the installation of wall telephones in Glenwood. The first operators were Harold and Walter Parkison, and the exchange was set up in Parkison's Pharmacy.

The diversion tunnel for the water system was completed in 1900. The new aqueduct carried water from Grizzly Creek through the intervening rock ridge into No Name Creek.

Two more buildings were completed in the 700 block of Grand Avenue; the one at 722 housed the Western Union Globe Express, taking the place of an outdoor bandstand. E. L. Peisar set up a jewelry store in the new building next door at 724 Grand. Both of the structures served a number of uses in later years. The Springs Sports Bar presently occupies 722 Grand, and Doc Holliday's Saloon is at 724 Grand.

Between the downtown area and the Roaring Fork River, an area known as the Park had been set aside for the cowboy sport of rodeo. (The old rodeo grounds is now the Vogelaar Softball Field.) Horse racing, roping contests, and "bronco busting," the riding of untamed horses, had been popular activities throughout the existence of Glenwood Springs, but by 1900 the Park was attracting world-class competition. The town even advertised the activities, offering prizes for the "World's Champion Bronco Buster."

Early in 1901, Vice President Theodore Roosevelt arrived in Glenwood Springs. Roosevelt, an outstanding naturalist, outdoorsman, and hunter, had come to western Colorado to hunt big game. From January 11 to February 14, he and his party hunted in White River country, north and west of Glenwood Springs. Among other trophy animals, the vice president was successful in killing the world's record mountain lion, a record that stood for a number of years. The lion was some eight feet long, and weighed in excess of 220 pounds. John Goff of Meeker was his principal guide during that hunt.

The silver cup won by the Glenwood Springs Polo Team in the 1901 championship match. (Courtesy of Frontier Historical Society)

F. H. A. "Hervey" Lyle and his polo team returned from Colorado Springs with a huge silver bowl that commemorated their victory in the Rocky Mountain Championship polo match. They won rather decisively, with a final score in the match of 11 1/2 - 1. The local newspapers praised the team highly.

Hyde Hall, on the western side of Cooper Avenue, had hosted just about everything in the years of its existence. It had seen citizens' meetings, talent shows, balls, church services, and prizefights. Surely one of the highlights of the great hall occurred in 1901 when the orchestra of John Philip Sousa played there. Among many other songs and marches, Sousa introduced "Hail to the Spirit of Liberty," and the orchestra played it for the first time.

The Spring Gulch Mine was located on the Grand Hogback almost directly south of Sunlight and north of John Osgood's Coal Basin. At approximately 6:00 P.M. on September 16, 1901, the mine was the scene of a huge explosion which killed six miners. The exact cause of the blast was never determined, but it traveled up two ventilation shafts that had been dug above the mine. Henry Coll, who had been born in Spring Gulch, reported that a watch belonging to Robert Bickerton was blown out of one of the air shafts. Bickerton was one of the casualties.

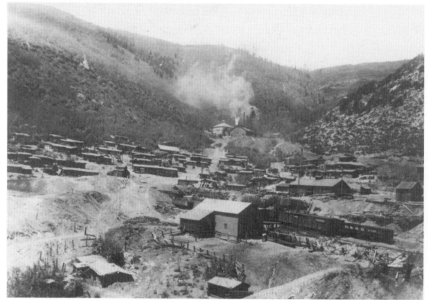

The coal town and mine at Spring Gulch. (Courtesy of Buzz Zancanella)

The Taylor State Road, from Denver to Grand Junction, was completed in 1902. The original appropriation had been $40,000, but the final cost of the project exceeded $60,000. Fully half of the total cost was spent in "the canyon east of Glenwood Springs." The *Glenwood Post* of May 17, 1902 quoted the designer of the project, J. J. McCune:

"Over a great portion, the road was cut out of solid rock, and as some factitious wag has said, there wasn't a bushel of dirt in the 20 miles."

H. B. Morrell, the contractor for the new road, was praised highly for his work by the reporter for the *Post*. It was said that it was necessary in places to lower the workmen down from the overhanging cliffs in order to drill the holes for blasting of the roadway.

Almost as soon as the new road was opened, it was traveled by noisy, strange-looking vehicles the likes of which had rarely been seen in western Colorado. The horseless carriage had arrived. One of the first was a broker named W. W. Price. Price left Colorado Springs in a Winton, one of the newfangled automobiles, headed for Leadville and points west. From the rarefied air of America's highest incorporated city, Price headed over Tennessee Pass and

An automobile on the bridge over Grizzly Creek, part of the Taylor State Road. (Courtesy of John Tindall)

One of the newfangled "horseless carriages." (Courtesy of Frontier Historical Society)

through the newly navigable Grand River Canyon. Arriving in Glenwood Springs, he reportedly annoyed the populace greatly by parading his "gas buggy" up and down Grand Avenue, "endangering people's lives by frightening their horses." Automotive tourism, for better or worse, had come to Glenwood. With a degree of relief, the residents watched Mr. Price leave town on his return trip.

Glenwood Springs returned to the relative quiet of horses and carriages, but the respite was not to last. The Colorado Automobile Association had just been formed in Denver, and the steadily improving roads throughout the state were beginning to attract the adventurous souls who were buying the new motorcars. Whereas previous travelers from Denver to Glenwood Springs had come by way of Cottonwood Pass, Independence Pass, or by train, they could now take a much more direct route, by way of the still primitive, but serviceable road through Grand River Canyon.

Fred Kaiser and his wife built their new home at 932 Cooper Avenue in 1902. Kaiser was an electrician with Glenwood Light and Power Company.

In 1903, the Citizens' National Bank was opened by B. T. Napier and George Yule, for whom the vast deposits of marble on the Crystal River were named. Napier was president, Yule was vice president, George H. Bell was cashier, and M. Waesall was assistant cashier.

The Board of Trade was organized in 1903. Horace Devereux was the driving force behind the formation of the organization, which was to become the forerunner of the Chamber of Commerce. The first president of the Board of Trade was Will Parkison. The Board was intended to promote not only Glenwood Springs, but also the remainder of northwestern Colorado. They sent displays both to the Colorado State Fair and to the St. Louis World's Fair in 1904, pointing out the ranching, farming, and tourism potential of the area.

In March of 1903, Teddy Roosevelt returned to Glenwood Springs on a whistle-stop tour of the western United States. He came as president this time. He had advanced to that office when William McKinley was assassinated. The assassination had occurred not long after Roosevelt's 1901 visit to Glenwood Springs. Roosevelt was only 43 years old when he became president.

Following their Rocky Mountain Championship in 1901, the Glenwood Springs polo team went on to win the World Championship in 1903 and 1904. They regularly played teams from Denver and Colorado Springs, as well as the U. S. Tenth Cavalry team from Fort Robinson, Nebraska. In 1903, the first year that the Glenwood team won the World Championship, they were defeated at home by the cowboy team.

The award as "The World's Champion Bronco Buster" had been won in 1903 by a South American named Grimsley. There was a suspicion of underhanded tactics in the victory, which was borne out the following year, at least to the satisfaction of the local cowboys. A local trick rider and horseman named Rich Thompson succeeded in riding rings around Grimsley, and they proceeded to strip him of his silver trophy belt and send him back to South America. The local cowboys apparently didn't put up with much. There were reports of a jockey from the Tenth Cavalry being shot and killed over a remark about the alleged "doping" of one of the Glenwood horses.

There were several developments on the health front during 1903. Doctor W. F. Berry, who had learned his medicine in Rochester with the Mayo Brothers, arrived in Glenwood Springs. He saw a need for a hospital in the still growing town. The St. Joseph's Sanitarium, which had been opened in 1899 by Sister Mary Agnes with the best of intentions, was just about to fail financially. In fact, the building was to be taken over later in the year by W. L. Lee, who was the manager of the Hotel Glenwood. The sanitarium was renamed the Grand, under the management of J. D. Phillipi, and reopened as a luxury hotel.

Meanwhile, Dr. Berry leased the second floor of the Deacon Building on Grand Avenue, to be used for his hospital. He converted the rooms so that they could be used for surgery and patient care. In addition, he started the Glenwood Nurses Training School, Inc. With the help of Dr. Paul Wiesel, surgeon and anatomy teacher, and Miss Buersh, his head nurse, he established a full three-year nursing school. After the three years of training in Glenwood Springs, the student nurses were qualified to take the State Board examinations for registered nurses in Denver.

Ella Barlow was still taking patients in her home hospital, but there were complaints that many of her "patients" were merely indigent rather than ill. Consequently, the Garfield County commissioners made the decision to buy the old Sisters of Humility Hospital which had been taken over by T. J. McDermott. They bought the building and the ten and one half acres from McDermott, with the intention of turning it into a County Poor Farm.

There was abundant incidence of smallpox in the valley at that time, and there was a real danger of infection if those afflicted were mixed with other patients. Smallpox was a virulent killer in the years before vaccination was perfected. After inhaling the virus, the infected person would suffer headaches and backaches, chills and high fever. After these symptoms abated, the patient would undergo a pronounced rash that changed to quite painful blisters. If the person survived, and many did not, the blisters would result in deep scarring.

In Glenwood Springs, it was felt that those already infected with the disease should be separated from the other inhabitants of the Poor Farm, as well as from the rest of the general populace. For this reason, a fourteen by twenty-four foot structure was built some distance from the main building. It was called the "pesthouse." Anyone with smallpox was placed there, regardless of sex or social position. Merchants and prostitutes, bankers and the unemployed shared the dismal little building. The first caretaker of the pesthouse was, interestingly, J. M. Schwarz, the mortician. He was paid fifty cents a day per patient.

The constant struggle against the disease and poverty was bad enough; the pesthouse was also filthy and infested with lice and other vermin. Bedbug powder was purchased by the barrel. To top things off, the little house of horror eventually gained the reputation of being haunted. Two of the later caretakers, John and Maggie Campbell, diagnosed the "ghosts" as woodpeckers.

In 1904, Senator Edward Taylor's home at 903 Bennett was finished. Taylor, in addition to being the father of the Taylor State Road, was also known as the initiator of the Taylor Grazing Act, which was to remain the law for grazing cattle on federal property to the present day.

The home of Senator Edward M. Taylor at 903 Bennett. (Courtesy of Frontier Historical Society - Schutte Collection)

The red sandstone and brick Denver & Rio Grande Railway Station was also finished in that year. It replaced the old Denver & Rio Grande depot on Pitkin Avenue. The new station was constructed across the street from the hotels and saloons of Riverfront, separated from the Grand River by the tracks themselves.

The opening of the new Denver & Rio Grande depot on the north side of Riverfront created the impetus for some major improvements to the neighborhood. A grocery store, four saloons, a restaurant, and a rooming house were closed, and Henry Bosco's wholesale liquor operation moved from the basement of one of the saloons to the ground floor. He then purchased several of the buildings and began remodeling them into the beginnings of the Star Hotel. At about the same time, Mr. and Mrs. Art Kendrick, who had been operating a rooming house called the Denver Rooms, began buying properties on the other end of the block. They purchased the Walter building at the corner of Riverfront and Cooper and converted it

The Denver & Rio Grande depot on the north side of Riverfront, built of red sandstone. (Courtesy of Frontier Historical Society)

into the Denver Hotel. Hervey Lyle and the Glenwood Springs polo team won the World Championship again in 1904, for the second year in a row. William Cross, whose taxidermy work had won him international acclaim, exhibited many of his mounted animals and birds at the St. Louis World's Fair.

President Theodore Roosevelt returned to western Colorado on April 15, 1905, for another big game hunt, arriving in Glenwood Springs on the Colorado Midland Presidential Limited train. It was powered by Engine No. 15, which had been decorated in red, white, and blue. "Our President" was emblazoned on each side of the coal tender. In addition to special cars for Roosevelt's Secret Service guards and Colorado Midland officials, the president had his own personal car, "The Rocket."

The Star Hotel in the center, the Rex Hotel to the left, and the Denver Hotel on the right. (Courtesy of Frontier Historical Society)

Lunchtime at Teddy Roosevelt's hunting camp. The president is at the head of the table. (Courtesy of Frontier Historical Society)

The train did not stop in Glenwood Springs, but Roosevelt was standing on the back platform of his car, and he shouted to the populace gathered along the tracks that he would see them after the hunt. Besides, it was common knowledge that the Hotel Colorado was about to become the "Little White House of the United States." Secretary of State William Loeb set up presidential headquarters in the east wing of the hotel with telegraph service to Washington, D. C., and a courier named Elmer Chapman rode on horseback between the hotel and Roosevelt's hunting camp with correspondence.

The train did stop in New Castle where school was let out, and almost the entire population gathered to welcome their leader. Like any good politician, Roosevelt spoke to the crowd, complimenting them on their attractive farms and irrigation projects. He challenged them to provide progressive education for their children, shook many hands, and mounted up for his ride to the hunting camp.

The hunting party set up at the head of West Divide Creek at an elevation of about 9,000 feet. There was an abandoned cabin on what had been the Bunn homestead, and the hunters utilized it for sleeping. As in his 1901 hunt, Roosevelt had chosen John Goff from Meeker to guide him. Jake Borah from Gypsum was also chosen, as was Al Anderson from Glenwood Springs. Goff had already guided hunters for many years, with some 100 bears and 350 mountain lions to his credit. In addition to the prominent guides, there was a large group of cowboys and other "hangers-on" who accompanied the president on the hunt.

Only two days later, on April 17, a large black bear fell to Roosevelt's gun. It was the first of ten bears and three lynx that were "harvested" by the hunting party. After hunting the Divide Creek area and along the Muddy River, they had planned to cross McClure Pass to Redstone. John Cleveland Osgood, coal baron and the founder of Redstone, had by that time built his castle a mile upriver from the town, and Roosevelt no doubt wanted to visit Osgood and Alma Regina Shelgrem Osgood, his second wife. However, the remaining snow was too deep, so the hunting party returned to the Grand River Valley and proceeded up onto the Flat Tops. They wound up hunting around the site of the old town of Carbonate.

As was the custom of the day, both bear and mountain lion were hunted with the aid of hounds. These were mostly large, rangy beasts, afraid of nothing. On this particular hunt, however, there was one dog that was smaller and weaker than the others. He was a fox terrier by the name of "Skip." Roosevelt took to him and made a habit of giving the small dog a ride behind his saddle when Skip became tired. They became great friends, and the president ended up taking Skip back to Washington with him.

President Theodore Roosevelt returning to Glenwood Springs after his 1905 hunt. (Courtesy of Frontier Historical Society)

After hunting for almost three weeks, Roosevelt reappeared in Glenwood Springs, riding an impressive white horse, and accompanied by his guides and the rest of the hunting party. That evening he was introduced by Mayor Will Parkison and spent some time working the crowd and shaking hands. Later, he hosted a stag banquet at the big hotel dining room for all of the men who had accompanied him on his hunt. Reportedly, he swore all of them to secrecy regarding the subjects of jokes and conversation.

The hides from the hunt were taken to Frank Hayes, local taxidermist, for tanning and making into rugs. It is said that Roosevelt posed on the front lawn of the Hotel Colorado with one of the larger of the pelts. His teenage daughter Alice suggested that the bear be called "Teddy." According to local legend, the president was later presented with a small toy stuffed bear made by the staff of the Hotel Colorado. A toy maker picked up the idea, and the "Teddy Bear" was born. There are those, including the Smithsonian Institute, who dispute this story, claiming that the first "Teddy Bear" was created in 1902 after Roosevelt declined to shoot a bear cub on a hunting trip in Mississippi. Whatever the truth, the legend persists that Glenwood Springs was the birthplace of the Teddy Bear.

On May 6, after walking from the hotel to the Presbyterian Church to hear the Reverend J. Wilson Currens, Roosevelt returned by way of Frank Hayes' White Elk Museum to admire the huge mounted albino elk that gave the establishment its name. That afternoon he again addressed the gathered crowd, this time from the balcony overlooking the open court of the hotel. Early in the evening, he returned to the "Rocket," in preparation for his return to Washington the next day. Having arrived by way of the Colorado Midland, he was to return on the Denver & Rio Grande tracks, so that he could see the canyon of the Grand River and also the Royal Gorge. The Denver & Rio Grande had designated Engine No. 720 to haul the president's train back toward the East. The engine was the first on the Denver & Rio Grande route to use an electric headlight.

While Roosevelt was meeting the hordes of people in Glenwood Springs, a motion picture photographer was busily filming the activities. It was the first "movie" to be filmed in Glenwood, as well as one of the first motion pictures of a United States President. Unfortunately, when the film was developed, it was discovered that it contained images of certain ladies of the evening meeting the president. Included in this group was reportedly one young lady who was attired in what has been described as an "indiscreet riding habit." Unfortunately for posterity, the entire film was ordered destroyed.

Harvey Logan, who became infamous as "Kid Curry," a member of Butch Cassidy's "Wild Bunch," had spent several years wandering the Rocky Mountain west, robbing banks and trains, stealing horses, rustling cattle, and generally raising hell. He was credited with killing almost a score of men during his career. On June 7, 1904, he and his current henchmen were surrounded in the mountains in the southwestern part of the county after robbing a Denver & Rio Grande train of $40,000. Kid Curry was wounded by Rolla Gardner, from whom they had stolen some horses as part of their getaway attempt. The "Kid" reportedly told his compatriots to go on without him and proceeded to end it with a bullet to his own head.

Kid Curry was buried in the Linwood Cemetery in Glenwood Springs. In fact, he was buried twice. There was some concern about his identity, even though his body had been viewed by many people prior to his interment. However, just to make sure, Pinkertons sent a detective named Lowell Spense to exhume the corpse on July 23, photograph it, and then rebury it.

In 1905, a home was built at 1001 Colorado Avenue for Dr. and Mrs. Marshall Dean. The house was to eventually hold a quite important place in the history of Glenwood Springs. After being purchased by a banker named George Edinger, the house was inherited by Churchill and Stella Shumate, Edinger's daughter and son-in-law. They in turn willed the building to the Frontier Historical Society in 1971, to be used as a museum.

Jack Vorhees ran a livery stable on Colorado Avenue for the care of the horses, tack, and buggies of customers. In 1905, he decided that his business needed one of the newfangled automobiles. He purchased a Winton, made by the Winton Bicycle Company of Cleveland. It was powered by a small gasoline engine, capable of propelling the vehicle at speeds approaching twenty miles per hour. "Try a spin in our automobile — better than a spring tonic," proclaimed his ads in the *Avalanche Echo.*

In the narrowest portion of the Grand River Canyon, a set of rapids had plagued both the railroad tracks and the wagon road for years. At high water, especially during spring runoff, the swift water would inundate the road and undercut the railroad grade. It was with a degree of relief, therefore, that those who maintained the transportation corridors learned that the Central Colorado Power Company was looking at the Shoshone Rapids as a possible source of energy for a hydroelectric plant.

Prior to the decision to build a dam and power plant near the center of the canyon, Shoshone had been the site of a railroad siding, Denver & Rio Grande section houses, a water tank, and a bit of ranching activity.

The Shoshone Plant after completion. The large building at the right was a boarding house for workers. The smaller houses at the left were for the plant managers. (Courtesy of Frontier Historical Society)

By 1905, construction of the plant was well underway. A smaller 1,000 horsepower plant was first built to provide power for the project. Myron R. Herrick, the head of Central Colorado Power, envisioned a network of hydroelectric plants in the Rockies, which would provide electricity to the entire state of Colorado. As it turned out, only two plants were actually built, the one at Shoshone and one near Boulder. Herrick went on to become governor of Ohio and eventually the ambassador to France. The economy of Glenwood Springs was to benefit from a payroll of nearly one thousand men during the construction period. That two year construction period claimed the lives of six workers, due to the dangers involved in working with explosives, heavy equipment, and countless tons of active river water. One of the casualties, a consultant named Colonel Higby, died when a broken hoist cable dropped a load of rock on him. A railroad siding across the river from the power plant was named for him.

Senator Taylor again introduced a bill in the legislature, this time to change the name of the river that ran through the canyon to the east of town. At that time, the Grand River and the Green River combined in Utah to form the Colorado River, which continued through Glen Canyon and Grand Canyon on its way to the Gulf of

California. It was reasoned that, since the Grand was the larger of the two rivers, it should adopt the name of the great river that it helped to form, the Colorado. Taylor sponsored the bill in 1907, but it was not to actually go into effect until 1921.

The International Order of the Odd Fellows, or IOOF, began meeting in a building at 825 Grand Avenue in 1905. The building has acquired a wooden facade since then, but the original brick still exists underneath.

Walter Devereux was still running his mining engineering business in New York and returning to Glenwood Springs in the summers. In the early morning of September 6, 1905, after attending a polo match the previous day, he suffered a paralytic stroke. Crippling him, it rendered his left arm useless. The stroke paralyzed his entire left side, but he did eventually learn to walk again. He was fifty-two years old at the time.

CHAPTER ELEVEN

From 1906 to 1910

"You have every sensation of being hurled through space. The machine is throbbing under you with its cylinders beating a drummer's tattoo, and the air tears past you in a gale. In its maddening dash through the swirling dust the machine takes on the attributes of a sentient thing...I tell you, gentlemen: no man can drive faster and live!"

Barney Oldfield, about 1905, on the occasion of achieving the frightening speed of sixty miles per hour in an automobile.

The twenty year franchises of the Glenwood Light and Water Companies were about to run out. Provisions in the original paperwork gave the city the option of purchasing the utilities, but no price had been set. Two factions formed, one in favor of municipal ownership, the other leaning toward renewing the franchises under private ownership. Hughes, the liquor distributor, aligned with the *Glenwood Post*, the First National Bank, and the Republicans of the town in favor of privatization. The opposition was made up of the Democrats, the Citizens' National Bank, and the *Avalanche Echo*. The Democratic group persuaded the city council to make an offer of $60,000 for the Glenwood Light Company. This offer was considered to be much too small, and only served to add fuel to the animosity between the two groups. The matter wound up in the courts, and the legal battles continued for some time, finally ending in the United States Supreme Court in 1910.

In the early days of automobiles, when Henry Ford was fighting the Winton factory of Cleveland for supremacy in the fledgling automobile industry, a young man by the name of Bernard Eli (Barney) Oldfield rose to prominence as a barnstorming race driver. Among other achievements, he was the first man to drive a car faster than a mile a minute.

Oldfield gained fame for traveling around the country, challenging all comers to a dirt track race, and beating them all. He was of course driving a race car, but he was apparently forgiven for that. He came through Glenwood Springs in 1906 during a run from coast to coast. In addition to adding to his own renown, the cross-country tour popularized the notion of road building. Soon there

was talk of a transcontinental highway. Many towns across the country sought the honor of being included as part of the final route. Glenwood Springs was no exception.

The Taylor State Road provided passage through the canyon, but it was still subject to the whims of Mother Nature. It was rarely open in the winter, and was inundated each spring when the

A driver navigates the Taylor State Road. Note the construction fill dumped into the river. (Courtesy of Frontier Historical Society - Schutte Collection)

The original configuration of the power company water supply, complete with a massive pipe running along the floor of the canyon. This was replaced with a tunnel through the canyon wall. (Courtesy of Frontier Historical Society)

snowmelt waters cascaded into the river. Even during the summer, it was a very high-maintenance roadway and subject to the occasional rockfall. The road would need improving before long, especially considering the growing popularity of the automobile, so it might as well become part of the inevitable transcontinental route.

Two of Walter Devereux's sons, William and Bourchier, went into business with him in New York in 1906, after his stroke the previous year. The business was then known as W. B. Devereux and Sons, Consulting Mining Engineers.

The construction was proceeding on the Shoshone Dam and on the power plant. A small city developed at the site of the plant, boasting a post office, a company store, a hospital, a commissary, apartments, and a school for the children of the construction workers. There were also a railroad depot, offices, and warehouses. The little settlement was named, appropriately enough, Shoshone.

The Shoshone Dam was not designed to produce electrical power in the normal way, that is, by creating a deep reservoir of water that could be released past turbines to provide the necessary energy. Rather, this dam was built to divert the water of the river into a huge pipe that ran over two miles along the north side of the river. At the lower end of the pipe, the deluge of water turned two huge turbines which in turn powered generators to produce electricity.

The mammoth pipe was certainly an eyesore. Little or no concern had been shown for the beauty of the canyon during the construction of the railroad, and even the Taylor State Road had done little to enhance the appearance. The two plus miles of corrugated pipe running along the river was apparently the last straw for the residents of the area. Even the White River National Forest got into the fray, finally taking credit for persuading the power company to try another approach. That approach resulted in one of the most unusual details of the system. They bored a tunnel that enters the north wall of the canyon, and carried the rush of water some 2.3 miles, 12,700 feet westward, following the natural slope of the canyon. At the lower end, the deluge turned two huge turbines, which in turn powered generators that produce the electricity.

The tunnel was laboriously drilled and blasted through the solid granite of the north wall of the canyon. The interior dimensions of the bore were sixteen by eleven feet, and it was lined with concrete. It had the capacity to carry 1,250 cubic feet of water per second to the waiting turbines. The weather did not affect the boring of the tunnel, for obvious reasons, but the dam was another matter. With no reasonable method of holding back the relentless flow of what was now the Colorado River, the dam builders worked in the dead of winter, when the water flow was the lowest. The entire construction site of the dam was covered by a huge, heated tent.

The existing Shoshone Plant was actually built as a temporary structure. Original plans called for the extension of the aqueduct on down the river, and the construction of a larger plant some four miles west of Glenwood Springs. However, the economic depression during the year of 1907 permanently delayed those plans, and the "temporary" sheet metal and steel structure still stands.

The various forest reserves in the United States were renamed in 1907. As part of the legislative action, the White River Timber Land Reserve became known as the White River National Forest.

The coal mine at Sunlight, up near the top of Four Mile Creek, was purchased in 1907 by Rocky Mountain Fuel and Iron. The Sunlight mine had been abandoned in 1904 due to the lower elevation and greater accessibility of the New Castle Mine. After the fire in the New Castle Mine, Colorado Fuel and Iron reopened Sunlight and operated it until 1904. Due to faults in the coal seams and the disrepair of the buildings and equipment, it was an expensive operation.

On Riverfront, Kendrick's Denver Hotel, and the Star, owned by Bosco, were separated by Ryan's Cafe. When the cafe burned in

The schoolhouse at the coal town of Marion. (Courtesy of Buzz Zancanella)

early 1908, it cleared the way for Kendrick to expand his hostelry by forty feet. Where Riverfront had held a motley collection of saloons, brothels, and gambling parlors, the block across the street from the depot now held the Sheridan House, the Star Hotel, and the Denver Hotel.

The coal mine and town of Marion had been experiencing difficulties for several years. The mine had several faults, making the extraction of coal difficult and dangerous, and was also subject to underground water problems. It had been closed in 1895 and reopened in 1907, operating again for little more than a year. The mine closed again, permanently, in 1908.

Dr. W. F. Berry, who had set up a small hospital and started a nursing school in 1903, built the Glenwood Sanitarium at Eleventh and Bennett. He hired his brother, E. A. Berry, as his business manager and set up a new medical clinic in the spacious quarters. The building featured a large ward for coal miners, another for railroad workers, and yet another for employees of the Shoshone Power Plant. The big clinic featured the most modern of equipment, and attracted many of the local physicians and surgeons. Agnes Bell was hired as the head nurse.

A doctors' convention arrived in Glenwood Springs just after the opening of the new sanitarium, bringing some 500 people to town. Dr. Berry's student nurses were privileged to observe the operating techniques of such luminaries as Doctors William and Charles Mayo from Rochester, Minnesota, Dr. Butler from Baltimore, and Dr. Lorenz of Vienna, Austria. The local patients also benefited from the level of expertise in town during the convention.

On Friday night, January 14, 1909, two Denver & Rio Grande trains, a westbound passenger train and an eastbound freight, collided about six miles east of Glenwood Canyon. Whether the accident was the result of a disregard of orders or simply an error in reading the correct time was a subject for conjecture. Whatever the reason, twenty-one men, women, and children died at the scene of the twisted wreckage, and five more died later as a result of accident-related injuries.

The same year, the citizens voted in favor of bonds for a new high school for Garfield County. The new building was to be constructed on the corner of Thirteenth and Grand in Glenwood Springs, and was to replace the old school at Eleventh and Blake.

The 1909 wreckage of two Denver & Rio Grande trains in Glenwood Canyon. (Courtesy of Frontier Historical Society)

The first Colorado State Highway Commission was formed the same year. The commission was originally funded with a total of $56,000.

The Shoshone Power Plant was finally finished. The total cost came in at $2,700,000. The big cables for the transmission of electricity had been set, leading to the east up and over the Continental Divide to provide electricity for eastern Colorado. As an added bonus from the construction, the notorious Shoshone Rapids and Falls on the Colorado River were finally controlled. Since the first crude wagon road had been hacked out of the north wall of the canyon, the rapids had periodically inundated the road.

Later in the year, the Citizens' National Bank, on the northwest corner of Eighth and Grand, was robbed. The robbers, who made off with $10,000, were apprehended and convicted in 1910. It was the largest bank robbery in the history of Glenwood Springs.

President William Howard Taft visited Glenwood Springs in September of 1909. He reportedly enjoyed his visit but declined an invitation for a dip in the Hot Springs Pool. Taft was rather portly, and according to the *Avalanche Echo* of September 23, 1909, he declined "because he was not built for public exhibition in a bathing suit." According to one story, Taft refused to leave the train at the new station on Riverfront, due to its proximity to the saloons and brothels on that infamous street.

The Devereux family returned to Glenwood Springs that summer. They did not reopen Cedarbank, but rather stayed in the Hotel Colorado. W. B. Devereux and Sons disbanded in 1910. Walter had spent most of the last four years traveling with Mary; William and Bourchier had been running the company. After the company ceased operations the two sons went out on their own. Mary Devereux died of "Bright's Disease," a kidney disorder, on September 10, 1910. Walter spent the remainder of his life at either his summer home in Perry, Maine, or his son William's home in California.

The population of Glenwood Springs in 1910 was 2,019. This landmark allowed the town to change its status to that of a city. Governor John Shafroth issued an executive order declaring Glenwood Springs a "City of the Second Class." Not an auspicious designation perhaps, but the little town had achieved a new standing.

CHAPTER TWELVE

From 1911 to 1915

"For the love of Mike, send me a supply of marriage applications. I am clear out of blanks and am having to type them for folks pestering me to get married Strawberry Day. Mail them out at once or send them Pony Express."
County Clerk Hubbard, in an urgent message to a
Denver printer just before the 1912 Strawberry Day

An ancient Ute Indian trail led from the south shore of the Colorado River to the summit of Lookout Mountain, the prominent peak just to the east of downtown Glenwood Springs. The trail had been improved during the early years of the twentieth century, and climbing the trail, either on foot or horseback, was another popular tourist activity. The trail led to magnificent views of Glenwood Springs and of the Colorado River Valley.

A round observatory, known as the Raymond Observatory or the "lookout," had been constructed on the top of Lookout Mountain. There are conflicting reports as to the material from which it was constructed, but an article in an 1894 edition of the *Avalanche* states that it was constructed of vertical logs, with no mention of the use of stone. The observatory assumed new importance in 1910 with the appearance of Halley's Comet. Unfortunately, the observatory caught fire just after that and burned to the ground. The flames were clearly visible from downtown Glenwood Springs. A large crowd from town had gone to the top of Lookout Mountain the previous morning in order to get a clear view of the comet, and it was theorized that sparks from one of their campfires might have ignited the wooden structure.

The comet, which was first

Guests of the Hotel Colorado ready for a trail ride. (Courtesy of Frontier Historical Society)

observed in 1531, was named for Edmond Halley, a prominent English astronomer. He accurately predicted its return to visibility from Earth in 1758. Halley was not to live to witness the accuracy of his own prediction, however. He died in 1742.

The litigation about the disposition of Glenwood Springs' utilities finally wound up in the United States Supreme Court in 1910. The high court ruled in favor of the Glenwood Light and Water Company. Unhappy with the decision, the city council threw their support behind a new player in the game. The Mutual Light and Water Company, a small, under-funded enterprise, proceeded to string wires throughout Glenwood Springs, frequently crossing the existing lines of the Glenwood Power Company. This of course led to even more litigation.

At that time, polo was still a popular sport for both the participants and the observers. The Glenwood team was still of world-class caliber, but they were defeated again by the local cowboy team.

Walter Devereux, who had suffered a stroke some five years earlier at a polo game, sold "Cedarbank," his mansion on the south bank of the Colorado River in 1910. The home, which Devereux had purchased from Captain Prey, was sold to Julius Wulfsohn. It became known as the "Wulfsohn Mansion." Devereux was not to return to Glenwood for any appreciable length of time after the sale. He wintered in California, and spent his summers in Maine.

Several of the area coal mines had closed in the previous few years, leaving empty buildings and dark, silent mine shafts scattered

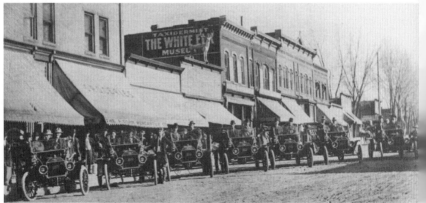

The members of the Glenwood Motor Club proudly display their brand-new 1910 Fords. (Courtesy of Frontier Historical Society)

about the hills. As the coal production dropped, so did the need for the long lines of ovens at Cardiff. By 1910, the production of the ovens had slowed drastically.

One of the early dentists in Glenwood was Dr. D. I. Pletcher. In 1910, he branched out into an unrelated field when he orchestrated the delivery of seven brand new Ford automobiles. He purchased one of the gas buggies for himself and sold the other six to Dr. W. F. Berry, H. O. Yewell, Jack Vorhees, and S. Hughes of Glenwood Springs, and to C. M. Donnell and W. H. Haley from Rifle. The seven men promptly organized the Glenwood Motor Club.

Also in 1910, a thirteen-year-old boy named Morgan Gavin made a drive from Carbondale, Colorado to Cincinnati, Ohio. The trip was a publicity stunt, aimed at continuing the emphasis on the need for decent roads through the western United States. Gavin traveled through Glenwood Canyon, over Tennessee Pass, through South Park, Colorado Springs, and Denver, and on east.

The new Garfield County High School that had been constructed at the corner of Thirteenth and Grand was accredited in 1911. The school charged no tuition, and many students from other parts of Garfield County attended.

Glenwood Springs, along with several other Western Slope towns, came under consideration for the site of a new college. Western State Teachers' College, along with the related eco-

The Garfield County High School, accredited in 1911. (Courtesy of Frontier Historical Society - Schutte Collection)

nomic benefits, was to be located in the town deemed most suitable for the educational and social benefit of the young teachers-to-be. Glenwood Springs, unfortunately, was still the home of Riverfront and its related side streets and alleys. The plethora of saloons, gambling halls, and brothels in and around the downtown area of Glenwood Springs apparently shocked and offended those upon whose shoulders the burden of the decision rested. They took a long look at the Glenwood Springs of 1911, a town of luxurious accommodations and medicinal hot springs on one side of the river and of dark, smoky dens of iniquity and general hell-raising on the other, and awarded the college site to Gunnison.

The vapor caves, as well as other properties, went into foreclosure proceedings. The properties were acquired by Fred Busk and B. Aymar Sands who formed the Glenwood Hot Springs and Hotel Company, incorporated in 1912. They bottled and sold the mineral water as a natural curative.

The Glenwood Polo Team again won the world's championship in 1912, under the leadership of Hervey Lyle. Lyle had lost an eye to an errant polo ball, but he still loved the game. Lyle had also taught most of Glenwood's elite to play golf on the course that the Devereux brothers had built adjacent to the polo grounds and race track.

Lyle also was appointed to the position of director of the new company that was formed when the Glenwood Hot Springs Company and the Hotel Colorado merged. He was to manage the operations through a very successful summer, notwithstanding some events that seriously affected many of Glenwood's businesses.

The Baha'i faith was founded by a man named Bahaulla. His son, named Abdu'l-Baha, visited Glenwood Springs in 1912. He reportedly stayed at the Hotel Colorado and enjoyed the Hot Springs Pool during the time he was in town. A plaque was placed on a boulder and a rosebush was planted near the main entrance of the Hotel Colorado to commemorate his visit.

The loss of Western State Teachers' College enraged many of the local residents, and there was a general outcry against drinking, gambling, and prostitution. Under pressure from the clergy and various women's groups, some of the neighboring towns became "dry." Then, Colorado laws were changed to totally prohibit gambling. As a result, all visible gambling devices, slot machines, poker tables, and the like disappeared from sight in Glenwood Springs

Part of the festivities related to the Basalt-to-Glenwood Springs Bicycle Race in 1912. Note the bicyclist on his way down the ramp. (Courtesy of Don Vanderhoof)

There is little doubt that the backrooms of many of the local establishments saw a continuation of wagering activity, but at least it was kept out of sight. Even though gambling activities were severely curtailed, there were still numerous activities to occupy the resident and the tourist alike. Strawberry Day was growing in popularity. For whatever reason, the year of 1912 was a huge year for marriages on Strawberry Day.

The Basalt-to-Glenwood Bicycle Race of 1912 featured a great many activities in addition to the race itself. There was a baseball game and a Wild West show. Bands from Grand Junction and from Marble performed. A tightrope walker successfully performed his balancing act across the Colorado River, and another daredevil performed a high dive from the top of the Grand Avenue Bridge into the river.

B. T. Napier, who owned the Napier Dry Goods Store and who also served as a Democratic state representative from the Ninth district, built his home at 930 Bennett Avenue in 1912.

When the Colorado Telephone Company and the Mountain States Telephone and Telegraph Company merged, they provided service to Glenwood Springs, replacing the lines that had been strung from Aspen in 1900 by the Colorado Telephone Company.

On Monday, September 9, 1912, F. H. A. "Hervey" Lyle collapsed during a dance at the Hotel Colorado ballroom and was taken to the Glenwood Sanitarium. He died about 8:15 that evening from an attack of appendicitis. As he was only fifty-two years old, his death came as a great shock to the people of Glenwood Springs. He had

A daredevil walks a tightrope across the Grand River in 1912. (Courtesy of Frontier Historical Society - Schutte Collection)

been a resident for some thirty-six years, and was held in high esteem by most of the populace. At the request of the mayor, all businesses were closed during his funeral. His body lay in state at the stone bathhouse for two days before his burial in Linwood Cemetery. His two polo ponies, riderless, followed the hearse up the trail to the old cemetery on the top of Jasper Mountain.

On November 20, 1912, Morgan Gavin, now fifteen, drove from Glenwood Springs to Denver on another publicity run. Accompanying him were two brothers, Stephen and Edmund Holland. Stephen

F. H. A. "Hervey" Lyle, Glenwood businessman and polo enthusiast. (Courtesy of Frontier Historical Society)

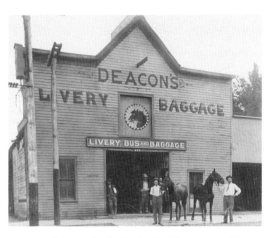

Deacon Livery, built in 1913. (Courtesy of Buzz Zancanella)

was fourteen, and Edmund was all of six. They drove through sixteen inches of snow on Tennessee Pass and survived a frozen water tank and a burned generator. Their route was subsequently proclaimed to be the Lincoln Transcontinental Highway. In 1914 that same route would become part of the Pike's Peak Ocean to Ocean Highway. On the return trip, with Morgan's father Austin Gavin driving, the group set a new record for driving time from Denver to Glenwood. They were delayed by a flood at Minturn, which defeated their attempt at a time record between the two towns, but their actual driving time was less than fourteen hours.

The original frame building on the southwest corner of Eighth and Grand that housed the Citizens' Bank was replaced with a larger concrete and brick structure in 1913. Also, J. F. McCoy constructed the building at 831 Grand Avenue, and the Deacon Livery Stable was erected at 818 Colorado Avenue. The Livery was rather unique in that it featured "basement parking." A ramp led to the lower level of the building, and the teams of horses and their wagons were backed down into the basement.

Also in 1913, The Central Colorado Power Company, the company that had built the Shoshone Dam and Power Plant and erected the power lines that marched to the east over the Continental Divide, went bankrupt. The assets of the company, including the power plant, were taken over by the Colorado Power Company.

Road building was still on the front burner for the Colorado Legislature, and $75,000 was appropriated in 1913 for the improvement of the road through Glenwood Canyon. The canyon road was designated to be part of the Pike's Peak Ocean to Ocean Highway the following year. Even with the fancy new designation and all the money that Colorado was throwing at it, travelers approaching the canyon in October of 1914 were greeted by a sign informing them that the Glenwood Canyon Road was "closed for the winter."

The Strawberry Day celebration of 1913 ushered in what was to become an integral part of the festivities. Miss Ruby Clark became the first Strawberry Day Queen. There were all of the trappings of the traditional beauty contest, a talent event, and the obligatory evening gown competition. Ruby Clark later became Mrs. Erle Hubbard.

Late in 1913, the Vulcan Mine near New Castle blew again. The tremendous explosion, the result of the methane pockets that hid in

Miss Ada Hutchings, crowned the Strawberry Day Queen of 1915. (Courtesy of Frontier Historical Society)

the coal veins of the Grand Hogback, killed thirty-seven men. Sadly, some of the dead miners were the sons of miners killed eighteen years before. Eight of the victims of the 1913 blast were found to be men who had been working at the Vulcan at the time of the 1896 explosion. They had cheated death the first time around, but the mine did not let them escape again.

In 1914, the official name of the canyon east of Glenwood Springs was changed from the Grand River Canyon to Glenwood Canyon. Work was proceeding on widening and improving the canyon road as part of the program that had designated it as a link of the Ocean to Ocean Highway. At least some of the work was done by convict labor, a form of state aid to the county, and the sight of prison stripes became common in the canyon.

The Glenwood Hot Springs and Hotel Company failed in 1914. Until his death in 1912, Hervey Lyle had acted as the liaison be

Glenwood Canyon (or Canon) after road improvement. (Courtesy of Al Maggard)

tween the hotel management and the English investors. Even then, the Hotel Colorado stayed open only in the late spring, summer, and early autumn months, as it had no central heating. Lord Rathbone, the leader of the investment group, had come to Glenwood to look over the situation. After staying at the hotel for a month, he reappointed Elmer E. Lucas as general manager and left his son, C. A. Rathbone, as the resident director. In 1914 a joint venture was formed with Charles Hughes and Charles McCarthy as principals, and they bought out the English investors. Elmer Lucas had an ownership percentage, and he remained as general manager. At about the same time, Jesse Dewey began providing transportation for the Hotel Colorado guests in the form of an electric bus. The new conveyance replaced the horse drawn carriages that had been serving the hotel.

The city of Glenwood Springs issued bonds in the amount of $110,000 to purchase the water plant, and an agreement was made that the Hotel Colorado would pay $2,250 per year for its water usage.

In a portent of things to come, the state of Colorado actually became "dry" by local option in 1914. This meant that, at the choosing of a particular town, the selling or serving of liquor became illegal. Accordingly, many of the surrounding towns became dry. Not surprisingly, Glenwood Springs chose to continue its old ways and persisted in the purveying of intoxicating spirits.

On June 28, 1914, Archduke Ferdinand of Austria-Hungary was assassinated in Sarajevo by a Serbian citizen. The accumulated tensions of some thirty years erupted, and Austria-Hungary invaded Serbia. This in turn started a chain reaction that soon drew other countries, including Russia, France, Germany, and Great Britain into the conflict. The United States remained neutral during the first stages of the conflict, but the effects of the escalating war reached everywhere. Glenwood Springs was no exception.

The Hotel Colorado and the pool and vapor caves had for a number of years drawn on England and Europe for at least part of their guest list. With the advent of the war, this source of income dried up almost immediately. The foreign visitors were replaced to a small extent by newly-wealthy Americans, but most of them were too busy making money off the misfortunes of their European contemporaries to spend much more than a hurried few days on a mountain vacation. Many local residents paid the admission fee of thirty-five cents to the pool, but they could not take the place of the former throngs of tourists.

With the decrease in the tourist activity and the decline of coal mining as an economic factor, it was time for the farms and ranches surrounding Glenwood Springs to step to the forefront. Farming and ranching methods had been improving for several years, and tractors were beginning to appear on the farms of the nation. Garfield County produced beef, mutton, pork, and various kinds of poultry, as well as grain, sugar beets, potatoes, and varied fruits.

A two horsepower threshing machine. (Courtesy of Frontier Historical Society)

An "overshot" hay stacker. (Courtesy of Frontier Historical Society - Schutte Collection)

As the war progressed in Europe, and the United States eventually became embroiled in the conflict, numerous young men of Glenwood Springs and Garfield County enlisted in the armed services. Many of them served with the Army's Eighty-ninth Division and saw action in Chatiau-Thierry and Verdun in France.

The farmers and ranchers of the area supplied a great deal of meat and produce to the war effort, and townsfolk planted what were known as "war gardens" for their own use and to lessen the demand for products so that more would be available to the war effort. The Strawberry Day celebration, which had been a popular annual get-together since its origin in 1898, was scaled back for four years during the war.

The war brought about a great many changes in the valley. The electric plant at Shoshone had been considered to be vulnerable to sabotage. For protection, a troop of soldiers under the command of Captain Lill was stationed at the plant. They lived in the boarding house on the plant site. In addition, the Denver & Rio Grande Railroad had been designated as an official route for the movement of troops and supplies, and was therefore also considered vulnerable. Troop trains frequently stopped in Glenwood Springs so that the troops could enjoy the Hot Springs Pool. The state of Colorado purchased the building at Ninth and Grand from J. F. McCoy and turned it into an armory. Company L, Third Infantry of the Colorado National Guard was formed with over one hundred local men. Their task was to guard the railroad. To assist them, and to help guard the town and bridges, a contingent of troops "of color" was billeted in the Kendrick Cottages.

In 1915 the Cardiff coke ovens were closed permanently. The small town of Cardiff had been built with one purpose, that of providing support for the coking operation, and the closing of the ovens predetermined the demise of the town.

CHAPTER THIRTEEN

From 1916 to 1920

"I thought he was crazy then, and I think he's crazy now."
Humbert Rees, referring to the "Human Fly" who scaled
two downtown buildings during the 1917 Strawberry Day.

The Mutual Light and Water Company which had gone into competition with the Glenwood Light and Water Company in 1910 was never adequately funded. Another court battle between the two companies was settled in favor of Glenwood Light and Water which drove Mutual Light and Water into bankruptcy. The surviving company was then able to take over the assets of their rival at little cost.

Buffalo Bill Cody in Glenwood Springs just days before his death in Denver. He is standing with his lifelong friend Dr. William Crook, prominent Glenwood physician. (Courtesy of John Tindall)

On January 5, 1917, Buffalo Bill Cody visited Glenwood Springs, staying at the home of his longtime friend, Dr. W. W. Crook. Cody was quite ill during his visit, and he subsequently died in Denver on January 10 of that same year. He is buried on Lookout Mountain just west of Denver.

During the early 1900s, actor Lon Chaney was an infrequent but impressive visitor to Glenwood Springs. Chaney had become famous in the silent movie days as "The Man With a Thousand Faces," due to his ability to portray crippled and deformed characters. He starred in *The Hunchback of Notre Dame, The*

The 1917 American LaFrance fire engine proudly displayed in front of City Hall. (Courtesy of Frontier Historical Society)

Phantom of the Opera, and many other movies. Chaney always arrived in Glenwood Springs in his private railroad car, one of the trappings of wealth in those days.

The State Highway Commission published a guidebook entitled "Highways of Colorado." In it they listed the Fairy Caves as one of the principal places of interest in Glenwood Springs. Notwithstanding that, the caves were closed in 1917 and remain closed as of the writing of this book. They did, however, reopen in 1999.

The Glenwood Fire Department received their first motor-driven fire engine in 1917. It was an American LaFrance, and cost $4,000. Between the troops stationed in town and in the canyon, and the modern firefighting equipment, it was felt that Glenwood Springs was ready for enemy attack, if and when it came. According to one story, three spies were in fact caught during this time of great apprehension. They supposedly possessed maps and pictures of the railroad, the bridges, and the Shoshone Power Plant.

The Strawberry Day celebration of 1917 featured a "human fly." The performer warmed up on the Citizens' National Building, and then scaled the outside of the Hotel Glenwood, according to Humbert Rees who grew up on a ranch near Rifle. Humbert was to become a columnist for the *Glenwood Post.*

As the war ended on November 11, 1918, there was hope on the part of the residents of Glenwood Springs that the well-heeled

The Federal Building at Ninth and Grand. (Courtesy of Frontier Historical Society)

European and American tourists would soon return. This was not to happen. Elmer Lucas was still the manager of the Hotel Colorado, and the United States Army approached him with the offer of converting the hotel into a hospital for physically and mentally disabled war veterans. Some consideration was given to the plan, but there was a great deal of opposition from the residents of Glenwood, and the conversion did not take place.

The Colorado Midland Railroad had originally been built to service the silver mines in the Aspen area and the coal mines that provided the raw material for their smelters. Consequently, the Midland had been seriously hurt by the Silver Panic and the resultant lowering of interest in mining. During the war years, the armed services had chosen the Denver & Rio Grande as the rail line to transport troops and war materials. This action further helped to seal the fate of the Midland. The rail line was forced into receivership in 1918 and ceased operations shortly thereafter. The Midland station in Glenwood Springs was torn down during that same year, and the Midland tracks were torn up in 1919.

The Vulcan Mine, outside of New Castle, blew again in 1918, this time killing three miners.

State Representative Edward Taylor had secured a position on the Federal Appropriations Committee, and he pushed through the allotment of $100,000 for a new federal building in Glenwood Springs. It was built at 900 Grand Avenue and completed in 1919. The building was to contain the United States Post Office and the Land Office. Prior to that, the post office had been located in Olie

Thorson's building on Grand, and the land office was in the second story of the Napier building. That same year, Tom Dever purchased the Kamm Mercantile building at Eighth and Grand, and converted it to the Dever Jewelry Store.

One of the great entertainments of the day was a show known as the "flying circus," a small number of airplanes that traveled from town to town giving exhibitions of aerial expertise. In June of 1919, Glenwood Springs had contracted for such a performance, and the polo field was designated as the landing strip. Eight men, flying four U. S. De Haviland biplanes, were to land at the polo grounds and then perform their air show. However, the pilots did not take into account the air currents in the relatively narrow Roaring Fork Valley. Only one of the De Havilands managed to land on the polo field. Another landed in a nearby hay field, the third wound up just north of Carbondale, twelve miles to the south, and the fourth landed just at the foot of Mount Sopris. The four planes finally were able to give the citizens of Glenwood Springs a brief show before departing for friendlier skies.

Joe Bair and two partners bought the big ranch at the east end of Glenwood Canyon, and Bair brought his Mormon family and some 2,000 sheep from their home in Alpine, Utah. The whole contingent came by train. The traditional hatred for sheepmen was alive in the Glenwood area, and there was word of armed cattlemen waiting for them at Dotsero. To avoid the conflict, Bair unloaded the family and the sheep from the train at the Shoshone Plant and

One of the wayward De Haviland airplanes that tried to land in Glenwood Springs in 1919. (Courtesy of Frontier Historical Society)

drove the sheep up the canyon to the ranch. They made the family home in a building that had been a stagecoach stop hotel at Siloam Springs. Some say that the building was moved to the ranch by train, some say by boat. Eventually, the partnership dissolved and Bair became sole owner of the big ranch.

As of the end of 1919, Glenwood Springs was somewhat dormant in relation to growth. The Hotel Colorado was still open only in the summer, and the city ended, for all intents and purposes, at Eleventh Street on the south. Elmer Lucas closed the polo field and extended the old golf course.

January 29, 1920 ushered in a new era. The changes affected not only Glenwood Springs, but also the entire United States. The Volstead Act and the Eighteenth Amendment implemented Prohibition as of that date, outlawing the sale or consumption of intoxicating beverages of any kind. The outlawing of liquor sales obviously dealt a death blow to Glenwood's many saloons. They had already lost the profits from gambling, and now the law changes were taking away their only other hope of making a profit. Saloons closed in droves. A few converted to pool halls, but they were dim visages of their former selves.

Gambling had been declared illegal, now liquor had followed suit, and this left the "ladies of the brick" on somewhat shaky ground. Prostitution had never been legal in Glenwood Springs. However, for as long as anyone could remember, the practice was for the authorities to fine the houses of "ill fame," for the penalties to be paid, thus providing money for the operation of the city, and for everyone to happily go back to their activities. However, a lot of pressure was put on the city leaders to enforce the existing laws, and the brothels gradually closed down. Supposedly, one madam set fire to her establishment for the insurance coverage. Whatever the truth, the face of Glenwood Springs was to change forever. The rip-roaring drinking, gambling, and "sporting" establishments of Riverfront were no more.

Like most other parts of the country, the advent of Prohibition produced a number of illegal stills in the ravines around Glenwood Springs. John Richardson, the owner of the Silver Club, proved to be quite adaptable when the new laws shut down his saloon operation. He turned his building over to a group that changed it into a garage and welding shop and became a Prohibition agent. He had his work cut out for him, as a number of "speakeasies" sprang up in town.

The Denver Hotel in approximately 1930. (Courtesy of Frontier Historical Society - Schutte Collection)

Art Kendrick took advantage of the new laws banning liquor, taking over the spaces that had held the Senate Bar and the Columbus Saloon and almost doubled the size of his Hotel Denver across from the Denver & Rio Grande train station. At the same time, Bosco's Star Hotel expanded in the other direction in the same block.

The building at 831 Grand Avenue had been built by J. F. McCoy in 1913 and taken over by the state for a National Guard Armory in 1917. In the early twenties, McCoy formed the Blossom Motor Company, the first Buick Dealership in town, and moved back into the ground floor of the building.

CHAPTER FOURTEEN

From 1921 to 1930

"The withered leaves of industrial enterprise lie on every side; farmers find no markets for their produce; the savings of many years in thousands of families are gone. More important, a host of unemployed citizens face the grim problem of existence, and an equally great number toil with little return."
United States President Franklin D. Roosevelt, speaking of the
Great Depression in his first Inaugural Address

The American public wasted little time finding alternative sources for alcoholic beverages after Prohibition was enacted in 1920. As mentioned, illegal stills sprang up in the country outside of most towns. People started experimenting with home brew of various kinds, which ranged from quite palatable to downright poisonous. Of course if something was in demand, and if that something happened to be illegal, the forces of organized crime were always willing to step in and lend a helping hand in providing it. Bootleg hooch was just such a commodity.

A whole new branch of the "mob" sprang up to handle the manufacture and distribution of liquor. The early twenties saw the start of a new attitude in America. The war was over, many people were experiencing a new prosperity, a lot of them had automobiles, and they were looking for a good time. The outlawing of liquor was completely out of step with the times. The "Roaring Twenties" were upon the land, and people were going to drink, regardless of the source of the product.

Two of the new breed of gangster chose the Glenwood Springs area for a part-time residence. Brothers named Bert and Leland "Jack" Varain, out of Chicago, purchased a log house on the shore of Sweetwater Lake. They leased the area from the White River National Forest, and set up residence there. There is still a degree of uncertainty as to whether they were using the Sweetwater facilities as a resort or as the rumor of the time would have it, as a hideout from the Chicago mob. If the latter were the case, if they were in fact hiding out, Jack apparently wasn't very good at it. He called himself "Diamond Jack Alterie," for reasons known only to him, and chose to habitually dress in flashy western outfits, complete with diamond rings, diamond shirt studs, diamond watches and belt buckles. To complete the picture, he was always armed with matching pistols worn in holsters hanging from crossed gun belts. He traveled nowhere without a goodly supply of armament and at least one bodyguard. He was also known as "Two Gun Louie," and at times, even "Three Gun Louie." He habitually traveled in a long, seven-passenger cream-colored Lincoln convertible.

At one time in his past, Diamond Jack had traveled the small town boxing circuit, fighting as a heavyweight under the names of Clyde Ways or Kid Haynes. After obtaining the Sweetwater property, he raised grain, hay, and cattle and ran a dude ranch during the summers. There are numerous reports of him or his henchmen expelling trespassers at the point of a gun.

"Diamond Jack" Alterie, Chicago gangster turned Colorado dude ranch operator. (Courtesy of Frontier Historical Society)

Jack and his brother were known to entertain others of their ilk at the Hotel Colorado. The infamous "Legs" Diamond was a guest on one occasion, and "Scarface" Al Capone visited at least once, taking the time to shop at Dever's Jewelry Store while he was in town. Capone was a very powerful figure in the underworld at the time, having gained much of his power thanks to the Prohibition Act.

Finally in 1921, the official name of the big river was changed from the Grand to the Colorado. Senator Edward Taylor had championed a bill in 1907 to change the name, but it was defeated. Colorado Senator Ollie Bannister pushed the bill through in 1921, and Governor Oliver H. Shoup signed it into law. Even then, an eighty mile stretch of the river in eastern Utah remained known as the Grand for some time, until it too was changed by the Utah legislature. Such place names as Grand Junction, Grand Lake, and Grand County retain the old name.

Rocky Mountain Fuel and Iron, which had purchased the Sunlight Mine in 1907, finally closed it in 1921. The demise and subsequent closure of the mine was due largely to the fact that the Midland Railroad had ceased operation.

A 1917 Supreme Court decision had declared the Denver & Rio Grande Railroad responsible for the payment of the principal and the interest on bonds that had been issued by the Western Pacific Railroad, a company that the Denver & Rio Grande had helped to finance. The decision drove the Denver & Rio Grande into receivership. The old company was dissolved in July of 1921 but reorganized as the Denver & Rio Grande Western Railroad.

During 1923, a great deal of work was done on the road through the canyon, which was in the process of becoming a part of the Pike's Peak Ocean to Ocean Highway. Both Garfield

Convict labor working on the canyon highway in 1923. (Courtesy of Frontier Historical Society)

County and the state of Colorado used convict labor on the highway. As many as 400 convicts who were normally incarcerated in Canon City worked to create the graded gravel surface of the new road.

In 1924, the Colorado Power Company merged its interest in the Shoshone Power Plant with the Public Service Company of Colorado. Colorado Power had kept the plant in good repair, and the new owners modernized it even further to bring it up to date.

Also in 1924, Glenwood Springs made two significant purchases of property. The Bailer family had owned a piece of ground south of town since the late 1800s. The city purchased the acreage for a new cemetery at a cost of $8,000, as the old Linwood

Hanging Lake, geological phenomenon on the north wall of Glenwood Canyon. (Courtesy of Frontier Historical Society)

Cemetery on Jasper Mountain was close to capacity. The new burial ground was to be called the Rosebud Cemetery.

The second purchase was a 763 acre patch of mountainside on the north wall of Glenwood Canyon which was to be a city park. The area, bought from the White River National Forest for $1.25 an acre, contained a geological phenomenon known as Hanging Lake.

Eons ago, the rock that cradles the lake broke away from the long valley that reaches to the edge of the canyon. The resulting depression caught and held the cold, clear water that drops from the rim of the canyon. Over the centuries the dissolved limestone in the water has built up a fragile rim that helps to contain the acre and one half of crystal clear water. It is some twenty-five feet deep in the center. Soon after its purchase by the city of Glenwood Springs, the lake was stocked with eastern brook trout.

Above the lake is a waterfall known as Spouting Rock, and the deluge creates another set of lacy falls as the excess water spills over the lower edge of the lake itself. Hanging Lake is reached by a steep trail that gains a thousand feet in just about a mile of length. The existing trail was built by the Civilian Conservation Corps in 1933. Hanging Lake is fed by the East Fork of Dead Horse Creek. The waterway was named by prospectors who lost a packhorse over a cliff in the area in 1881.

Spouting Rock above Hanging Lake. (Courtesy of Frontier Historical Society

Beginning in the 1920s, a resort grew up in the canyon at the base of the Hanging Lake Trail. It featured a restaurant, a service station, and a small motel operation. Hanging Lake Resort enjoyed success as a pleasant rest stop for motorists, as well as the jumping-off place for hikes up to the lake.

The United States Land Office in Glenwood Springs was one of the busiest in the United States. In 1925, an economy move by the federal government closed the land office in Montrose and moved all of the records to Glenwood Springs. For a brief time, the Glenwood Office was among the largest in the nation. Three years later, another economy move closed the Glenwood office and moved everything to Denver. Representative Edward Taylor fought the move, but to no avail.

On April 22, 1925, a huge fire destroyed roughly one-third of what had become the world's largest marble mill in Marble. About forty barrels of oil had been stored in the mill which helped to feed the flames. The fire occurred during somewhat antagonistic efforts to unionize the mill, and there were rumors, never proven, that arsonists were at fault. The light and color of the fire were reflected on the underside of the clouds, clearly visible in Glenwood Springs.

At the urging of Loi Pratt, the head of the Lions Club in Glenwood, the first radio broadcast from Glenwood Springs occurred on September 17, 1925. Director Robert Quick and the Hotel Colorado Trio played a concert that was transmitted to Denver by telephone. The sound was then broadcast over KOA Radio in Denver.

C. W. "Doc" McFadden began his practice as a chiropractor in 1926. McFadden was later to purchase the vapor caves.

The falls below Hanging Lake. (Courtesy of Frontier Historical Society - Schutte Collection)

The summer of 1926 would be a memorable one for the people of Glenwood Springs. Tom Mix, famous for his starring roles in numerous "horse operas" or western movies, came to town with his wife and his entire movie company to film in Glenwood Springs and Glenwood Canyon. They actually filmed location shots for two movies while in Glenwood: *The Great K & A Train Robbery,* and *The Canyon Light.* Little is known about the subject of the second film, but *The Great K & A Train Robbery* involved bad guys, thrilling horseback riding, and, of course, a heroine. His leading lady in the film was Dorothy Dawn. Mix was one of the early kings of the western melodrama. It is said that John Wayne worked on *The Great K & A Train Robbery* as a prop man, his first job in the movies.

Around fifty-five people made up the cast and crew of the production, and they arrived in town on two special Pullman train

cars. Most of the company stayed at the Hotel Colorado, and special trains with open observation cars carried spectators into the canyon each day to watch the proceedings. At one point Tom Mix rode his horse Tony across the narrow top of the Shoshone Dam, and then he proceeded to jump onto a moving train in his pursuit of the evildoers. Several locals joined the cast, including a young man named Wyrick Juhan. As the story goes, Wyrick borrowed a gray horse from his father (without his father's knowledge or consent) and proceeded to ride it across the Colorado River during the filming. This fact was revealed only when his father saw the film.

Tom Mix on location in Glenwood Springs. (Courtesy of Frontier Historical Society)

During the summer of the filming, Tom Mix and his company entertained the populace with rodeos and prizefights, and exhibitions of fancy riding and marksmanship. They also staged a variety show in the junior high school auditorium and appeared at the Odeon Theater on Seventh Street. Mix was a Mason, and helped to raise money for the construction of the Glenwood Springs Masonic Lodge. In appreciation for the summer of entertainment, the townspeople made Mix the Guest of Honor at the Strawberry Day celebration that year.

In addition, the citizens of the town were entertained that summer with Roman races, parachute jumps, Charleston contests, and in August with the Barnum and Bailey's Big Top Circus.

The Rock Gardens Campground was built in 1926, two and one half miles east of Glenwood Springs. It was built just outside of No

Name on a gentle hillside leading from the highway down to the banks of the Colorado River.

Chipeta, widow of Ouray, the great Ute Chieftain, died in 1926. She had returned to the ways of her people and lived her final years in Bitter Creek, Utah. She was blind during the last few years of her life. Chipeta was buried in Montrose, Colorado.

The economic recession that was beginning to take a grip of the rest of the country began to affect Glenwood Springs. The traveling public was still coming to town, but they seemed to have less money to spend. Buster Gardner,

Tom Mix and his horse Tony.(Courtesy of Frontier Historical Society)

one of the actors in the Tom Mix movie, decided to stay in Glenwood. He and C. R. McCarthy built the first of a number of motor courts at No Name Creek. They were the forerunners of motels, small cabins for the motoring public that were somewhat more affordable than the larger hotels. John Noonan built another set of the small buildings on his land called "Noonan's Grove." The adjacent bridge across the Roaring Fork became known as "Noonan's Bridge."

Elmer Lucas, the man who had begun as a room clerk and worked his way up to owner of the Hotel Colorado, died in 1927. His widow sold half interest to Charles E. Hughes, and the two of them continued to operate the hotel in the summers. Jonas Lindgren, the first man to commercially utilize the hot springs with his hand hewn tub also died in that year.

The recession was in full swing by 1928. The *Avalanche Echo* was absorbed by the *Glenwood Post*, small banks in neighboring towns were closing, and more and more men were out of work. There was activity, however. The Mountain States Telephone and Telegraph

Company constructed their building at 921 Grand Avenue. The Denver & Rio Grande roundhouse and the old shops were removed, and work was done on the tracks through town. Massive Mallard steam engines replaced the smaller freight and passenger engines.

The courthouse that had been constructed at Eighth and Pitkin had included a jail that was approximately twenty-two by twenty-five feet. There were an inordinate amount of escapes, and the jail and the courthouse itself were replaced in 1928 by the large county courthouse building which occupies the block bordered by Seventh and Eighth streets and by Colorado and Pitkin avenues. Originally the Masonic Temple stood on that site.

The Denver, Northwestern and Pacific Railroad had been organized in 1902 by Denver banker David H. Moffat and reorganized as the Denver and Salt Lake Railroad after Moffat's death in 1911. The route was often referred to as the Moffat Road. The company completed what was to become known as the Moffat Tunnel in 1928. The tunnel was an effort by the railroad to avoid the steep grades and winter weather problems of their original route over Rollins Pass. The railroad was never financially strong, however, and the Denver & Rio Grande Western negotiated an agreement to use the Denver and Salt Lake tracks through the tunnel. That move, coupled with the laying of new track from Dotsero north to near Bond, cut some 175 miles off the Denver & Rio Grande Western route from Glenwood Springs to Denver. Later, the Denver & Rio Grande Western was to acquire all of the assets of the old Moffat Road.

Other improvements were planned for the town. Up until the late 1920s, the streets of Glenwood Springs were still unpaved. Consequently, they tended toward muddy when it rained, dusty when it did not. The first paving began in 1929, and when Grand Avenue was finished the next year, the town threw a May Day party that included roller-skating and a street dance.

Two of the more prominent hotel owners died in 1928 and 1929. Charles E. Hughes, who had purchased half interest in the Hotel Colorado when Elmer Lucas died in 1927, was killed by careless smoking in December of 1928. An investor from Leadville, Frank H. Zaitz, acquired his interest in the hotel. Henry Bosco, owner of the Star Hotel passed away in 1929 and the ownership of the hotel on Seventh Street passed to his heirs.

Doc Holliday's old friend Wyatt Earp survived the good doctor by a great many years. He died January 13, 1929 in Los Angeles and is buried in the Hills of Eternity Memorial Park in Colma, California.

Engineers at the Shoshone Power Plant discovered in 1929 that injecting air above the water flowing through the 12,450 tunnel from the dam to the plant would increase the flow by about twelve percent, up to 1,408 cubic feet per second. The practice has been continued to the present day.

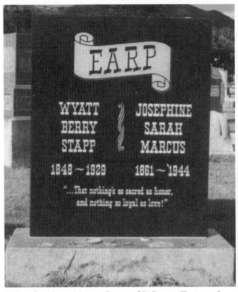

The final resting place of Wyatt Earp, close friend of Doc Holliday. (Photo by the Author)

In October of 1929, the United States Stock Market crashed. October 24, known as "Black Thursday", was the beginning. By Tuesday, October 29, the total drop in the value of securities was more than 26 billion dollars. By the end of 1929, the total loss in value nationwide was in excess of 100 billion dollars. The stock market collapse was the beginning of what became known as the Great Depression.

In 1930, Frank Mechau painted a mural in the main stairwell of the Federal building at 900 Grand Avenue. Mechau was an internationally acclaimed painter who had grown up in Glenwood Springs. He lived and painted in Paris for three years prior to returning to the Glenwood area.

As an indication of the state of the general economy and especially the economy of Glenwood Springs, the population of the town dropped between 1920 and 1930. The total count fell by some 400 people between the two dates, the only period before or since when that has happened.

CHAPTER FIFTEEN

From 1931 to 1940

"A community has not ceased to be essentially law-abiding merely because it refuses to practice literal obedience. There is such a thing as orderly disobedience to a statute, a disobedience which is open, frankly avowed, and in conformity with the general sense of what is reasonable."

Walter Lippmann, speaking against prohibition

In March of 1931, the *Glenwood Post* reported that a site near Rifle had been chosen for the location of an oil shale plant. The facility was to cost $1,500,000.

Economic conditions were still grim in the early thirties. The Citizens' National bank closed in 1932, forced into receivership. It was a terrible blow to the town.

In early 1933, the state opened Glenwood Springs' first unemployment office. The first day saw 108 applicants. Unemployment was rampant, and it was not helped by the fact that every train into town seemingly carried a new supply of transients, the "hobos" who traveled the country during the Depression. They would drift into a town and go door to door, begging food in return for work, if necessary. The city set up a location where they could cut wood in exchange for a voucher good at any of the stores or restaurants in town. They earned twenty-five cents in value for every two hours of work.

The hot springs along the Colorado River attracted the migrants, and it was not long before Glenwood Springs was the home to a flourishing "hobo jungle." The County Poor Farm, as it was called, was rapidly filling up with indigents. The sanitary conditions had not improved greatly since the days of the smallpox epidemics and the "pest house." The place was still overrun with lice, bedbugs, and other pests. Nonetheless, it was needed to shelter those who had nothing else.

Then just as they were most needed, the sprawling group of ramshackle buildings burned to the ground. No one was killed in the fire. Works Progress Administration (WPA) labor was introduced at about that time which provided gainful employment for many of the jobless. The governmental program would later become known as the Work Projects Administration. A new county hospital was constructed, with the help of a $9,000 federal grant. It was a far cry from the old facilities which had fought smallpox, diphtheria, and typhoid fever for so long without the benefit of the new immunizations that were becoming available. WPA labor was also used to build a sewage disposal plant and to improve street drainage and install curbs and gutters. They also converted an old livery stable that had been owned by Yewell and Vorhees into an American Legion auditorium.

As another reflection of the state of the economy, the Hotel Colorado was open only three months during 1933. The Glenwood Sanitarium and Nurses' Training School that had been started and operated by Dr. Berry was forced to close. Many of the patients were unable to pay for their care, which finally drove the operation out of business.

On December 5, 1933, after nearly fourteen years, Prohibition was repealed. It had been a bad law, a law that was routinely ignored, broken, ridiculed. It served to accomplish little except the enriching of a significant segment of organized crime and the creation of a new breed of lawbreaker, the average American. When the Eighteenth Amendment was finally repealed, Glenwood Springs was so far down economically that it initially made little difference.

The old Grand Hotel, which had been constructed as the Hotel Barlow, changed to the Hotel Yampa and later to the St. Joseph's Sanitarium, had shifted on its foundations and it was decided to raze the building. It was torn down in 1934.

The WPA provided work for the older generation of unemployed, but it did little or nothing for the ranks of young men who were seeking work. Consequently, the CCC, or Civilian Conservation Corps, was set up by the government. Its target was the youthful worker, its aim was the improvement of forests, campgrounds, and whatever other projects were needed.

In Glenwood Springs, Camp SP 10 C was set up in the area that is now Sayre Park, just off south Grand Avenue. Five long barracks were built as well as an administration building, a recreation hall, a mess hall and a bathhouse. The facilities were capable of housing 240 young men. The CCC workers in Glenwood did a great deal of work in the White River National Forest, building roads and trails, establishing campsites with picnic tables, shelterhouses, restrooms

Civilian Conservation Corps encampment in the area that is now Sayre Park. (Courtesy of Frontier Historical Society)

and fireplaces. They helped to fight forest fires and replanted burned areas, built the Grizzly Creek Campground, and reconstructed the trail up to Hanging Lake. The workers also helped to clear the brush from Red Mountain so that a ski tow could be built there and assisted in the construction of the first runway for the new Municipal Airport.

In late 1934, word reached Glenwood Springs that Walter Devereux, the man responsible for much of the town's early glamour, including the construction of the Hot Springs Pool and the Hotel Colorado, had passed away. He died on November 19, 1934 at the home of his son in California. He was one month shy of his eighty-first birthday.

State funds helped to improve the road that led west toward Rifle, which was now known as Highway 40. Representative Edward Taylor was still making every effort to obtain funds for the improvement of the highways through Glenwood Springs. He was responsible for a huge grant from the federal government, some $36 million, to be spent on a new federal highway across the state. He sponsored the legislation for the construction of the federal highway from the Kansas border west to the Utah line. A million and one half of the funds was set aside for further improvements through Glenwood Canyon. The construction began in 1936 and lasted until August 1 of 1938, at which time the new federal highway 5 & 24 was dedicated. During construction, much of the normal canyon traffic was detoured over Cottonwood Pass, one of the early stagecoach roads into the valley.

The highway construction followed the rules that had originally been set forth for the Taylor State Road. Existing vegetation was to be protected whenever possible, and advertising billboards were not to be allowed. The Shoshone Power Plant lost some of its buildings to the widening of the highway, including the office building, the superintendent's house, and the boarding house.

"Diamond Jack" Alterie was still ruling his little kingdom in the Sweetwater area. He had been known to fire upon other residents who ventured too near his stronghold. There were rumors that the Internal Revenue Department was after him, and that he was behind on payments on the Sweetwater Resort. After wounding three innocent bystanders during a drunken brawl at the Hotel Denver, Alterie was finally arrested for attempted murder. He was judged to be guilty, and fined $1,250. He was also given the choice of spending five years in prison or permanently leaving the state. He chose to depart Colorado and was reportedly killed by rival gangsters.

Sadie Korn, Glenwood Springs' first female attorney, set up practice in 1935 and purchased the house at 1008 Colorado Avenue, built in the early years of the century by the DeRemer family.

Theodore Von Rosenberg, the architect of the stone bathhouse at the pool, the pool itself, and the bridge over the Grand River, died in Glenwood Springs on March 20 of that year. Since the time of the construction of his magnificent buildings, he had held offices as city engineer, county surveyor, and state irrigation division engineer.

Judge John Noonan had established a group of motel units in what was known as "Noonan's Grove," at the confluence of the Roaring Fork and the Colorado rivers. He had also built a business building in the downtown area, on the north side of Eighth Street which still bears the "Noonan - 1912" identification high on the south side of the building. John Noonan had died the previous December after being gored by a bull.

In 1935, Bill Noonan, John's son, also met his death. Bill Noonan had incurred the ire of Harvey Taylor, a janitor. Taylor's wife was at the time working for the younger Noonan as a housekeeper, and his daughter served as Noonan's secretary. One morning, Taylor confronted Noonan outside of the Noonan Building and proceeded to shoot him eight times in the stomach with a .32 automatic handgun. Taylor then threw the gun down, walked to the sheriff's office, and turned himself in. Noonan was transported to Dr. Porter's Hospital over the First National Bank Building, where he died.

The Bair family built a swinging bridge over the Colorado River in 1936. Prior to that time, the family caught a train to get to and from Glenwood Springs and crossed the river either by boat or horseback. If they needed to bring a wagon onto the ranch, they would contact the Shoshone Dam and ask that they lower the water level of the river.

Quite a bit of new money moved into Glenwood in the late thirties. Frank Kistler came from the oil fields of Wyoming and purchased the Hotel Colorado, the pool, and the vapor caves for a total of $165,000.

George Sumers had been an investment broker from New York City. He had survived the great financial crash of 1929 and was now seeking a new, quieter life for himself and his family. He purchased the old Citizens' National Bank Building and most of the all but abandoned town of Cardiff, south of Glenwood Springs. He built a large, luxurious mansion near the Roaring Fork River and donated the area between the now silent coke ovens and the river to the city for the site of the Municipal Airport.

Henry P. Williams, known locally as "Hank," moved to town and purchased the home of the Baxters on Main Canyon Creek. Williams, the heir to the Williams Shaving Cream fortune, built a home on the creek known as "Rock 'N Pines." He developed a herd of brown Swiss cattle and opened a restaurant called "The Den."

Mr. and Mrs. George Traver purchased the area known as Echo Park, where they built a summer residence and bred Hereford cattle.

J. E. Sayre had made money in the oil fields of Oklahoma, and he spent a good deal of it in the Glenwood Springs area. He invested in oil leases around Carbondale and purchased land south of downtown Glenwood that he leased to the CCC camp and later donated to the city for a park. Sayre also purchased the northern slope of Red Mountain, which he also donated to the city for a ski area. After the Glenwood Sanitarium closed, he bought the building and converted it into an apartment house. It became known as the "Elms."

The Storm King Ranch above Mitchell Creek, which had been developed by the Devereuxes, had passed into the hands of Joe Bershenyi, who in turn sold it to Curtis King. King originally intended to create another polo field, but that was not to be. He did build a large home on Mitchell Creek and laid out a road up onto the Flat Tops to Coffee Pot Springs where he owned a summer cabin.

Wilderness areas had been set up within the White River National Forest. To the north of Glenwood Springs, the Flat Tops Wilderness Area is a high, wild area of lakes, streams, canyons, and forests. The Maroon Bells-Snowmass Wilderness Area, near Aspen, is higher and more heavily forested, more inaccessible. Both of the wilderness areas are without roads or improvements of any kind. They are accessible on foot or by horseback only. In 1938, the American Forest Association began organizing trail rides into the wilderness areas; horse pack trips of a week or more. Rich Thompson, a former forest ranger, took responsibility for furnishing horses, camping gear, and food for the trail ride participants.

Marcus C. "Mike" Bosco and Henry, his son, were able to meld the Denver Hotel and the Star Hotel into one unit in 1938. They added a new lounge called the Riverside Room.

Even though the Glenwood Municipal Airstrip had been deemed too small to participate in National Defense funds, a federal grant came through for $108,500 for construction of the airport. Two hangars and a maintenance building were built, and cinders from the old Cardiff coke ovens were used to surface the runways.

In 1940, six new houses were constructed south of Eleventh Street, still nominally the south city limits. Julius Wulfsohn's store was moved to a new location in the corner of the Hotel Glenwood, taking the place of Parkison Drug. Parkison, on the other hand, moved into Wulfsohn's former location at 810 Grand Avenue.

A former visitor to Glenwood who had not been seen since late 1887, "Big Nose" Kate, who was then going by the name of Mary K. Cummings, died in the Pioneer Home in Prescott, Arizona, on October 2, 1940. The former saloon girl, prostitute, and paramour of John Henry "Doc" Holliday was ninety years old when she passed away.

That same year, Glenwood Springs was poised on the edge of becoming a ski town. An enthusiastic group of young men, who called themselves the Winter Sports Club, began looking for a location for a ski run. The Spring Valley side of Lookout Mountain was considered at first, but then Sayre donated the north slope of Red Mountain, which made up their minds. Dr. Earl Garland headed a holding company whose purpose was to acquire a ski lift. A mining company in Ouray had a tow line available, and the city helped them purchase it. With the help of the WPA and local men, wooden towers were constructed, and the tow was set up for operation. The

The Red Mountain Ski area just to the west of downtown Glenwood Springs. (Courtesy of Frontier Historical Society - Schutte Collection)

first chairlift in western Colorado was in operation, on a ski hill that was visible from downtown Glenwood Springs.

One of the first passengers on the new lift was tossed out and fell hard, suffering a concussion. R. Morris "Buck" Buckmaster recovered from a coma and underwent extensive rehabilitation and eventually became a ski instructor.

CHAPTER SIXTEEN

From 1941 to 1950

"A sincere tribute goes out to all the firefighting volunteers, who were on the job until the fire was under control, and finally extinguished, disregarding the authentic danger they were in. They put up a gallant and effective fight."
The *Glenwood Post*, reporting on the 1948 oil tank explosions.

United States Representative Edward T. Taylor, who served as Colorado state senator from 1896 to 1908 and then went on to serve seventeen terms in Washington, was eighty-two, and was not well. He was known for his ceaseless work in water resource and agricultural legislation, as well as his support of the Taylor State Road through Glenwood Canyon. On September 3, 1941, word reached Glenwood Springs that he had died. He was buried in the Rosebud Cemetery in Glenwood.

The world was again at war. As of the beginning of 1941, the United States was not officially a participant in the various conflicts, but America was supplying war materials to Great Britain and had sanctioned Japan and Germany for their hostile acts in various locations throughout Europe and the East. Then on December 7, 1941, the United States was plunged into World War II by Japan's surprise attack on Pearl Harbor.

As during the First World War, many of Glenwood's young men enlisted in the armed services. The youths who were in town as residents of the Civilian Conservation Corps camp were no exception. The CCC Camp closed not long after the beginning of American's involvement in the war.

The war transformed Glenwood Springs. The town was subjected to rationing of sugar, gasoline, and rubber tires, and to the loss of its young men, like all other American cities. However, due to some special features of the little mountain town, it was affected in other ways, as well. The Hotel Colorado was commissioned as a Navy hospital in 1943. Trainloads of doctors, nurses, and wounded sailors began arriving almost immediately. The boilers from the Corwin Placer plant on Treasury Mountain

The Hot Springs Pool showing the Quonset hut housing hydrotherapy treatments for the Navy wounded. The pool was closed to the public during most of World War II. (Courtesy of Frontier Historical Society - Schutte Collection)

above Marble were moved to Glenwood to be used in the hotel since the hotel did not have central heating.

The Hot Springs Pool and the vapor caves were closed to the public, and taken over for the rehabilitation of the wounded servicemen. School children were allowed into the pool only under the direction of Red Cross swimming classes. The stone bathhouse was converted to a clinic and laboratory, and the Navy erected a Quonset hut at the east end of the pool for hydrotherapy.

The influx of servicemen into town led to the necessity for a United States Organizations (USO) facility for their entertainment. The people of Glenwood lent furniture to the USO, and they eventually leased the American Legion Auditorium. There were home-baked cookies and dances, and the famous USO road shows. Dinah Shore came to town to entertain the troops, raising quite a stir in Glenwood Springs.

There were war bond drives and Red Cross drives and salvage drives for paper and metal. The people of Glenwood opened their hearts and their homes to the servicemen. Trainloads of soldiers and sailors would stop off in town to relax in the pool or the caves for a bit before going about their duties, wherever they might take them.

Camp Hale was opened on Tennessee Pass not far from Leadville. It became home to the Tenth Mountain Division, who trained in the mountains of western Colorado as ski troops. Some

The American Legion Building, which was taken over by the USO for entertainment of the troops. (Courtesy of Don Vanderhoof)

of the military families of the Tenth Mountain troops lived in Glenwood, and many of the soldiers took advantage of the pool, the caves, and the hospitality.

The Navy did a great deal to repair and modernize the Hotel Colorado. They replaced the old wiring and plumbing and installed an automatic fire protection system. They also redecorated much of the hotel.

The local chapter of the Veterans of Foreign Wars was established in Glenwood in 1944. The Kiwanis Club was also formed in that year, one of the first service clubs to be established in town.

John Vanderhoof, who was in later years to become governor of Colorado, was brought to the Hotel Colorado to convalesce after being shot down in the Pacific. He had been a Navy pilot. He convinced his parents, who were living on the Front Range of Colorado, to move to Glenwood Springs. They made the move in 1945, and Roy "Vandy" Vanderhoof opened Van's Sporting Goods with the help of John and his other son, Don.

During the later years of the war, the old CCC Camp was utilized for quite a different purpose. The barracks were converted for use as a prisoner of war camp for Nazi Storm Troopers. They were marched on Grand Avenue under heavy guard and introduced soccer to Glenwood Springs. The prisoners played what they called "foosball" for recreation, and the residents of Glenwood Springs watched and cheered them on.

The war and related activities took the forefront of the minds and the hearts of the people of Glenwood during the first years of the 1940s. However, other events also affected the area. An infestation of bark beetles destroyed in excess of 670,000 acres of Engelmann Spruce in the western part of the country. The Forest Service established Mt. Sopris Nursery between Carbondale and Basalt, some 200 acres of seedling trees to replace those that had been killed.

The Red Mountain ski area was open and operating during the first part of the war, and more and more of the Glenwood Springs residents were experimenting with the new winter sport. Some of the ski troops who were training on the slopes at Aspen came to Red Mountain to ski for fun in their leisure time. The relatively low elevation of the ski area, however, resulted in undependable snow conditions. The area was closed after two years of operation, because two of the wooden towers were found to be defective, and Glenwood Springs was again without a ski area for the duration of the war.

On December 15, 1943, Dr. W. W. Crook died at the age of seventy-nine. Crook was a longtime Glenwood Springs physician and surgeon as well as a good friend of Buffalo Bill Cody.

In May of 1945, after years of war that had involved a great deal of the world, Germany surrendered to United States. Hitler had been reported dead, and the back of the Third Reich had been broken. The war continued in the Far East, and more and more pressure was put on Japan to surrender. The fight continued, however, and it was not until the United States dropped the world's first atomic bombs on Hiroshima and Nagasaki that they finally surrendered formally on September 2.

On September 14 of that year there was a mass observance in Glenwood Springs to celebrate the end of the war and to recognize those who did not return from the conflicts. After the end of the war, Glenwood Springs gradually returned to the status of a quiet mountain town. The Navy occupied the Hotel Colorado until February of 1946, when they turned it back over to Frank Kistler. The medical equipment at the pool's bathhouse was turned over to a business called the Glenwood Hospital and Clinic, who ran it as a hospital for the next several years.

During 1945, three national forests merged into one. The White River, Holy Cross, and Sopris national forests joined under the name of the White River National Forest, creating the largest national forest

The hulk of the Hotel Glenwood after the disastrous 1945 fire. Five people lost their lives. (Courtesy of Frontier Historical Society)

in Colorado and the second largest in the nation. It totals over 2,300,000 acres, and stretches from the Continental Divide west to Rifle and from Aspen north to Meeker.

Mrs. Lucas, the former owner of the Hotel Colorado and the owner of the Glenwood Light Company, died the same year. She had created a provision in her will that allowed the city to purchase the company after her death, and they did so, at a cost of $225,000. The city then signed a contract with the Public Service Company to purchase power from the Shoshone Plant. The light plant was converted to city maintenance shops.

Shortly after midnight on December 14, 1945, one of the city's oldest and largest landmarks burned. The Hotel Glenwood, at the northwest corner of Eighth and Grand, was consumed by fire. There was some delay in searching the ruins because of snowfall and ice from the water used to fight the fire, but newspaper accounts spoke of two confirmed deaths and two others who were known to be missing. The bodies of Charles Marshall and C. C. Brown were the first to be recovered, and Charles Williams and an unknown "transient" were found later. Mrs. Henry Hart died a short time later from pneumonia and from injuries which she sustained in jumping from the third floor of the hotel to the roof of an adjacent building.

Only a small part of the structure survived. A small room to the north of the hotel proper, which had originally been used as a sample room for traveling salesmen, somehow escaped the blaze that left only a skeleton of the old hotel standing. That portion of the building had been used as a barbershop at the time of the fire. The fire was so intense that the windows in all of the nearby stores were cracked or broken from the heat.

In the mid 1940s Marie Holloway became the first female county judge in Colorado and one of the very first in the entire western United States. She had been born in Missouri, but her family moved to Colorado when she was three years old. Holloway attended a women's college in Missouri and obtained her law degree from the University of Southern California. She was to serve as Garfield County judge for almost twenty years. During her years on the bench she developed a reputation for her work with juvenile offenders. She insisted that the youthful transgressors apologize for their misdeeds and make financial amends to the injured parties.

In 1946, Cran Rader, Jr. leased the airport and added a service facility and new hangars. At the time he owned a four-seat Stinson Voyager, and he set up a charter service and a flying school.

Frank Mechau, the internationally known mural painter who had painted the mural in the Forest Service Building on Grand Avenue, died in 1946 of heart failure. He was forty-two years old.

Glenwood Springs adopted a city manager form of government in 1946 and elected the first city council members in November of 1947.

At that time, Frank Kistler owned the Hotel Colorado, the Hot Springs Pool and bathhouse, and the vapor caves. He decided to split his holdings, selling the hotel to A. J. Crawford and Frank Houes. The new hotel owners converted the facility back into a luxury hotel and promptly resold to Shay Hotel Corporation, run by Philip Shaiman. The new owner replaced the fountain in the south courtyard with a swimming pool to compete with the big pool owned by Kistler. Kistler promptly built two luxury motor lodges and converted the bathhouse/hospital into the main building of the new Hot Springs Motor Lodge. Lost to the renovations were the wildlife refuge and a great deal of the landscaping.

There was a small stir of excitement in 1947 when Continental Airlines landed a DC-3 at the Glenwood Airport. They apparently landed and took off successfully, but there is little report of that sort of thing happening with any regularity. It can probably be assumed that it was a bit of a tight squeeze.

The Red Mountain Ski Area was handy to town, but the snow conditions were never dependable. The Vanderhoof family, who owned Van's Sporting Goods in Glenwood, had

A Continental Airlines DC-3 which landed at the Glenwood Springs airport in 1947. (Courtesy of Frontier Historical Society)

purchased surplus skiing equipment from Camp Hale after the Tenth Mountain Division stopped training there. Since the gear had been meant for fighting in the snow, most of it was white. In the interest of finding a better location for a ski area, the Vanderhoofs investigated the Walck Ranch some ten miles up Four-Mile Creek, past the site of the old coal mining town of Sunshine, later Sunlight. There were significant slopes available on Compass Peak, and the additional elevation resulted in heavier, more reliable snow conditions.

The Vanderhoofs cleared trees and brush off of what was to become known as Holiday Hill. The resultant slope was about 3,800 feet

Holiday Hill, opened by the Vanderhoof family on the site of the present Sunlight Ski Area. (Courtesy of Don Vanderhoof)

Smoke billows from a massive oil tank fire on May 15, 1948. (Courtesy of Buzz Zancanella)

in length and was served by a rope tow. The tow was powered by a 1930 Dodge pickup truck. The Vanderhoof family ran the fledgling resort for two years.

In 1948, there was another huge fire in Glenwood Springs. A series of oil storage tanks caught fire and exploded, sending massive sheets of flame up and over the town. The explosions were described as giant mushrooms of fire, shooting up hundreds of feet into the air and spreading out to cover several square blocks. Only a fortuitous lack of wind and the quick and heroic action of the Glenwood Volunteer Fire Department saved the town from serious damage. Over one hundred persons were estimated to have suffered burns from the tremendous heat of the blast. Some of the injured were several blocks away from the exploding tanks.

Lawrence "Bugo" Zancanella was burned badly in the fire, receiving second and third degree burns on his face, head, and hands. His lungs were also burned. He was not expected to live, but he did recover and continued to serve on the fire department. Several other firemen, including Don Paterson, Albert Lewis, John Fish, Wayne Burdge, and Harry Hughes were seriously burned, but there were no fatalities.

Harry Truman had ascended to the Presidency on April 12, 1945 when Franklin D. Roosevelt died. On September 23, 1948, President Harry Truman came through town on a "whistle-stop" tour of the western United States. He was cheered by enthusiastic crowds.

The first radio station came to Glenwood in 1949 when Rex and Charles Howell of Grand Junction formed KGLN. They built a tower in north Glenwood in 1950, but the original location of the station was at the southeastern corner of the old polo field. The first broadcast was on Mother's Day of 1949.

The Denver and Rio Grand Railroad began service with the California Zephyr in 1949. The train was the latest in luxury and featured new Vista Dome coaches. The dining car boasted fine linen and tableware, Colorado carnations, and five chefs. The passenger cars sported windows that reached up and over the roofs, affording magnificent views of such scenery as Glenwood Canyon. In fact, the idea for the Vista Dome roofs was sparked by a trip through the spectacular scenery of Glenwood Canyon. The cars also featured reclining seats, carpeting, and music from wire recordings. The advertising motto of the Zephyr was "We put the See in Scenery." Continental Trailways instituted service with their big new buses the same year. The American public was beginning to travel again, which boded well for Glenwood Springs.

In 1950, a "monument to an idea" was erected in Glenwood Canyon. A man-made stone arch supported a nine-foot-long, 500 pound replica of a

The "Monument to an Idea" in honor of the Californie Zephyr Vista Dome. The monument sat near the presen Grizzly Creek Rest Area. The Zephyr itself is in the background. (Courtesy of Frontier Historical Society Schutte Collection)

Vista Dome car. The monument was located near the present site of the Grizzly Creek Rest Area.

The Civil Air Patrol set up headquarters in Glenwood Springs. It was meant to be an emergency and rescue patrol and was monitored by the United States Air Force.

During 1950 and 1951, Joe Juhan leased the Red Mountain Ski Area and spent over a million dollars on it. He installed steel towers and converted the chairlift from single chair to double. He also put a degree of pressure on the city to eliminate his competition by closing Holiday Hill. The city agreed. The ski area up Four Mile Creek closed, and the skiing action again shifted to the lower elevations.

After all of the work on the Red Mountain area, the refurbished ski area struggled to make a profit. Years of sparse snow and warm conditions hurt the operation. Juhan built trails and a picnic area toward the top of the mountain and ran the lift in the summers. Later, Margaret "Cap" Smith, who owned a ranch above the ski area, was to open a short ski run at the very top of Red Mountain called Mountain Meadows. It was served by a poma lift, but it only lasted for one season. The road that accessed the area wound up the side of Red Mountain and was described as "terrible."

The Hopkins Hospital in about 1927. It closed in 1950. (Courtesy of Frontier Historical Society)

Cran Rader, Jr., who owned the Glenwood Airport, purchased the Rifle Airport in 1950. He hired Betty Clark to operate the Rifle facility. Clark introduced crop dusting to Garfield County.

When the stone bathhouse at the pool was converted from a clinic back to use as part of the Hot Springs Pool operation, there was a need for a hospital. The Garfield County Hospital Association was formed with Harold Parkison as its president. The city still owned the four and one half acres that had held the County Poor Farm, and they donated the land to the cause. Over $525,000 was raised for the hospital project, part from private donations and part from a federal grant under the Hill-Burton Act. The new facility was thoroughly modern and held thirty-six beds. It was called Valley View Hospital. It was originally administered by the Mennonite Board of Missions and Charities. Of the remaining private hospitals, the Hopkins Hospital closed when Dr. Hopkins died, and the Porter Hospital when Valley View Hospital opened.

The population of Glenwood Springs in 1950 was 2,412.

CHAPTER SEVENTEEN

From 1951 to 1960

"The sale of this beautiful resort property to the business leaders of Glenwood Springs will assure continuation of the traditions of hospitality and the 50-cent admission which has made this naturally-heated pool one of the great tourist attractions of the United States."

Frank Kistler, on the occasion of the sale of the
Hot Springs Pool to a group of businessmen

The Rocky Mountain Savings and Loan, an industrial bank, opened in 1951. The post-war economy was showing signs of life. More and more travelers were coming to Glenwood Springs, and it appeared that the dark days of the Depression were over.

On June 1, 1951, Jerry and Marcie Fitch took over the management of radio station KGLN. At that time, the station featured local news and announcements, music, and commercials. The station was one of the main sources of news and sports for the valley, given that the *Glenwood Post* was still a weekly newspaper published every Thursday.

The cottonwoods that lined south Grand Avenue prior to widening the street in the early 50's. (Courtesy of Buzz Zancanella)

The old incandescent streetlamps were replaced with modern mercury-vapor lights, the old Von Rosenberg-designed bridge across the Colorado River was replaced, and Grand Avenue was widened. Unfortunately, the improving of south Grand Avenue necessitated the removal of the big old cottonwood trees that had been planted when the polo field was built. However, travel on Colorado Highway 82 toward Carbondale and on to Basalt and Aspen was increasing, and Grand Avenue had become the north end of Highway 82. Examination of the trees revealed that the trunks were largely rotten, and would have had to be removed anyway.

In 1953, Doctor C. W. McFadden purchased the Glenwood Hot Springs Company, which included the vapor caves but not the pool. McFadden, an osteopath, had been practicing in Glenwood since 1926. Under his ownership, the caves began offering chiropractic services and massage therapy.

A new high school was built in Glenwood Springs in 1953, and Colorado Rocky Mountain School, a private coeducational boarding school, was formed just north of Carbondale. CRMS was organized by Mr. and Mrs. John Holden, and the work-study institution was housed in converted farm buildings.

The Vanderhoof family, who had been operating Van's Sporting Goods and who were instrumental in the opening of Holiday Hill, founded Glenwood Industrial Bank in 1955. Don Vanderhoof would become president of the bank.

Doc Holliday had come to Glenwood Springs in May of 1887 and died in November of that year. There seemed to be little need to point out to the world the fact that Glenwood Springs had been the temporary home and final resting place of what many considered to be little more than a foul tempered drunk. However, *Doc Holliday*, a book by John Myers Myers was published in 1955. To quote Myers:

"He was one of the coolest killers ever to snatch a gun from hiding. He was a gambler of enough parts to make two. He was a con man....and equally deft at dodging the passes which the law often made in his direction. He drank enough liquor to earn a place on John Barleycorn's calendar of saints."

Suddenly, here was a book that introduced Doc to new generations as the type of scoundrel that Americans love. For nearly seventy years, he had rested in relative obscurity. That was all to change. Al Axtell was the city manager at the time, and he quite correctly assumed that the grave of Doc Holliday might just serve as an attraction to tourists.

There was of course a small problem related to the marking of the grave. No one knew where it was. One version of the events, following his death in November, stated that he had been buried somewhere on Palmer Avenue as a temporary measure, given that the trail up to the Linwood Cemetery was impassable that late in the year. Supposedly his remains were disinterred the following spring and moved up to the cemetery. Another rendering of the tale says that no one was willing to pay the necessary expenses to move the body, and that he is in fact still somewhere near Palmer Avenue.

Whatever the truth, a monument was needed so that the anticipated tourists would have a subject for their photographs. Axtell took both C. W. McFadden and Wallace Bryant, two men who professed to know the truth about the burial site, up to the cemetery and turned them loose. They both identified the same general area as the proper place, and a specific location was chosen. An impressive monument, which had been carved and donated by Snyder Memorials of Grand Junction, was set up on a location overlooking the Roaring Fork Valley. Later another marker was added, stating that Doc's remains are buried "someplace in this cemetery" The monument states incorrectly that Holliday graduated from Dental School in Baltimore, (in fact, he graduated from the Pennsylvania College of Dental Surgery), misstates his date of birth, (the stone says 1852—he was born in 1851), incorrectly lists his birthplace as Valdosta instead of Griffin, and misspelled Valdosta, but the stone does sport crossed six-guns and a poker hand.

The monument to Doc Holliday erected by the City of Glenwood Springs in 1955. (Courtesy of John Tindall)

In 1956 a group of twenty-two Glenwood Springs businessmen formed the Glenwood Hot Springs Lodge and Pool Company. The new corporation purchased the pool complex from Frank Kistler for a reported one million dollars. They began a program of remodeling which covered the next five years and spent another several hundred thousand dollars. The project included removing the Quonset hut that the navy had erected as well as a group of cabanas. Also removed were the old firebrick paving and sandstone walls. The pool itself was deepened and enlarged, winding up as 405 feet long and tapering from forty-four feet to 110 feet wide. A new hot pool was added at the east end of the big pool, containing water of 104 degrees. The main pool, which after the renovations held a total of 1,071,000 gallons of water, was maintained at between ninety and ninety-five degrees. The big pool completely changed water every six hours, and the hot therapy pool underwent a changeover every two hours.

A new filtration system and underwater lighting were added, plus children's wading pools. The old wooden bathhouse was torn down and replaced with new dressing rooms, a swim shop, and a poolside coffee shop. One of the casualties of the renovations was the old cold water fountain at the west end of the pool.

When the Shoshone Dam was finished, it created a unique piece of river between the dam and the power plant. In the summer and fall, the two mile length of river can be almost dry, a narrow, V-shaped canyon with a lot of rocks and very little water in the bottom. However, during spring runoff, the stretch becomes an unbelievable maelstrom of white water, churning madly between the boulders. It forms two class VI rapids, the most dangerous kind. One is known as Cottonwood Falls, the other as Barrel Springs.

In May of 1956, three adventuresome men from Aspen chose to challenge this boiling tangle of water. They used a borrowed war surplus raft twenty-five feet long and made of heavy neoprene and canvas. Motorists stopped to watch. With over 200 spectators, they launched the raft into the river. The water grabbed the raft, spun it down Cottonwood Falls, and sucked it under the surface. When the river spit the raft back out, there was no one in it. One of the men managed to swim to shore with a dislocated shoulder. Another was washed down the river and was ready to give up the fight when his feet touched bottom, and he was pulled out by spectators. The body of the third man was found a month later, thirty miles downstream. The rapids between the Shoshone Power Plant and Grizzly Creek at high water have been called "some of the toughest in the state,"

Modern adventurers challenge the white water of the Colorado River. (Courtesy of Blue Sky Adventures)

with names like Upper and Lower Superstition, Man-Eater, Tombstone, and The Wall.

In that same year, Mid-Continent Resources began mining operations in Coal Basin. The Coal Basin Mines had originally been opened and worked by Colorado Fuel and Iron under the direction of John C. Osgood. CF&I operated the mines from 1898 to 1909. Two coal seams originally showed in the Mancos Shale cliffs; one at 10,000 feet in elevation and the other at 10,500 feet. The coal sought by Mid-Continent was the same high quality coking coal that had originally attracted Osgood's attention. The high elevation and the presence of methane pockets increased the normal dangers of mining coal from deep within the earth, but it was felt that the uniqueness of the coal deposits justified the extra risk.

The city of Glenwood Springs was creeping south. Annexations added the area around Valley View Hospital, the land just south of Hyland Park, and several other tracts along and on both sides of south Grand Avenue. Up to 1956, Cooper Avenue ended at the Twelfth Street ditch. During that year, a bridge was constructed which allowed the street to continue on south. At about the same time, work was begun on the tract of land which had once held the old CCC Camp and the prisoner of war camp. The resultant expanse of grass and trees was to be known as Sayre Park.

The Mountain States Telephone and Telegraph built a new building on Grand Avenue to house the equipment necessary to convert Glenwood Springs' telephone network to a dial system. The modernization was part of a nationwide conversion to a telephone system that would eventually allow a person to dial any other number in the country.

The timber on Grizzly Peak, just inside the west end of the canyon, caught fire from a lightning strike in 1958. The people of Glenwood Springs watched as the smoke from the fire billowed into the sky. A Rocky Mountain bighorn ram who had frequently been seen on the mountain was not seen again.

All of the schools in Basalt, Carbondale, and Glenwood Springs combined into one school district in 1959. It was known as RE-1. A bond issue came to a vote to raise $1,500,000 to combine all of the high schools into one big school, but it was defeated. The next year another bond, $950,000 this time, was approved to build schools in all three towns.

The Wulfsohn Mansion, which had been built by Captain Prey, purchased and named "Cedarbank" by Walter and Mary Devereux, and most recently owned by Julius Wulfsohn, was purchased by Union Oil Company. The purchase price for the house, buildings, and about 500 acres was $175,000. In 1959 all of the remaining art objects were removed from the old mansion and the building was razed.

In about 1960, John Higgs purchased much of the private land near Compass Peak including the former site of Holiday Hill. He formed an investment group and reopened the area. They bought the poma lift from Margaret Smith's Mountain Meadows Ski Area and obtained a special use permit from the White River National Forest in order to expand the ski area to some 3,000 acres. They installed a Riblet double chairlift and opened over fourteen miles of trails, ranging from beginner to expert.

In 1960, President Dwight Eisenhower signed the necessary legislative documents to authorize the appropriation and expenditure of funds for a segment of interstate highway between Denver and Cove Fort, Utah. Congress had approved the establishment of an interstate highway system four years earlier in 1956. Eisenhower had been a proponent of the interstate system for several years, both for peacetime use and for the transport of armed services personnel and equipment in case of war.

A young civil engineer named R. A. "Dick" Prosence was assigned the task of formulating the original cost estimates for high-

Fire from the explosion of a 17,000 gallon oil tank on June 15, 1960. (Courtesy of Buzz Zancanella)

way construction between Dillon, Colorado and the Utah state line. This was his introduction to the monumental undertaking of designing and building the interstate highway through Glenwood Canyon. Prosence, a former Glenwood Springs resident, was to become the Colorado Department of Transportation District Three Engineer in charge of the exceptionally lengthy process which was to result in the Interstate 70 project through the canyon.

On June 15, 1960, a massive explosion rocked Glenwood Springs. A 17,000 gallon oil tank exploded and burned, having been ignited by a heater used to soften the heavy asphalt road paving oil which was being transferred from a railroad tank car to the big city storage tank. Two of the three workmen at the site of the explosion were literally blown clear of the resulting fire. Miraculously, one of these men was the only burn victim in the incident. He suffered a superficial burn to his neck.

Lawrence "Bugo" Zancanella was the fire chief and one of the men who had been seriously burned in the 1948 oil tank explosions. Zancanella, covered by his hose crews, again displayed remarkable courage when he climbed into the railroad car to shut off the valves and stop the flow of oil.

Cave explorers discovered a small hole at the back of the known reaches of the Fairy Caves in 1960. The hole, known as "Jam Crack," vastly extended the explored areas of the cave network. The Fairy Caves, which are located inside Iron Mountain just north of the Hotel Colorado, had been closed to the public in 1917 and remained closed as of 1960.

The population of Glenwood Springs in 1960 totaled 3,613.

CHAPTER EIGHTEEN

From 1961 to 1970

"Whether our river is ushered through town within concrete retaining walls or a natural water bank, whether we view our streets, our pool, our town through a chain link fence or through a glade of trees, or grass, or weed, is a decision not encompassed within the responsibility of the highway department, but only ourselves."
Floyd Diemoz, in a letter to the Editor of the *Glenwood Post,* July, 1965

The Hotel Colorado was still having difficulty turning a profit. To help make ends meet, part of the old hotel was turned over to junior high school classes when the junior high building was condemned. The classes continued at the hotel while the new school was being built.

Rocky Mountain Natural Gas Company had been drilling exploratory wells in the mountains to the south and east of Glenwood Springs. In 1961 they signed an agreement with the city to furnish natural gas from their producing wells. They ran lines to Glenwood as well as up and down the Roaring Fork River. The vast majority of homes and businesses that had been utilizing coal for decades converted to the cleaner, and much more convenient, natural gas.

A new wing was added to Valley View Hospital in 1962, doubling the capacity of the facility, and there was an addition to the high school.

Eleanora Malaby, who had been the first bride in Glenwood Springs and who had entertained Colorow and other Ute Indians in her home in the very early days of Glenwood Springs, died in 1962. She was ninety-five years of age.

That year, the George Sumers home south of town was given over to the Holy Ghost Fathers for a novitiate. The mansion was converted for use in the instruction of young Catholic men who aspired to the priesthood.

Another annual event was started in 1962. The Glenwood Art Guild, a local organization of artists, held the first Glenwood Springs Fall Art Festival. The festival to was to grow over the years to attract artists from all over the United States.

Floyd Diemoz, a member of one of the pioneer families in the Glenwood Springs area, first became involved in Colorado Department of Transportation issues in 1963. At that time, public input was requested concerning the possible construction of twin tunnels at the west end of the canyon. The tunnels were to bypass the Horseshoe Bend area of the river, a massive meander of the Colorado just before it breaks out of Glenwood Canyon. Public sentiment overwhelmingly favored the construction of the tunnels, since they would replace one of the most dangerous sections of highway in the canyon. The curved roadway was shaded much of the year, resulting in the formation of ice patches during the winter. The tunnels were approved with little opposition.

At that time, there existed little in the way of environmental awareness regarding the prospect of fitting a standard four lane interstate highway within the narrow confines of the canyon. Diemoz was to remain involved in the debates, the design processes, and the construction of the highway for the next thirty years.

The Glenwood Springs Roping Club, the primary organization behind rodeo activities in the area, orchestrated a cooperative effort with the city to build a new rodeo grounds near the airport. The city donated the land and the labor involved in building bleachers. The combined efforts of the Roping Club, the 4-H Clubs, and local businessmen brought the new arena into being.

A new building was erected at Eighth and Cooper to house the various offices of city government. It included city council chambers, the office of the city manager and the planning department, the city utility departments, the police department, the library, and the headquarters and equipment garages for the volunteer fire department.

A new federal building and post office were also constructed in 1964 at the corner of Ninth and Colorado Avenue. The old federal building on Grand Avenue was by then almost filled with personnel of the White River National Forest.

The Frontier Historical Society was formed in 1964. It was founded through the cooperation of valley pioneers, the Glenwood Springs School District, the city of Glenwood Springs, the chamber of commerce, and the Forest Service. Area residents and organizations donated a wealth of artifacts and memorabilia to the society.

The twin tunnels east of Glenwood Springs, the first segment of four lane highway in the canyon. (Courtesy of Frontier Historical Society)

The twin tunnels at the west end of the canyon were completed in 1965. The highway between No Name and Glenwood Springs that ran through the tunnels became the first section of four lane road in Glenwood Canyon.

Mid-Continent Resources had taken over the operation of the old Coal Basin mines, enlarging and modernizing them. The mines offered well-paying, if somewhat dangerous, jobs to many of the residents of the valley. It was not at all unusual to see men of the area wearing the mark of the mines, the black-rimmed eyes, a result of working amidst the coal dust. On December 31, 1965, a methane explosion killed nine of those miners.

The Glenwood Springs Rotary Club, the local chapter of Rotary International, was formed in 1966.

In the mid-sixties, the building at 724 Grand Avenue began its present incarnation as the home of Doc Holliday's, a saloon and restaurant dedicated to the memory of the "Deadly Dentist." It contains a good deal of memorabilia from the late 1880s.

In 1966, the federal government determined that Highway 70, later to be known as Interstate 70, was to run through Glenwood Canyon and along the north side of the Colorado River through town. It was to be four lanes wherever possible, and as straight as they could make it. This necessitated moving the Denver & Rio Grande Railroad tracks to the south side of the river within

Glenwood. This move also served to clean up the old freight yards and switching tracks that were cluttering Glenwood Springs along the north side of the river.

As the construction progressed from the Traver curve in west Glenwood toward the twin tunnels at the end of the canyon, controversy built from a whisper to a crescendo. The visual results of the process, the massive cuts into the hillsides to the north and the fills into the river, brought on an environmental awareness and concern that would halt further construction in its tracks.

On January 15, 1967, the Glenwood Restaurant and Lounge was destroyed by fire.

When the Hotel Colorado was originally built, an ornate stone causeway was constructed over the wagon road that existed in front of the hotel, a pathway from the hotel to the Hot Springs Pool and back. When Highway 40 and then Highway 6 & 24 replaced the old wagon road, the causeway was retained. However, by 1967 the height of over-the-road trucks had increased so much that the old structure had to be removed.

An addition to the old grade school building was completed in 1967 and named for Wilbur J. "Skip" Bolitho. Bolitho, who started teaching math and physical education in the Glenwood Springs school system in 1931, had become principal of the grade school in 1951.

The western campus of Colorado Mountain College was established in Spring Valley in 1967. It was formed as a two year college, or junior college, and was a sister campus to the CMC campus in Leadville. The school combined regular two year curriculums with a community continuing education program which allowed local residents to take courses in a wide range of subjects in classrooms in Glenwood Springs, Aspen, Basalt, Rifle, and New Castle. The college expanded to include resident campuses in Glenwood Springs, Leadville, and Steamboat Springs, covering an area of some 12,000 square miles.

In February of 1968, the Colorado General Assembly passed Senate Joint Resolution Number Sixteen. The resolution addressed the potential for damages to the beauty of Glenwood Canyon by construction of a four lane highway. It also instructed the highway commission to form an advisory committee, to be made up of citizens concerned with the environment. The committee was to review and comment on the planning process, with an eye toward the final visual and recreational aspects of the highway construction. The resolution was aimed toward a highway that would be "so designed that, to the fullest possible extent, the wonders of human engineering be tastefully blended with the wonders of nature."

After Rex and Charles Howell successfully opened KGLN, the first radio station in Glenwood Springs, they began investigating the possibility of a television station. The installation of the necessary equipment became a community project with the cooperation of Mountain States Telephone, the Glenwood Springs Electrical Department, and Holy Cross Electric. The completed signal booster offered three channels of television to the town. In 1967 Rex Howell installed the additional equipment for Glenwood Cable Television, offering two more channels.

The observant traveler through Glenwood Canyon will notice, at about mile marker 124, an American flag on a pole high on a pinnacle to the south of the highway. The flag was originally erected and has been maintained since by Steve Kibler and Mike Paddock. The two men, graduates of Palisade High School, spent much of the summer of 1967 rock climbing in the canyon. In 1968 they put the flag in place as a tribute to the previous summer.

Glenwood Medical Associates, a consortium of doctors and support personnel, built the Glenwood Medical Clinic across Blake Avenue from Valley View Hospital in 1968 to complement the hospital's services.

John B. Shutte died on March 4, 1968. Ten years earlier, Shutte had been honored at a testimonial dinner to commemorate a total of fifty years with the United States Postal Service. He started with the postal service in 1908, and was appointed assistant postmaster in 1923 and postmaster in 1940. Shutte was and still is known for his outdoor photography. His collection of excellent photographs has been turned over to the Frontier Historical Society. A number of his photos are included in this work.

On March 29, 1968, the engineer of an eastbound California Zephyr hit the emergency brakes on his train to avoid boulders that had fallen onto the tracks. The lead engine derailed, sending it and the second engine into the river. Two more engine sections, the diner, a baggage car, and three coaches also derailed but did not go over the embankment. There were no injuries among the 189 passengers.

The first comprehensive history of Glenwood Springs was published in 1970. It was *Glenwood Springs: Spa in the Mountains,* written by Lena M. Urquhart.

The Colorado Highway Department hired a consulting firm in the summer of 1970 to assess the environmental impacts of routing Interstate 70 through Glenwood Canyon. At about the same time, the highway commission appointed a seven person advisory committee to review the initial plans for the canyon highway. Several of the advisory committee members expressed dissatisfaction with the plans, and it was suggested that alternative routes such as Cottonwood Pass be investigated. A number of environmental groups immediately jumped into the pending conflict, and the situation rapidly developed into a widening rift, with highway engineers on one side and environmentalists on the other. There are no records of additional meetings by the advisory committee.

Two alternate routes for the interstate were investigated early on. One of these routes would have taken the highway over the Flat Tops, leading north from Dotsero to near Deep Lake, and then west and south to Rifle. That route would have taken the road to 10,000 feet in places, as well as adding forty-two miles to the finished highway. It was estimated that the Flat Tops route would cost up to five times as much as a highway through the canyon.

Another possibility would have the route cut south from Gypsum, climb over Cottonwood Pass, and descend into the Roaring Fork Valley south of Glenwood Springs. That route would increase the total length of the construction by over nine miles, and like the Flat Tops route, would subject drivers to severe winter conditions part of the year. Even if Cottonwood Pass could be used as a detour during construction in the canyon, a great deal of expense would be necessary to bring the rough trail over the pass to two lane highway standards.

The directors of the Glenwood Springs Chamber of Commerce adopted a resolution calling for the routing of the interstate through Glenwood Canyon, under three conditions: that the highway design be developed by outstanding national or international designers, that drawings, models, and renditions be prepared to demonstrate the design concepts, and that local public hearings and a citizens' advisory committee review every stage of the planning, pursuant to the General Assembly Resolution of 1968.

The next few years saw a great number of heated public debates between the factions for and against a canyon highway. It would have been difficult to find anyone without a strong opinion about the fate of Glenwood Canyon.

CHAPTER NINETEEN

From 1971 to 1980

"I'm the most cold blooded sonofabitch you'll ever meet. Sometimes I feel like a vampire."

Ted Bundy

Stella and Churchill Shumate willed their home at 1001 Colorado Avenue to the Historical Society for use as a museum, and the society's collections of artifacts and memorabilia were moved there in 1971.

In the 1970s, many Rocky Mountain bighorn sheep were being killed by traffic in Glenwood Canyon. Residents who had built homes in the canyon had planted apple trees which drew the big animals down off of their usual high haunts. The Division of Wildlife trapped the remainder of the resident herd and relocated them elsewhere.

In October of 1971, public hearings about the routing of Interstate 70 were held in Glenwood Springs and Denver. The meetings drew huge crowds, predictably polarized in their opinions. Four members of the Glenwood Springs Chamber of Commerce Transportation Committee spent some $3,000 of their own money and ten months of their time producing a twenty-five minute film showing their recommendations for the design of the highway. Floyd Diemoz, Jerry Brown, Ed Mulhall, and Jim Rose created "I-70: Where and How?" The film looked at all three alternatives; Glenwood Canyon, Cottonwood Pass, and the Flat Tops route.

Italian mountain road construction techniques were shown, using photographs sent to the filmmakers by Dean Moffat. Moffat, later to become a Glenwood Springs architect, was living in Italy at the time. The photos of the autostratas of Northern Italy demonstrated that highway spans could be efficiently constructed high above the ground, thus freeing the floor of the canyon for wildlife and recreation. The thrust of the film was that the interstate highway should be built through the canyon, but that it should be done in such a way as to preserve its beauty. Between August 1971, and June 1972, the film was shown to over forty-three private, civic, and

An early picture of the canyon, illustrating the difficulties involved in constructing a four lane interstate highway through it. (Courtesy of Frontier Historical Society)

governmental groups from Hawaii to Washington, D.C. At the conclusion of the October 1971, meeting in Glenwood Springs, twenty-six organizations supported the canyon route, and two groups opposed it. After the Denver meetings, forty more organizations lined up in favor of the canyon route, and eleven more came out against it.

The Hotel Colorado was still struggling. In the early seventies it was again remodeled, and the name was changed to the "Village Inn." The rooms were updated, the Presidential Suite was converted to a business office, and a new bar called the Red Garter Room took over the area once occupied by the north dining room with the indoor waterfall.

The Readmor Bookstore, next to the First National Bank Building on Grand Avenue, burned in 1973. There was real danger of the fire spreading to other downtown buildings, but again, the valiant efforts of the volunteer fire department prevented a further disaster.

John Vanderhoof served as the governor of Colorado from 1973 to 1975. He had come to Glenwood Springs as one of the injured Navy personnel during World War II. With his father Roy, he opened Van's Sporting Goods in Glenwood Springs in 1945.

In 1974, Dr. McFadden came to an agreement to sell the Vapor Caves to Dr. Richard Renn. McFadden retained ownership for the next five years, but Renn took over operation of the caves.

On March 23, 1974, Marcus "Mike" Bosco died at the age of eighty-one. Bosco was the longtime owner of the Hotel Denver on Seventh Street, as well as a member of the Glenwood Springs Volunteer Fire Department. He served on the city council for eighteen years.

Another annual celebration was founded in the mid-seventies. Ski Spree was established as the brainchild of Don Vanderhoof and Bob Zanella, who was then president of the Jaycees. It is a winter celebration which helps to promote tourism and is, according to Vanderhoof, a therapeutic winter celebration for the locals.

By 1975, the Interstate Highway System was well on its way to criss-crossing the country with wide, four-or more-lane ribbons of asphalt. Interstate 25 was complete from the New Mexico border up through Pueblo, Colorado Springs, and Denver to the Wyoming line. Interstate 76 was almost complete from Denver to Kansas. Interstate 70 was creeping westward from Denver toward the Continental Divide, where the Eisenhower Tunnel was completed and waiting. Understandably, concern was beginning to grow on several fronts about the inevitability, indeed the possibility, of building a four lane interstate highway through Glenwood Canyon.

As of the end of 1975, over one million dollars had been spent over a nine year period in studies and design concepts for the stretch of interstate highway which might, or might not, be built through the canyon. A study of the existing Highway 6 & 24 through the canyon by the Colorado Department of Highways revealed that accident rates in the canyon were over thirty percent higher than that of comparable two lane roads, and that the fatality rate was some 300 percent higher.

Three design firms had submitted conceptual designs for a possible canyon highway. Of these, the concept submitted by Edgardo Contini of Victor Gruen Associates from Los Angeles seemed to receive the most favorable comments from the various factions. The Gruen organization stated that there were two main issues involved in designing a highway for Glenwood Canyon: the objective of moving traffic safely and quickly, and the objective of protecting and/or maximizing the scenic and recreational aspects of the canyon.

Several environmental groups raised objections to any construction in the canyon, especially construction of any sort of a four lane highway. Among the most visible and vocal was a group known as Citizens for a Glenwood Canyon Scenic Corridor Committee headed by Mark Skrotzki. Among others, he enlisted singer and Aspen resident John Denver and former Interior Secretary Stewart Udall to help publicize their cause. One of the main concerns of Skrotzki and others was the seeming impossibility of performing any sort of meaningful construction in the canyon without leaving permanent scars on the majestic rock formations. In 1974, John Denver threw a rock across the Colorado River to emphasize the narrowness of the canyon and its unsuitability for an interstate highway. It reportedly took several tries.

In December of 1975, the Federal Highway Administration recommended Glenwood Canyon as the route for the interstate. In 1976, the United States Department of Transportation designated the canyon as the official corridor for the highway. An amendment was attached to the Federal Highway Act which allowed variations from the standard construction standards and "four-or-more-lane" configuration for interstate highways. The amendment stated that the variances would be allowed when necessary for protection of the traveling public, of the environment, or to preserve the historic or scenic values of Glenwood Canyon. The factions which opposed the canyon interstate hailed the amendment as a sign that a four lane highway might be averted. Whatever happened, whatever configuration that stretch of interstate highway might take, it was now clear that Glenwood Canyon would be subjected to several years of highway construction. That realization, coming some thirteen years after the first public hearing in Glenwood Springs, was met with reactions ranging from elation to horror.

In May of 1976, a new Citizens' Advisory Committee was formed. It was composed of seven members: Floyd Diemoz, Sam Caudill, Henry Faussone, Mary Hoza, Mark Skrotzki, Allen Koeneke, and Blake Chambliss. The group included architects, environmentalists, engineers, contractors, and business owners from several Western Slope communities. The group was to meet many times over the next few years in order to review virtually every inch of the highway construction.

At about the same time, another segment of the design team was formed. It was known as the Technical Review Group, and was made up of members representing the Federal Highway Administration, the United States Geological Survey, the Denver & Rio Grande Western Railroad, the Division of Wildlife, the United States Forest Service, the Bureau of Land Management, Public Service Company of Colorado, the United States. Bureau of Outdoor Recreation. They were to review every aspect of the pending construction, ranging from noise data to fish habitat. Both the Technical Review Group and the Citizens' Advisory Committee held public workshops which explored the myriad questions and concerns from the general populace.

In December, the city of Glenwood Springs received a formal request from Susan McKey Thomas, a descendent of the Holliday family, for the exhumation and return of Doc Holliday's bones to what she considered to be his rightful resting place, beside his mother in Valdosta, Georgia. It was explained to Thomas that no one was really sure where the good doctor was in fact buried, and that it would therefore be rather difficult to accede to her wishes. After two years of negotiation, the Colorado attorney general ruled against the Georgia contingent, and they were forced to give up.

In 1976, the grand old hotel built by the Devereuxes, once again known as the Hotel Colorado, was declared to be a National Historical Monument.

The Hotel Colorado became a National Historical Monument in 1976. (Courtesy of Frontier Historical Society)

The Defiance Community Theater Company was organized in that year. It was set up as a non-profit organization to provide community theater to Glenwood Springs. The organization purchased the old Silver Club Building on the 700 block of Grand Avenue and converted it from a welding shop to a dinner and dessert theater. The organization truly operated on a shoestring, to the extent of offering free admission on opening night to anyone who brought and donated a wooden kitchen chair. The opening production, on Strawberry Days weekend, was *A Funny Thing Happened on the Way to the Forum.*

In the late 1970s, a great deal of interest began to be shown in the development of the vast oil shale deposits in the western part of Garfield County. The federal government, as well as Exxon, Occidental, Unocal, Gulf, Mobil, and others, all expressed varying degrees if interest in the shale deposits. Oil Shale originates from fine-grained mud deposits on the bottom of ancient oceans and lakes. They are rich in primordial organic matter. High temperatures over the millennia have changed the organic matter in oil shale into kerogen, a material that is neither organic matter nor oil, but rather something in between. When oil shale is heated to 662 degrees Fahrenheit (350 degrees Centigrade), the kerogen turns to oil. Heated oil shales commonly yield twenty-five to thirty gallons of oil per ton of shale. Oil shale deposits are known to be huge and are thought to be capable of producing more crude oil than can conventional oil reservoirs. However, they are very expensive to mine and heat. Also, disposing of the shale after the oil has been removed poses environmental problems. At least one extraction process required a barrel of water for every barrel of shale oil produced. In a semi-arid area where water had always been precious, it was suddenly invaluable.

The interests of both the federal government in tracts C-a and C-b, and Union Oil and Exxon in properties north of Parachute, generated an ever-increasing degree of economic excitement in the area. Battlement Mesa was formed by Exxon on the mesa south of Parachute. It was to be a company town, holding a projected 25,000 people by the 1990s. Parachute, population 200, was expected to well to some 40,000, and the other towns up and down the Colorado River were to experience growth, economic benefits, and skyrocketing real estate prices.

Glenwood Springs was not directly affected by the oil shale activities, most of which were west of Rifle, but the collateral effects of the activities certainly benefited the Glenwood economy.

Estimated budgets for some of the proposed shale projects ranged up to five billion dollars. As the projects progressed, a lot of new people and new money flowed into the area. Housing costs and the expectations of businessmen soared throughout the Garfield County section of the Colorado River Valley.

In January 1977, the process of selecting a design firm for the Glenwood Canyon interstate highway was well underway. Out of nine firms that submitted design proposals, two were finally chosen. Edgardo Contini of Gruen Associates, who had formed a sub-contract agreement with Nelson, Haley, Patterson, and Quirk, a Greeley engineering firm, would design the highway for the east half of the canyon. Joseph Passonneau, of Daniel, Mann, Johnson, and Mendenhall was to do the same for the west half. Passonneau was quoted in the July 5, 1977 issue of the *Glenwood Post*. He stated that the final alignment of the highway would be the result of six factors: "Ecology, appearance of the highway, recreation and other interests, highway engineering and other safety standards, costs, and very serious construction problems."

In April of that year, Ted Bundy was transferred to the Garfield County Jail. Bundy had been accused of several murders of young women throughout the western United States, and was awaiting trial on the murder of Caryn Campbell in Aspen. He had some legal background, and he fired his defense attorney and insisted on defending himself. While performing legal research in the courthouse library in Aspen in June, he escaped by jumping out of a window. He eluded capture for six days, stealing food and sleeping in vacant cabins around Aspen. Finally, he was spotted leaving town in a stolen car and was put back in the Garfield County Jail in Glenwood Springs.

On December 30, Bundy would again escape. He made his way from his cell up into the ceiling area and found an opening into the closet of a jailer's apartment. He waited for the apartment to be empty and casually walked out of the jail. By the time his escape was discovered, he was well on his way to Chicago. From there, he made his way to Florida where he killed three more young women including a twelve-year-old girl. In all, Bundy confessed to the murders of eleven women in Washington, eight in Utah, three in

Colorado, one in California, two in Oregon, two in Idaho, and three in Florida. Many who followed the accounts of the serial murders believe that the true total of his victims was much higher.

A new feature was added to Strawberry Days in 1978. The Strawberry Shortcut, featuring both a 5K and a 10K run was added. Both runs were open to the amateur, the professional runner, or the social walker. The event attracted 232 participants the first year and has grown since then.

In 1979, Dr. Renn assumed ownership of the vapor caves, and formed the Glenwood Vapor Caves, Baths and Massage, Inc. He then promptly sold the cave operation to Ron Hoban and Patty DeFries. Doctor C. W. McFadden, who had owned the caves for many years, retired the following year.

In 1980, construction began on the interstate through Glenwood Canyon at No Name. The project cost was estimated at close to 300 million dollars. The plan was to begin the construction at both ends of the canyon, working toward the more difficult center sections. The construction of the canyon highway bolstered the economy of Glenwood Springs for the next ten years or so.

Construction begins on Interstate 70 through Glenwood Canyon. (Courtesy of Casey Peter - Colorado Department of Transportation)

In February of that year, Dave Grounds resigned as a state employee. Grounds had been the design-project manager for the Glenwood Canyon highway project. He was replaced by Ralph Trapani, a highway engineer who had been active in the construction of the Vail Pass Interstate 70 Project. There was still a great deal of controversy over the design and construction of the canyon highway, including threats of lawsuits by environmental groups and concern over the costs of the project. Dick Prosence, District Engineer, was still deeply involved in the interstate project. Prosence had by then been generally acknowledged as "Father of Glenwood Canyon's I-70 Project."

That April 1, Valley Bank and Trust opened on south Grand Avenue in Glenwood Springs. It was the fourth bank in a system that included locations in Carbondale, Snowmass, and Basalt. Bob Young headed the banking group, Steve Connolly was president of the Glenwood Springs operation, and Kris Gardner was cashier.

CHAPTER TWENTY

From 1981 to 1990

"Of course, not all motorists reacted quite so predictably to the flaggers. Some travelers left their vehicles, strolled down to the river or hiked as far as a mile away to observe the construction and admire the canyon. Some dozed off and napped in the warm summer sun. Others produced culinary items and fixed picnic lunches complete with charcoal burners, card tables, lounge chairs, beer and frisbees. Still others allowed their children and pets to climb the canyon walls, wade in the nearby river, climb into strangers' cars or become too dispersed to move when the time came."
John Haley, speaking of canyon motorists during I-70 construction in
Wooing a Harsh Mistress: Glenwood Canyon's Highway Odyssey

The B & M Hardware store was located just across Grand Avenue from the Readmor Bookstore that burned in 1973. In 1981, the B & M building caught fire, burning the store and second floor residential quarters to the ground. Again, the adjacent buildings were saved by the fire department.

Two inmates of the Garfield County Jail sued the county in 1981 for conditions that they deemed "cruel and inhumane." Following the suit, an estimated half-million dollars worth of improvements were made to the jail facility, enlarging the booking area and adding a visiting area and a holding cell.

Mid-Continent Resources was working the coal seams that had originally been discovered by John Osgood. The old mining tipple and the miner's houses at Coal Basin had been replaced with modern machinery and equipment. The Mid-Continent mines used highly efficient long-wall equipment, extracting amounts of coal from the mountains above Redstone that would have staggered the old coal barons.

Unfortunately, one thing about the mines had not changed in the intervening years; the coal seams were still laced with pockets of highly volatile and poisonous methane gas. The Dutch Creek No. 1 mine was very productive, generating trainloads of coal. It was also quite "gassy." It has been estimated that the No. 1 mine released a million and a half cubic feet of methane every twenty-four hours.

Twenty-two men were working in the Dutch Creek No. 1 mine

on the afternoon of April 15, 1981. They were somewhat scattered up and down the thirteen-degree shaft, but some of them were as deep as 7,200 feet from the surface. At about 4:15, there was a massive explosion deep within the mine. The tremendous blast knocked out both the communication system and the ventilation for the shaft, which made the initial rescue efforts extremely hazardous.

Not long after the explosion, three men emerged from the mouth of the mine, shaken but uninjured. Before long, a rescue team brought out four more, suffering from varying degrees of injuries or burns, but also alive.

There were fifteen men still missing. As word of the disaster and the names of the missing circulated throughout the area, families of those still unaccounted for set up vigils around campfires on the mountainside below the mine entrance. The waiting was interminable. Then, a day and a half after the explosion, word flew through the waiting crowd that nine miners had been found, deep within the mine. It appeared that they had all died instantly. As one miner put it, "Being near a methane explosion in a mine would be like being in an exploding gun barrel." Hope dimmed for the relatives of those still missing.

Finally, three hours later, another five bodies were found, and the fifteenth and last body was discovered after another three hours of searching. The vigil was over, and the mourning for the fifteen miners could begin. Of the fifteen dead miners, six were from Glenwood Springs. The fifteen were:

Loren H. Mead	Age thirty-five
Kyle Cook	Age thirty-three
Kelly B. Greene	Age twenty-five
Glen William Sharp	Age thirty-one
Terry E. Lucero	Age twenty-eight
John Ayala	Age forty
Richard D. Lincoln	Age twenty-two
Thomas Vetter	Age twenty-four
William E. Gutherie	Age thirty-two
Daniel Litwiller	Age twenty-one
Brett Tucker	Age thirty
John D. Rhodes	Age twenty-nine
Ronald W. Patch	Age thirty-four
Robert H. Rogle	Age twenty-nine
Hugh W. Pierce, Jr.	Age twenty

May 2, 1982 became known as "Black Sunday" up and down the Colorado River, from Glenwood Springs to Rifle, to Parachute, and on to Grand Junction. It was on that day that Exxon announced that it was pulling out of the oil shale development in Colorado and ceasing operations immediately. Suddenly, literally overnight, people were out of work, investments in land and businesses lost a great deal of their value. Roughly $85 million in annual payrolls for the residents of western Colorado evaporated overnight. Many of the people who had come to the valley to work in the oil shale industries simply left again; they had no other choice. Every rental truck and trailer within ninety miles of Parachute was spoken for within four days. Over 2,100 people left the area in the next two weeks. All of a sudden, rental properties stood empty, mortgages went unpaid. It was estimated that the pull-out cost Colorado some 10,000 jobs.

The federal government had pulled out of the western Colorado shale development earlier, and Union Oil was operating on only a limited basis, so Exxon had been the big player in the game for some time. The pull-out was a devastating blow to the entire area.

Dick Prosence resigned from the Colorado Department of Transportation in 1982. During his tenure as District Engineer in Grand Junction, he helped to develop 185 miles of interstate highway system. At the time of his resignation, almost all of Interstate 70 had been completed; the unfinished stretches included seven miles of De Beque Canyon, and of course, about twelve miles of Glenwood Canyon. However, his efforts over his twelve years as District Engineer had laid the groundwork for an almost universally approved environmental and engineering master plan for the Glenwood Canyon highway.

In April of 1982, groundbreaking ceremonies were held for the new West Glenwood Springs Mall. The mall was to be built on ground that had formerly been occupied by a drive-in theater and a horse pasture.

Scott McInnis, Glenwood Springs attorney, began his political career in 1982, after gaining a thirteen vote margin of victory over Kathleen Sullivan for the legislative seat for District 57. McInnis was to go on to become a United States Congressman.

The population of Glenwood Springs in 1982 was approaching ,600.

In 1983, the United Lumber Company at Eighth and Pitkin, also known as UPL, was destroyed in a spectacular blaze. The fire was fed by the wood stocks in the yard and by the paints and solvents in the headquarters building. Once again, a potentially disastrous fire was subdued by the volunteer fire department.

Garfield County celebrated its centennial in 1983. Various celebrations were held to commemorate the first hundred years of the county. *Garfield County, Colorado: The First Hundred Years 1883-1983,* was published by the Grand River Museum Alliance. The book, which had been written by the Alliance, was edited by Andrew Gulliford.

Valley Bank, along with its sister banks in Carbondale, Basalt, and Snowmass, officially became Alpine Banks in 1983.

Lena Urquhart Doose, the author of *Glenwood Springs: Spa in the Mountains, Cold Snows of Carbonate, Roll Call: The Violent and Lawless,* and *Colorow — The Angry Chieftain,* died in 1983.

On April 24, 1983, the Vista Dome railroad cars, the California Zephyr of the Denver & Rio Grande Western made their last run through Glenwood Canyon, after thirty-four years of service. The route was taken over by Amtrak.

After final approval by the State Highway Department and input by the Glenwood Springs Citizens' Committee, the pilot bores for the Hanging Lake tunnels were bored in 1983. In 1984, the Highway Department took possession of certain parts of the Bair Ranch for

The east portal of the Hanging Lake Tunnels in Glenwood Canyon. (Courtesy of Casey Peter - Colorado Department of Transportation)

The self-propelled gantry works to place sections of the new highway as traffic continues below. (Courtesy of Casey Peter—Colorado Department of Transportation)

the interstate highway construction project. In return, they built a concrete bridge across the Colorado River for the use of the ranch. The spring of 1984 saw unusually high runoff, the Colorado River swollen by the melt water from heavy winter snows, and the old footbridge was washed away not long after the completion of the new bridge.

In all, the completed canyon highway would include forty bridges and viaducts. While some of the bridges were cast in place using traditional methods, many of the elevated portions of the highway were built with the use of a French-built self-propelled gantry. The 350 foot gantry "walked" from pier to pier on eight legs, hoisting and placing forty to fifty-ton precast concrete sections which were then epoxied and "post-tensioned" into place. Thus, it was possible to erect massive spans of elevated roadway while minimizing the impact on the canyon floor.

The Hotel Denver, under new ownership, underwent a major remodeling project in 1984. The new decor of the hotel was "Art Deco," and included a three-floor atrium in the center of the building. The same year, the First National Bank Building was redone, including a new brick facade.

In January of 1984, KCWS-TV went on the air. It was located in a large building just off Highway 82 south of Glenwood Springs.

The station began to experience financial problems almost immediately, filing for reorganization under the bankruptcy laws in June of that year, and closing not long after.

By 1984, traffic delays due to construction in Glenwood Canyon were becoming an increasing problem. With years of highway construction ahead, it was obvious to all concerned that the traditional methods of traffic control through construction zones were simply not going to work. There were numerous projects going on in the canyon at any one time, involving many different companies and individuals. If any sort of traffic control scheme was to work, it would have to include the cooperation and coordination of all of the involved entities.

The resultant system included the combining of all of the traffic control functions under one command, an extremely sophisticated communications system to deal with the impossibility of line-of-sight communication within the twists and turns of the canyon, and a pilot car operation. The innovative concept of traffic control revolved around a rather complicated dance between construction equipment and the normal canyon traffic. Since there was little room for detours within the narrow confines of the canyon, the task of the pilot car drivers and the flag persons was to move the two groups past each other with a minimum of delay for either.

Once the new traffic control system was in operation, very few delays exceeded thirty minutes. In addition, the flaggers walked up and down the waiting lines of vehicles, informing the motorists of the estimated time of delay and answering questions about the construction. Most of the stopped motorists took the waiting period in stride, using the time to stretch and admire the canyon.

Just two years after the Garfield County Centennial celebration, Glenwood Springs observed its hundredth birthday. The theme of Strawberry Days reflected the pioneer days of the community, and *Glenwood Springs: Spa in the Mountains,* by Lena Urquhart, was republished.

In 1985, Congress dealt the already weakened oil shale industry another crippling blow. They abolished the Synthetic Fuels Corporation, which had been created to assist in the financing of synthetic fuels such as oil shale.

The Glenwood Springs area has had perhaps more than its share of disasters, coal mine explosions and the like. However, coal mining is a dangerous profession, and a certain number of serious injuries or deaths are not surprising. It was with a great deal of shock, therefore, that the citizens of Glenwood Springs received the news that the Rocky Mountain Natural Gas office building had exploded. It was December 16, 1985, just nine days before Christmas. The building, which also housed the warehouse, sat on the south side of the Colorado River. A propane tank on a flatbed truck had been parked in the maintenance garage in the lower part of the building. The pressure gauge on the tank was removed, creating a leak. The propane gas, being heavier than air, flowed across the floor of the garage until it was ignited by a water heater pilot light. The resulting explosion took much of the building with it. The walls and ceilings of the structure collapsed, fifteen people were injured, and twelve were killed. They were:

Teri Luetke	Age thirty-four
Cindy Cowling	Age twenty-four
Brian Carroll	Age twenty-nine
Shelby Jackson	Age twenty-three
David Neal	Age thirty-three
Larry Hutson	Age forty-five
Tom Bolin	Age fifty-four
Barbara Feld	Age thirty-eight
Jim Joslin	Age thirty-six
Harley "Dick" Eckert	Age fifty-three
Allen Rhodes	Age fifty-five
Rex Rhodes	Age thirty-four

In 1987 a celebration was held to mark the 100th anniversary of the death of John Henry "Doc" Holliday. There was a staged shootout, country/western music, and a night of poker games at the Hotel Denver. Other activities included a procession/wake winding through the streets of Glenwood Springs, headed by a horse-drawn wagon. On the wagon was an open casket containing an actor dressed as the "deadly dentist."

In the late 1980s, there was a move by some one hundred petitioners to place Colorado Mountain College under state control. Dennis Mayer was the president of CMC from 1987 to 1993, and in his words,

"The College Board decided to raise taxes, which raised the spirits and the hackles of everybody in the district. I received a call one day that said, 'We've fired other presidents, and we're going to get you!'"

After a prolonged battle, including public hearings in Glenwood Springs, Leadville, and Steamboat Springs, the move to place the college under state control was defeated.

In 1989, *U.S. News and World Report* published a ranking of some 1,200 community colleges across the nation. In that ranking, Colorado Mountain College was listed in the top twelve.

On January 24, 1989, Ted Bundy was executed in Florida. Bundy, the confessed murderer of thirty young women, had escaped from the Courthouse in Aspen and from the jail in Glenwood Springs in 1977. He had been sentenced to death a total of three times, the last time for the murder of twelve-year-old Kimberly Leach in Florida.

Lawrence L. "Bugo" Zancanella died on August 22, 1989. Zancanella worked as a mechanic for thirty-four years, but he distinguished himself in his service to the community as a volunteer fireman. He served on the Glenwood Volunteer Fire Department for fifty-one years, twenty-five of those years as fire chief. He was eighty years of age.

In 1990, the Yampah Hot Springs Corporation purchased the vapor caves from Patty DeFries, who had assumed sole ownership in 1986. The new corporation was owned by Bruce Kendall and Patsy Schwennesen, and they renamed the operation the Yampah Spa and Vapor Caves. They extensively remodeled the spa operation.

The Colorado Division of Wildlife decided to reintroduce the Rocky Mountain bighorn sheep into the Glenwood Canyon. They have transplanted some 300 to 400 animals from the Gunnison area and from Estes Park, offering the bighorns a new home in the canyons leading down to the Colorado River.

In August of 1990, a methane gas-fueled fire began in one of Mid-Continent's mines in Coal Basin. It was extinguished, only to start up again. The miners fought the fire for several months, and it was eventually extinguished, but it brought mining operations to a halt in October of that year. Without any coal production, the company soon reached a critical financial situation. They were unable to pay the workman's compensation payments for the 433 paid employees. Suddenly, the mines shut down with no warning, and a huge payroll which had helped to support the entire area was gone. The mine buildings have since been removed, and reclamation projects are underway to restore the Coal Basin area to some semblance of the valley which first fired the imagination of John Osgood.

A number of public hearings were held during 1990 regarding a proposal to build a desalination plant in Glenwood Springs. The idea was to reclaim a part of the thousands of tons of salts that are poured into the Colorado River each year by the numerous hot springs. The plan would also have helped to clean up the Colorado River below Glenwood, rated as one of the saltiest anywhere. The proposal was heavily opposed, and was finally withdrawn.

CHAPTER TWENTY-ONE

From 1991 to 2000

"Cycling up the Champs-Elysee is the dream for anyone who cycles. The Tour can be good and then bad and then good. But at the end it is good."
Bobby Julich, after placing third in the 1998 Tour de France

During the early 1990s, Colorado Mountain College moved from the ranks of junior colleges by becoming affiliated with Regis College in Denver. This association offered, for the first time, the opportunity for CMC students to earn a full four year bachelor's degree.

In 1991, an effort of court political correctness led to a change in the nomenclature for the traditional Strawberry Days royalty. It was felt that "Strawberry Days Queen" was insulting, demeaning, and quite possibly chauvinistic, so it was decided to change the title to "Strawberry Days Ambassador." That moniker was met with something less than total enthusiasm, so it was changed again the next year, this time to "Miss Strawberry Days Ambassador." That proved to be even more unwieldy, so it was ultimately shortened to "Miss Strawberry Days."

In 1991, a lawsuit was brought by the American Civil Liberties Union on behalf of an unnamed citizen regarding the lighted cross on Red Mountain west of downtown. The cross had traditionally been lit during holidays or in cases of special remembrance. The lawsuit had to do with separation of church and state, as the cross was located on public land. The ACLU and the anonymous citizen won, and the cross was permanently dimmed. However, a new, larger cross was quickly erected on private land at the top of Red Mountain, and it took over the cherished traditions of the old one.

In March of 1992 a new, unique organization came into being in the Roaring Fork Valley. It began as a program of the Aspen Substance Awareness Project and was conceived as a support function for the valley's growing Latino population. It was to be known as Asistencia Para Latinos, and an office was opened in Glenwood Springs.

The need for some manner of Latino support organization was becoming more and more obvious. The population of valley residents with Spanish, Mexican, or Central American ancestry in 1988 was estimated at 1,000. As of 1996, that figure would mushroom to over 12,000 with no indication that the Latino population growth rate was slowing.

The dramatic change in the racial composition of the area was due in large part to the booming local economy. The national economy was healthy, leading to an increase in tourism. In addition, the general population of the area between Rifle and Aspen was growing. This growth created a demand for housing, fueling the need for construction and landscape workers.

The influx of immigrants was not without problems. It is impossible to inject several thousand new people into a reasonably small area without a degree of discord. When there is an accompanying diversity of language and customs, that discord can be exacerbated. The prevention or resolution of that conflict is one of the aims of Asistencia Para Latinos. In the words of the Executive Director, Silvia Barbera:

"The main goal of Asistencia Para Latinos is to connect people and cultures. We act as a bridge between both communities. The Latino community is privileged to have an organization exclusively dedicated to their population in the Roaring Fork Valley. Our services are diversified and they change constantly, according to the needs of the population we serve."

Wilbur "Skip" Bolitho died on July 14, 1992. He had retired from the educational system in 1973 after serving as a teacher and a principal of the school that had been named for him, Bolitho Elementary. Bolitho had also served as football, basketball, and track coach and ran the "Learn-to-Swim" program for some years. He was eighty-six.

Jeanne Golay of Glenwood Springs qualified to ride in the bicycle road race in the Barcelona Olympics in 1992. Golay, who had been competing internationally for several years, finished sixth in the race.

On October 14, 1992, at 10:00 A.M., a ribbon-cutting ceremony marked the official opening of the new interstate highway through Glenwood Canyon. It had been twelve years since motorists could travel the entire length of the canyon with no anticipation of construction delays. The final touches, the landscaping, cleanup, and erecting of signs would take most of another year, but the final link in the Interstate Highway System was complete at long last. It would be referred to as the "Crown Jewel of the Interstate System."

The total price tag of the canyon highway was very close to $500 million. To quote Floyd Diemoz, long-standing member of the Citizens' Advisory Committee and the man chosen to officiate at the opening of the canyon interstate:

"My friends, we have preserved the gift God has so graciously bestowed upon us. Glenwood Canyon remains one of the most beautiful sites in all America."

The formal opening of the canyon interstate brought into play one of the most sophisticated control centers ever to monitor a highway. When the twin tunnels were drilled across the river from the trailhead to Hanging Lake, it was decided to incorporate a four-story building into the tunnel construction to house the command center for the canyon highway. In fact, the high tech equipment at the center monitors Interstate 70 from the bottom of Vail Pass to the Utah border, and other highways as far south as Montrose and as far north as Rio Blanco County. However, it is the Glenwood Canyon highway and the tunnels themselves that receive special scrutiny.

Television cameras watch the traffic from a mile west of the tunnel to the Bair Ranch Exit. Overhead wires within the tunnel monitor heat readings from the vehicles passing beneath. Sensors

The main control room at the Hanging Lake Tunnel control center. (Courtesy Casey Peter—Colorado Department of Transportation)

check for over-height vehicles, excessive speed, or icy conditions. Strips buried in the roadbed of the tunnels track each vehicle, and computers alert human operators if a car or truck does not register on following strips.

The control center building, the largest building in Garfield County, also contains four huge 300 horsepower fans which can move 240,000 cubic feet of air per minute. The lower level, behind the massive doors in the sides of the tunnels, hide the support vehicles and shops for the tunnels. There is a fire truck with a roof-mounted water cannon that can fire 750 gallons of water per minute, a flatbed vehicle-carrying truck, various support and fire fighting vehicles, and a short-wheel-base tow truck that is capable of hauling any vehicle that might venture by.

The tunnels contain a rebroadcast system that allows motorists to continue listening to their car radio while motoring through the tunnel. In addition, the system also allows the control center operators to communicate with those same motorists over their car radios in case of an emergency.

The twin Hanging Lake tunnels, each some 4,000 feet long, are lined with 2.5 million ceramic tiles. The purchase of the tiles was subject to a bidding process, with the low bid submitted by a company in Germany. Interestingly, the stock of replace-

Overview of a section of the completed Glenwood Canyon Interstate Highway, showing the east and westbound lanes, the bike/hiking path, the railroad, and even a raft in the river. (CP-6 Courtesy of Casey Peter—Colorado Department of Transportation)

ment tiles stored in the control building are marked on the back as to their country of manufacture. They say, "Made in the USA."

After lengthy negotiations between the Forest Service and the three remaining bands of Ute Indians, a historic powwow was held in Glenwood Springs in May of 1993. It was the first meeting of the remaining three bands in over 130 years. The leaders of the Ute Mountain Utes, the Southern Utes, and the Unitah and Ouray Utes worked with the Forest Service personnel to identify numerous "sacred sites," locations of vision quests and other religious ceremonies in the forests surrounding Glenwood Springs. The unique gathering was to be repeated for the next two years.

With the help of the Ute elders and volunteers, the Forest Service has located and mapped the ancient Ute Trail across the Flat Tops. The trail begins near the east end of the Glenwood Canyon at Dotsero and meanders northwest to the area of the South Fork of the White River, near the site of Meeker's agency. The trail was used by hundreds of generations of Indians to access the game animals of the high country, as well as the quarries for toolmaking rock. Later it provided a crude trail for the hopeful prospectors who populated Carbonate. The trail, some fifty miles in length, approaches 11,000 feet elevation in some places. It was dedicated to Frank "Slats" Olson, who was instrumental in its recognition and development at a ceremony on October 4, 1992. The sign at the Dotsero Trailhead states:

> *"Remember, you are walking on ground sacred to the Utes. They have blessed*
> *this trail to preserve their heritage on your public lands. Take care of all your*
> *resources by leaving everything as you find it. Let rich memories be your only*
> *souvenir and enjoy your trip back in time."*

The No Name Rest Area, just east of Glenwood Springs in the canyon, opened in July, 1993.

In the early 1990s, scattered skeletal remains of a human being were found deep in a cave in the White River National Forest. The cave was found at an elevation of close to 10,000 feet. The cave was secured, and both the cave and the bones were studied by federal government researchers, as well as scientists from Washington University of St. Louis. In 1993 partial results of their study were released. DNA tests showed that the man was related to some North

A portion of the Ute Trail leading up and across the Flat Tops. (Courtesy of Bill Kight—United States Forest Service)

American Indian tribes. He stood about five feet five inches tall, died at roughly forty years of age, ate a diet heavy in meat, carried heavy loads on his back, and did considerable walking on steep terrain.

Most surprisingly perhaps, was the discovery of the age of the remains. The man died approximately 8,000 years ago. The Southern Ute Tribe was the closest geographically, so the bones were turned over to them for burial according to their customs.

In March, 1993, most of the old coke ovens at Cardiff were destroyed to make way for proposed light industrial property development. The fifty-two ovens that

One of the few remaining coke ovens at the old townsite of Cardiff. (Photo by the author)

survived were mostly in a state of disrepair. Ten of them were deeded to the Frontier Historical Society, and the site was later to be placed on the Colorado State Register of Historic Places.

On the early evening of July 2, 1994, a dry lightning storm moved slowly over the west of Glenwood Springs. This is not an unusual occurrence, but 1994 happened to be one of the driest years in memory in western Colorado. There had been scant snow the previous winter, and the low snowpack, combined with a drier than normal spring, had resulted in tinder-dry conditions in the scrub oak brush, juniper, and pinon pine on the hills around Glenwood.

By the early days of July, numerous forest fires were burning on the Western Slope of the Continental Divide. More than forty new fires had been reported in the Bureau of Land Management's Grand Junction District in just the two days prior to July 2, 1994. Fire fighting teams had been called in from all over the western United States.

At about 6:30 P.M. on July 2, a lone finger of lightning snaked down from the low clouds and struck a tree near the top of a ridge on Storm King Mountain, just to the west of Glenwood Springs and north of Interstate 70. The tree ignited, spreading flames to brush and other trees nearby. The small fire, only one of hundreds across Colorado, was on a knoll overlooking the Colorado River and Interstate 70. The fire was noted by authorities, but the wind was blowing from the north, and the only way for the fire to expand was down toward the river and the highway. Since down is not a common way for a fire to travel, little concern was applied to the now three acre blaze.

There were plenty of other fires in progress, fires that showed danger of spreading or

A Helitac helicopter heads toward Storm King Mountain in the background. (Courtesy of the Glenwood Post)

of threatening property, and those received priority. However, two days later, the fire had spread to about eleven acres, and as it was visible from Glenwood Springs, a degree of concern was beginning to be expressed by the residents. A crew was sent to the mountain on the afternoon of the July 4 to deal with the still small blaze. The crew knew that it was a two and one-half hour hike up the mountain to the site of the fire, so it was decided to wait until the morning of the July 5 to begin fire fighting efforts.

A seven person crew made up of Forest Service and Bureau of Land Management personnel hiked up to the fire, began a fire line, and cleared a landing area for a helicopter. A slurry bomber made a drop during the day, but the fire was still burning by that evening. The crew left the site to repair their equipment and were replaced by eight smoke jumpers who parachuted into the area and worked the fire lines until about midnight. The fire had overrun the original fire lines, so they constructed new ones farther down the mountain.

On the morning of July 6, they were joined by the Bureau of Land Management/Forest Service crew and eight more smoke jumpers. There were more drops of slurry and water, but the fire had a foothold on the thick stands of gambel oak, pinon pine, and cedar that covered the steep slopes of Storm King Mountain, and the fire shrugged off the efforts to control it. The crew was joined later in

The Prineville Hotshots prepare to do battle with the Storm King Mountain fire. (Courtesy of the Glenwood Post)

the day by members of a Hotshot crew from Prineville, Oregon, and the entire contingent worked on building fire lines to try to contain the now raging fire. The massed firefighters

Observers search for signs of life after the mountain blows up. (Courtesy of the Glenwood Post)

would gain precious ground, only to be forced back by another flareup.

By that time the forces on the mountain included BLM personnel, Forest Service firefighters, smoke jumpers from several western states, Helitack crew members, and the Hotshots. Some of America's finest young firefighters, both male and female, faced a fire that was out of control, and which was about to become an inferno.

At 3:20 P.M. on the sixth, the weather suddenly changed; a cold front moved in, and the winds shifted and intensified. The winds had been bad all along, and a fire of any size will create its own winds, but the weather front brought with it the makings of a disaster. The fire was by that time quite extensive, and there were personnel in several different locations. When the fierce new winds caught the fire, the steep drainage on the west side of Storm King Mountain literally exploded. A wall of flame blasted up the hill with incredible speed, covering some 1900 feet in two minutes. Twelve fire fighters were overrun by the flames as they tried to make it to the ridgeline, and two others were trapped as they tried to escape along that same ridge.

It was obvious to the people of Glenwood Springs that something extraordinary was occurring on Storm King Mountain on the afternoon of July 6, 1994. The billowing clouds of brownish-gray smoke all but blocked out the sun, giving the light an eerie quality. Flakes of gray ash fell over the town as the ponderous shapes of the slurry bombers, the quicker spotter planes, and the darting helicopters appeared and disappeared in Glenwood's normally quiet skies.

Homeowners in the western part of West Glenwood trained garden hoses onto their roofs as they watched the fire advance ever closer to the edge of town. Travelers and commuters creeping along Interstate 70 west of Glenwood saw tongues of fire reaching down the gullies on the south side of Storm King Mountain. At about 4:30 P.M. the entire top of the mountain blew up. It resembled a gigantic volcanic eruption, the flames and smoke shooting straight up thousands of feet with unimaginable force. The knowledge that there were people up there was chilling.

When the rumors started flying, the word came down that fifty firefighters were missing, then thirty, and finally fourteen. That last figure unfortunately proved to be accurate. Four young women and ten young men died in the performance of their jobs, fighting wildfires and protecting the lives and property of others.

Kathi Beck	Age twenty-five
Scott Blecha	Age twenty-seven
Robert Browning	Age twenty-eight
Terri Hagen	Age twenty-eight
Robert Johnson	Age twenty-seven
Don Mackey	Age thirty-four
Jim Thrash	Age thirty-one
Tamera Bickett	Age twenty-five
Levi Brinkley	Age twenty-two
Douglas Dunbar	Age twenty-three
Bonnie Holtby	Age twenty-one
Jon Kelso	Age twenty-seven
Roger Roth	Age thirty-one
Richard Tyler	Age thirty-three

It is to these fourteen courageous young people that Storm King Mountain will always belong.

The realization of the tragedy hit the residents of Glenwood Springs like a fist. Glenwood Springs has had its own share of disasters and untimely deaths. When it was learned that nine of the Hotshots had come from another small town, Prineville, Oregon, Glenwood Springs felt an immediate kinship. Someone came up with the idea, and within hours, most of the populace was wearing a purple ribbon to commemorate the fallen young people.

The summit of Storm King Mountain after the fire (Courtesy of the Glenwood Post - Photo by Casey A. Cass)

The day after the blowup, the city council created the Storm King Fourteen Monument Committee. The committee consisted of fourteen members, including the Glenwood Springs mayor, representatives from the Forest Service and from the BLM, local artists, and others who felt that they could make a contribution. Each of the committee members adopted one of the families of the fallen firefighters. They did their best to help the family members through the terrible days following the catastrophe. As one member said, "I wanted to do something. I wanted to say something in some way."

The committee also met weekly to bring about the establishment of a memorial to the fallen fourteen. Two Rivers Park was chosen as the site of the monument. The park is within the city limits of Glenwood Springs, the town that the firefighters were working to save, but it commands a clear view of Storm King Mountain. The committee called for entries for the design of the monument, and Joyce Killebrew of Sedona, Arizona was chosen. Killebrew herself worked with the Forest Service for some twenty years as a fire lookout and fire fighter. Her life-size bronze sculpture depicts a smoke jumper, a Helitack crew member and a Hotshot — two men and a woman. It sits atop a marble base in the west end of Two

Monument to the fourteen firefighters who lost their lives on Storm King Mountain. (Photo by the author)

Rivers Park. Surrounding the monument are fourteen boulders, each with a picture and a brief biography of one of the fallen firefighters.

The fire was not controlled until July 16, and was not completely extinguished until August 5. A total of 452 firefighters, seven tanker planes, and five helicopters were used to finally defeat the fire.

A rough footpath up the west side of Storm King Mountain was widened and improved by volunteers. Originally used by the families of the victims to reach the sites where the bodies of their loved ones were found, the trail was deliberately left steep and rugged. It was felt that visitors to the site should gain some idea of the terrain faced by the firefighters. The developed path leads to an observation point from which may be seen the granite crosses which have been erected, one for each of the fourteen firefighters. Each of the crosses is engraved with the names, birth dates, and fire fighting unit insignia of the deceased. The fourteen crosses are identical in shape, except for the one dedicated to Terri Hagen. Terri was a Native American, and the horizontal bar on her cross is lower, forming a representation of the four sacred directions of Indian theology. Also, a steel representation of a Native American "medicine wheel" was erected by Terri's cross.

A restoration project at the Hot Springs Pool in 1994 restored much of the original grandeur of the stone bathhouse. After the renovation, the building housed the corporate offices and facilities of a health club.

In August, 1994, an annual celebration of the Old West was started. It was a weekend known as "Doc Hollidays," and the activities centered around western history in the early 1880s. The Downtown Business Association sponsored the event, which featured historical tours, a showing of *The Great K & A Train Robbery*, Tom Mix's film that was shot in the Glenwood Canyon, and frontier dress for all who care to do so. The centerpiece of the weekend was a reenactment of the Gunfight at the OK Corral, complete with real guns, fake bullets and blood, and a great deal of noise. It was, of course, an excuse for a group of grown men to dress up and play cowboy, but the event drew huge crowds.

In September, 1994, a heavy rainstorm drenched the burned-over slopes of Storm King Mountain. With little vegetation left to slow it, a wall of mud rolled down the southern slopes of the mountain, engulfing several hundred yards of Interstate 70. The slide trapped five cars and injured two people. The highway department managed to clear one lane in either direction by the next afternoon, but it took an additional two days to completely clear the highway. Later that fall the Bureau of Land Management air-dropped several thousand pounds of seed on the denuded slopes in what turned out to be a successful attempt to revegetate and stabilize Storm King Mountain.

In July, 1995, Two Rivers Park was the gathering place for over 2,000 people, relatives and friends of the fourteen young people who had fallen a year before on Storm King Mountain, survivors of the killer fire, and spectators. The occasion was the dedication of the memorial monument to the firefighters. On the same day, the residents of Canyon Creek Estates subdivision to the west of Storm King Mountain dedicated another memorial, consisting of fourteen boulders with plaques located at the entrance of the housing development. The subdivision was threatened by the fire and was also the location of the base of operations for the firefighters.

The Glenwood Health Spa was torn down in 1995.

In 1995, *Apparition Manor, True Ghost Stories of the Hotel Colorado*, by Kathy Rippy Fleming, was published. The collection of stories deals with accounts of ghostly encounters by hotel guests and employees. It seems that certain occupants of the old hotel chose, for reasons known only themselves, not to leave.

There have been repeated reports of dishes and lamps moving, seemingly of their own volition. Doors unlock and open by themselves, and elevators move between floors with no visible passengers. Male guests have awakened in the middle of the night to find a young woman bending over them. A young girl, dressed in fashions of the late nineteenth century, has been seen in the halls playing with a large ball. A sweet perfume is frequently detected in the Devereux Room, the main dining room. The smell of cigar smoke, with no apparent source, has been reported for years in the main lobby area. Various figures in period dress appear and disappear in unusual places at odd moments.

Hotel employees have named the most prominent of the male apparitions "Walter," after Walter Devereux, the man responsible for the creation of the Hot Springs Pool and the Hotel Colorado. It is known that Devereux enjoyed his cigars. However, others believe that the cigar-smoking ghost is that of F. H. A. "Hervey" Lyle, one-time manager of the hotel and one of the men who introduced polo to Glenwood Springs. Another popular theory claims that it is Elmer E. Lucas, controller, general manager, and eventually owner of the hotel.

In 1995, Bob Young was named as Colorado's Outstanding Philanthropist in honor of his contributions to Human Services organizations in Glenwood Springs and throughout Colorado. Young is Chairman of the Board of Alpine Banks.

The population of Glenwood Springs in 1995 was close to 7,200.

Jeanne Golay, who had competed in the bicycle races at the Barcelona Olympics, qualified for the United States Senior National Bicycling Team in 1996. She thereby qualified for the Olympic Games in Atlanta. In the years of her international bicycle racing, she has been a nine-time national champion and a three-time world championship medalist. She won the road race in the 1995 Pan American Games, won the Colorado Cyclist Classic, was second in the Powerbar International, and was first overall in the Fresca Cup.

Peter Jennings, of ABC News, named Alpine Bank and Norm Franke "Person of the Week" in January of 1996, when Alpine Bank offered interest-free paycheck loans to federal employees when Congress failed to approve a budget.

In May, 1997, the citizens of Glenwood Springs voted to keep their airport. Glenwood Land Company, which owned 150 acres in south Glenwood Springs, urged the city council to put the question of the airport closing on the ballot. According to the company, the closing of the airport would allow the building of a development which encompassed the amenities most desired by the city: commercial space, ball fields, and affordable housing. Three-quarters of the votes cast were to retain the airport.

With the increases in housing costs in the entire Roaring Fork Valley, more and more of the workers from Glenwood Springs to Aspen have resigned themselves to a daily commute. They come from the communities along Interstate 70, travel through Glenwood, and on up Highway 82 toward their jobs in Aspen. This has resulted in the Western Slope's equivalent of traffic jams twice a day; several thousand cars heading up-valley each morning and back down in the evening. With the view that the transportation problem would only get worse in subsequent years, there has been a great deal of conversation regarding possible solutions. A rail corridor which runs up the Roaring Fork Valley has been acquired, and the city of Glenwood Springs is participating in the Roaring Fork Railroad Holding Company. The Holding Company is a consortium of state and local entities that raised $8.5 million to secure the land and rights-of-way for the rail corridor and is continuing to investigate the possibilities of some manner of high speed transit system. There is also talk of using the rail corridor through Glenwood Springs for the construction of a vehicle bypass and a bike/walking trail in addition to the rails.

In 1997, the Colorado Department of Transportation proposed replacing the old Grand Avenue Bridge with a wider, more modern structure. The old bridge had never been designed to carry four lanes of traffic, and is therefore several feet too narrow to meet modern standards. The proposed new bridge would have been paid for with money available from the federal government which had been designated for highway bridge replacement. However, the proposal was turned down by the Glenwood Springs City Council at the urging of many of the downtown businesses. They cited disruption of the downtown area during construction, aesthetic impact to the area, and the possibility of increased traffic on an already beleaguered Grand Avenue.

A survey of clients by Asistencia Para Latinos in 1997 revealed some interesting facts about the Latino population of the area. Of those surveyed:

72 percent were originally from Mexico
15 percent were from El Salvador
28 percent spoke English proficiently

45 percent spoke a little English

22 percent spoke no English at all

55 percent were documented

9 percent were in the process of obtaining legal residency documents

31 percent were undocumented

To the probable surprise of no one, fully 42 percent of the Latino clients work in Pitkin County, but only 8 percent of them live there.

Interior of a coke oven, showing the glass-like melted surface of the fire bricks. (Photo by the author)

In 1997, the Colorado Historical Society provided a grant for test excavations and structural assessments of the remaining coke ovens at the old townsite of Cardiff. It was discovered that at least some of the coke ovens featured an underground flue system. A similar flue system was developed in Wales in the mid 1800s, to capture waste heat and increase the production of coke. It is possible that the Cardiff ovens were the only ones in the United States to have such a system.

The Garfield County jail has been located just north of the County Courthouse at the edge of Glenwood Springs for many years. With the increases in population in the county, the jail predictably suffered from overcrowding. As of the beginning of 1997, the city of Glenwood Springs and Garfield County were in agreement that a new jail would be constructed on the site of the old one.

In the late summer of 1997 it was announced that, for the first time in many years, Glenwood Springs High School would not field a varsity football team. This was a very emotional issue in Glenwood, considering that the Glenwood Demons had made the state playoffs six times between 1978 and 1990, bringing home the championship twice. Craig Denney, the Demons coach, made the decision to eliminate the varsity program. He felt that it would be impossible to put together a team without putting some of the students at risk of injury. The reactions from the parents and the local populace was largely favorable. Arrangements were made for some of the more talented players to compete on other area teams. The varsity program was reinstated in 1998. Incidentally, the 1998 version of Demons football won their first game of the season with a rather decisive 35-24 victory over the Meeker Cowboys.

Later in 1997, the city Planning and Zoning Commission turned down the county's sketch plan for the new jail, laying the groundwork for many months of dispute, disagreement, and strained relations between the Glenwood Springs City Council and the Garfield County Commissioners. Several other locations were suggested for the new facility, including the former location of the United Lumber Company just west of the present location, and at least two locations in Rifle. Also considered as a possibility was the Wulfsohn Ranch property, former site of Cedarbank, home of Walter Devereux and his family.

The population of Glenwood Springs in 1997 was 7,829. The average sales price for a single-family residence in Glenwood for 1997 was $222,030, not quite twice the amount that Walter Devereux paid to Isaac Cooper in 1885 for the ten acres which included the hot springs.

Another newspaper made its appearance in Glenwood Springs on February 10, 1998. It is called the *Glenwood Independent* and is published five days a week. The publisher is Martha Cochran, and the editor is Jon Klusmire.

Nellie Duffy died in August of 1998 at the age of 90. Nellie was a newspaper reporter for much of her life as well as a poet and a historian. She co-authored *Glenwood* in 1978 with E. H. Goodwin and Jim Henderson. She was the last person to ever be buried in the old Linwood Cemetery on Jasper Mountain overlooking Glenwood Springs.

On August 2, 1998, Bobby Julich placed third in the Tour de France. Julich, a graduate of Glenwood Springs High School, entered the world of professional bicycle racing soon after his graduation. He placed seventeenth in the 1997 Tour de France, his first attempt at the world-class race. His third-place finish made him one of two Americans, along with Greg LeMond, to ever finish in the top three positions of the race.

In August of 1998, Glenwood Independent Bank merged with Weststar Banks, and the Glenwood Springs location became a branch

One of the massive formations inside the Glenwood Caverns. (The old Fairy Caves) (Courtesy of Glenwood Caverns, Inc.)

of the Weststar system. At the time of the merger, Don Vanderhoof stepped down as president of Glenwood Independent Bank. In his years as a banker, Vanderhoof was also extremely active in various civic organizations and volunteer groups. He served as mayor and as a member of city council, as well as chairman or committee member of the Strawberry Days Committee, the Drums Along the Rockies Committee, the city Transportation Committee, the Defiance Community Theater Company, and many, many others. He is also a prominent and influential member of the Republican Party.

Also in August of 1998, it was announced that the old Fairy Caves, high on Iron Mountain north of the Hotel Colorado, were to be reopened to the public. Steve Beckley, an engineer and cave enthusiast from Littleton, Colorado made plans to reopen the caves in 1999 under the name of Glenwood Caverns. Beckley leased the caves from POW, Inc., a corporation that had purchased the cave property in 1961.

The Fairy Caves had been closed in 1917. At that time, they had been measured at some 1,000 feet in length. However, in the 1960s, a small crack was found at the back of the cave which led to the discovery of additional caverns, extending the overall explored length of the caves to nearly two miles. Also, the previously undiscovered lower regions of the caves revealed two of the largest cave rooms in the state of Colorado. The Barn is a cavity some forty feet wide and 300 feet long whose ceiling height exceeds that of a five-story building, and King's Row exhibits a variety of unusual and beautiful formations along its entire length.

An example of the delicate crystalline formations within the caves. (Courtesy of Glenwood Caverns, Inc.)

On August 23, 1998, the Hotel Colorado polo team defeated the Roaring Fork polo club in the annual Centennial Cup match. The contest was played at the Roaring Fork Polo Club facility at Cozy Point, not far from Snowmass Village, instead of at the old polo grounds in Glenwood Springs. Nonetheless, it can be hoped that the ghosts of Hervey Lyle and the Devereux brothers enjoyed the match.

A new, 38,000 square foot academic center was completed on the Spring Valley Campus of Colorado Mountain College in August of 1998. The new center took some thirteen months of planning and construction. The building boasts a thirty-foot high rotunda with a pyramidal skylight, faculty offices, a technology center, and a theater. The technology center includes a computer center, photo lab, and so-called "smart classrooms" for the study of biology, veterinary technology, chemistry, geology, nursing, police sciences, and fine arts. The building is known as the James C. and Conni L. Calaway Academic Building.

In September, 1998, it was announced that an organization known as Aspen Springs Ranch, LLC, had purchased the 5,830 acre Spring Valley Ranch from Waleed Zahid of Saudi Arabia. The reported purchase price was $17 million. The Spring Valley acreage has been approved by the county for single-family and multi-family homes, golf courses, a hotel, and commercial space.

As of December, 1998, the Garfield County Commissioners and the Glenwood Springs City Council had made no firm decision as to the location for the new Garfield County jail. Sites in both Glenwood Springs and in Rifle were being considered. Then, the Garfield County Commissioners voted on January 12, 1999 to construct the new county jail facility on a forty acre site near the county airport, just outside of Rifle. This action was taken after over two years of unsuccessful attempts by the commissioners to obtain approval from the Glenwood Springs City Council to build a new jail near the courthouse. This decision caused a great deal of consternation on the parts of Glenwood Springs officials and residents alike. After a great many more meetings, cost studies, and letters from concerned citizens, the commissioners changed their vote and decided to build the new jail in Glenwood Springs, adjacent to the courthouse. As of this writing, those plans appear to be holding.

As it moves inexorably toward the twenty-first century, Glenwood Springs has established a distinct identity. It has become a regional trade center, an attractive residential community, and, perhaps most importantly, a world-class resort. During the late 1800s, it was the pool, the vapor caves, the recreational opportunities, and the magnificent scenery that brought the tourists to Glenwood Springs. As the 1900s draw to a close, it is those same attractions that bring the modern tourist to the valley. Walter Devereux had the right idea.

Acknowledgments

This book has been a labor of love. I am not one of the rare Glenwood Springs natives, but I have lived roughly half of my life here. In that time, I have seen a great many changes to my adopted hometown. My first office was in a log cabin that sat under a giant weeping willow tree, located approximately where Alpine Bank's drive-up window now resides. The only radio station available at that time was KGLN-AM, and it went off the air at sundown.

During the intervening years, Glenwood Springs has been very good to me and to my wife Mary. We have met and befriended a remarkable array of people, many of whom have labored to make Glenwood Springs what it is today. It would be a fitting tribute to them and to the generations who came before, to mention each of them, for each of them has in some way shaped our community. Unfortunately, even in a work of this scope, it is impossible to hit much more than the high spots. Many thousands of people have populated Glenwood Springs since its beginnings back in the days of James Landis and Colorow. It must suffice to express my heartfelt gratitude to all of them, past and present, for providing me such a wonderful place in which to live.

* * *

A number of people deserve my thanks for their assistance in the research and polishing of this book. Janet Riley and Willa Soncarty consented to review the entire manuscript, and their additions and corrections have been duly included. Thanks also to the expertise of Floyd Diemoz on Glenwood Canyon, Bill Kight on the Utes, and Bill Shettig on the geology of the area. Buzz Zancanella, Al Maggard, Don Vanderhoof, John Tindall, Scott Leslie, Casey Peter and the *Glenwood Post* were kind enough to give me access to their photo collections. Special thanks to Ann Roberts, Willa Soncarty and Sue Plush of the Frontier Historical Museum for putting up with me for most of two years, and for the use of the museum's extensive photo collection.

Jim Nelson

Bibliography: Glenwood Springs, Colorado

Books/Pamphlets

Allan, Alice. 1998. *Glenwood Springs — Circa 1957.* Glenwood Springs: Old Timer Publications

Athearn, Robert G. 1976. *The Coloradans.* Albuquerque: University of New Mexico Press

Bancroft, Caroline. 1958. *Glenwood's Early Glamour.* Boulder: Johnson Publishing Co.

Benson, Maxine. 1994. *1001 Colorado Place Names.* Lawrence: University Press of Kansas

Carhart, Arthur H. 1932. *Colorado.* New York: Coward—McCann, Inc.

Cassells, E. Steve. 1983. *The Archaeology of Colorado.* Boulder: Johnson Books

Ellis, Richard N. 1989. *The Ute Legacy.* Ignacio: Pinon Press

Fleming, Kathy Rippy. 1997. *Walter B. Devereux, The Legend The Man.* Glenwood Springs: Twin Aspen Publishing

Fleming, Kathy Rippy. 1995. *Apparition Manor, True Ghost Stories of the Hotel Colorado.* New Castle: Twin Aspen Publishing

Goodwin, E.H., Duffy, Nellie, and Henderson, Jim. 1978. *Glenwood.* Glenwood Springs: Gran Farnum Printing & Publishing Company

Gulliford, Andrew. 1983. *Garfield County, Colorado: The First Hundred Years 1883-1983.* Glenwood Springs: Gran Farnum Printing & Publishing Company

Haley, John L. 1994. *Wooing a Harsh Mistress: Glenwood Canyon's Highway Odyssey.* Greeley: Canyon Communications

Johnson, Anna and Yajko, Kathleen. 1983. *The Elusive Dream.* Glenwood Springs: Gran Farnum Printing & Publishing Company

Marsh, Charles S. 1982. *People of the Shining Mountains.* Boulder: Pruett Publishing Company

McDonald, Kae, Metcalf Archaeological Consultants, Inc. 1998 *Archaeological Testing at the Cardiff Coke Oven Site (5GF461)*

McGregor, Heather. 1992. *A Guide to Glenwood Canyon.* Glenwood Springs: Pika Publishing Company

Myers, John Myers. 1955. *Doc Holliday.* Lincoln: University of Nebraska Press

Nelson, Jim. 1998. *Glenwood Springs—A Quick History.* Fort Collins: FirstLight Publishing

Nelson, Jim. 1998. *Marble & Redstone—A Quick History.* Fort Collins: FirstLight Publishing

Pettit, Jan. 1982. *Utes—The Mountain People.* Colorado Springs: Century One Press

Schader, Conrad F. 1996. *Glenwood Canyon—From Origin to Interstate.* Golden: Regio Alta Publications

Shoemaker, Len. 1965. *Pioneers of the Roaring Fork Valley.* Denver: Sage Books

Shoemaker, Len. 1973. *Roaring Fork Valley—An Illustrated Chronicle.* Silverton: Sundance Publications, Limited

Shoemaker, Len. 1965. *Pioneers of the Roaring Fork Valley.* Denver: Sage Books

Tindall, John. 1985. *Glenwood Springs Centennial History.* Glenwood Springs: Tineagle Publishing

Traywick, Ben T. 1984. *Tombstone's Deadliest Gun: John Henry Holliday.* Red Marie's Books on the West

Urquart, Lena M. 1967. *Cold Snows of Carbonate.* Denver: The Golden Bell Press

Urquart, Lena M. 1967. *Roll Call: The Violent and Lawless.* Denver: The Golden Bell Press

Urquart, Lena M. 1968. *Colorow—The Angry Chieftain.* Denver: The Golden Bell Press

Urquart, Lena M. 1970. *Glenwood Springs: Spa in the Mountains.* Taylor Publishing Company

Waters, Frank 1946. *The Colorado.* Rivers of America Series. New York: Rinehart and Company

Werner, Fred H. 1985. *Meeker—The Story of the Meeker Massacre and Thornburgh Battle September 29, 1989.* Greeley: Werner Publications

Videotapes

Glenwood Canyon—Ancient Treasure, Modern Marvel. 1993. Colorado
    Department of Transportation
Highways and the Environment—Innovative Mitigation. Viewfinder
    Productions, Inc., for the Federal Highway Commission
I-70 - Where? How? 1972. Jerry Brown, Floyd Diemoz, Edward
    Mulhall, Jim Rose

Index